WAKE UP!

WAKE UP!
Awakening through Reflection

A 10-DAY LIFE LESSON WORKSHOP

Book One of the Up! Trilogy

SUZANNE ROSS

Sacred Dragon Publishing
Los Angeles, California - Sedona, Arizona

WAKE UP!
AWAKENING THROUGH REFLECTION

Second Edition, Copyright © 2021 Suzanne Ross
ISBN-13: 978-1-7366793-2-6

Cover design by Ida Jansson of Amygdala Design

Scared Dragon Publishing
Los Angeles, CA
www.SacredDragonPublishing.com

TABLE OF CONTENTS

DEDICATIONS

I want to express deep gratitude to my mother for her never-ending faith in my strength and courage. Growing up, she would wake me up every morning by saying, "You are the bravest, smartest and prettiest girl there ever was!" I am also grateful for her absolute love of books which inspired me to read, read some more and now write!

And to my big sister who taught me how to read and write while I was still in diapers! After school, she would prop me up and teach me everything she learned that day. As an adult, she introduced me to the beautiful teachings of Buddhism which awakened my soul and inspired my spiritual quest.

And finally to Scott, the love of my life, my true knight in shining armor, who has supported me with pure love and devotion for the last 20 years. He has truly been there for me in the most transformational moments of my life. For that, I express my eternal gratitude and infinite love.

I am driven by one singular motivation
~ To encourage others to explore
The true breadth and depth of their existence.
If I can inspire one person to
Expand the breadth of their consciousness
And peer into the depth of their soul,
I will have served my divine purpose.

~Suzanne

READER DISCOUNT

Purchase audio recordings of the
Up! Trilogy guided meditations referenced in this book at
SuzanneRossTransendence.com.

Enter promo code **WakeUp!44** at check-out for your reader discount.

PREFACE

LIFE

Meaning: To Create
Purpose: To Evolve

I am blessed to have found my true calling in the field of wellness. It has given me the opportunity to improve the lives of hundreds of people over the last twenty years. Helping others realize what they are truly capable of has been extremely gratifying. For most of my career, I have been primarily focused on the physical well-being of my clients but have always made a sincere effort to uplift them on an emotional level as well. Giving positive feedback and helping my clients have a brighter and more optimistic perspective, especially when faced with difficult challenges, has been the most fulfilling aspect of my career. Over the last five years, I have taken this to a whole new level. I began a spiritual quest as the result of a life-changing experience and as I did, my clients began to notice a marked change in my attitude and outlook on life. I gradually became more calm, patient and joyful and as they watched my transformation, they took an interest in my journey.

Responding to their inquiries, I shared with them how my spiritual practice was bringing me a profound sense of peace. Several of them asked if I would consider guiding a weekly meditation. Due to their enthusiastic response and heightened interest in spirituality, I became inspired to share my personal revelations with others. I wanted everyone, my clients, friends and family, to experience the same feelings of pure joy and inner peace that I had discovered along my path. When you start to see the world from a more enlightened perspective, you want to share it with everyone! It comes from a place of love and compassion for all of humanity. The bliss is so profound that you want others to realize it as well. I was inspired by a powerful motivation to bring this full realization forth so others could benefit from it as well.

It had become clear to me over the last few years that the path toward reaching one's full potential had to include comprehensive, or integrative, wellness. In a state of total well-being, revelations about human potential and spirituality could be fully realized. So I put together a program of integrative wellness where participants could discover a profound sense of physical, mental and spiritual well-being. This would enable them to realize their full potential!

For the body aspect of the program, I incorporated a nutritional detoxification with a clean-eating program. I designed "Metabolic Empowerments" that offered participants a more intuitive approach to eating. For the mind, I designed "Thought Awareness Workshops" that would challenge students to expand their consciousness and open to the greater possibilities of life. The workshops were designed to help participants harness the power of their thoughts so they could turn their dreams into reality. I taught them how to use the emotional force of their intentions to manifest their desires. I encouraged them to embrace their lives by expressing more joy, love and compassion.

I would open the workshops with "Dynamic Movement" which included a series of bending, reaching, opening and expanding exercises culminating in an awe-inspiring nature visualization. The visualization would incorporate their five senses and encourage them to express gratitude and love for all of the blessings in their life. For the soul, my dear friend, Janet Myatt, who is a Spiritual Counselor, agreed to teach meditation classes. In addition to guiding deep meditation, she would teach the students special techniques so they could learn to meditate on their own. We also co-created the content for the "Thought Awareness Workshops" and decided to teach it together. This turned out to be a powerful approach. It was an exciting time for me and I knew that I had been blessed with this manifestation of my desire to share my joy and inspiration with the world! In the process, I had realized my own potential!!

The program is a success! Each participant had their own unique story but the overriding theme was the desire to find more meaning and purpose in their lives. Most were business people trying to survive in the corporate world. They wanted to reduce their stress, improve their health and explore their spirituality. In general, they wanted to enhance the quality of their life! I had planned to start out with a presentation about the importance of open-mindedness but as each of the participants shared their stories, it became apparent to me that they were already wide open to thinking about life in a new and more inspired way. They were ready to expand their consciousness and attain new insight. As it turned out, the program had such a profound impact on the lives of the participants that they wanted to continue beyond the 30-days! We actually stayed together as a group for the next four months! We explored the power of the mind on a deeper level and I was amazed at the profound impact these workshops and classes were having on the lives of the students, both personally and professionally. Here are a couple of the testimonials they shared:

"The mindfulness that started with food choices has carried over to all aspects of my life. I've learned to accept myself and let go of past negative thoughts. I want to continue to bring calm and light into my life."

"This program has given me the tools I need to continue on a healthy path.

It was an incredible experience to work with such caring and knowledgeable women. So many seeds were planted – I will continue to grow in the light!"

The more research I did to prepare for the weekly presentations, the more I became inspired to write. What took place over the course of that incredible four month period encouraged me to write this book. I began to think, "If I can help this group in such a powerful way, maybe I can reach out and inspire many others!" I realized that I enjoyed writing and people complimented my work. So I began compiling as much research as I could. I read everything I could get my hands on from spirituality and religion to quantum physics and ancient philosophy. During meditation, I would get insights about the best way to inspire others, "Share your journey!" was the message I kept hearing over and over. I started to ask myself: "How did I go from being engulfed in the distractions of life's pressures and demands to living from a place of pure joy and inner peace? How did I start living a life so full of love and compassion, meaning and purpose?"

On my nature walks, I would have epiphanies about the design and structure of the book. I knew I wanted to present it as a 30-day program of progressive evolution. Then the idea of three 10-day books unfolded into a nutritional program for detoxifying the body, a life-lessons workshop for liberating the mind and an outdoor adventure for unveiling the spirit. These books for the mind, body, and spirit would be called *Wake Up!*, *Lighten Up!*, and *Rise Up!* The "Up! Trilogy" was falling into place and as it did, I became more enlightened and empowered. All along I knew I was being guided by a higher source of knowledge and pure wisdom.

For me, there is a process and it is a joyful path. First, there is the research and practice. Second, there is contemplation. Third, a personal interpretation develops which represents the truths that resonate from within. Fourth, a strong belief begins to flourish as fragmented truths fall into place beautifully and become one unified whole. Then finally, a knowing occurs deep within your soul that is profound and complete. You have an experience of becoming one with the truth as it resonates within the very core of your being. The spiritual essence, or true nature, of your reality begins to permeate your body, mind and soul. As you come into this self-realization, your whole perspective becomes enlightened and you are naturally compelled to bring forth your highest self in every thought, word and action. You are also compelled to share this realization with others out of love, compassion and a true desire to enhance their well-being. You are inspired to treat yourself, others and Mother Earth with a great deal of consideration and respect. Compassion and patience, as well as peace and joy, radiate from your being and are expressed in every moment of every day with this enhanced appreciation for life! You come to find that you are eternally grateful for this precious opportunity to create and evolve, which is after all, the meaning and purpose of life.

It's both simple and miraculous at the same time.

Workshop Format

Awakening through Reflection

First of all, you are already perfect in every way. Each of us is inherently perfect, regardless of the apparently imperfect conditions of our body or mind. Regardless of what we have been told or led to believe, inside each and every one of us is a faultless being just waiting to be revealed in all of its glory, power, and unlimited potential. Have faith that there are no limitations, physical or mental, that can prevent this perfection from manifesting. All you need is a strong desire to bring forth the creative potential that lies within you. You also have to be willing to make the effort, of course, but I can tell you that it's much easier than you might think!

When you come to realize that all creation is perfection in motion and you are a created being, then you can recognize that you are perfection in motion as well. To reinforce this belief, all you have to do is look at the natural creation around you. Look at a rose in full bloom: so perfect, so beautiful. And the rose is compelled to become just that! From the moment it springs forth from the earth, it is determined to become a perfect work of art! It reaches for its source of life, the sun, knowing with certainty that all it will ever need to survive will be provided for. The rose has only one purpose: to manifest itself for the benefit of others. All that is required is that nothing interferes with its natural process of divine expression. Interference is the only thing that could possibly stand in the way of nature expressing its pure and perfect potential. The potential for perfection is there from the beginning, just like it is in you.

This pure and unlimited potential to create lies within each and every one of us, here and now. It is just waiting to be realized and set into motion. Once it is, the possibilities are endless! But it's natural to ask: *Why all the interference?* Why is it so challenging to realize our full potential? Why do so many obstacles have to be overcome before we are free to fully express ourselves as perfectly created beings? I believe it's because the world is a kind of classroom in which our obstacles teach us important life lessons on our way to a realizing a higher way of being. Without interference or diversity, there would be no comparative, no learning experience. In order to experience and appreciate happiness, one must know sadness. In order to experience and appreciate health, one must have sickness.

Fortunately, we can choose happiness instead of sadness, and we can choose to improve and sustain our health. In the face of interference, we can

1

choose to surrender and transcend, or we can choose to become a victim of our circumstance. Whether we realize it or not, we are manifesting all of our experiences for the purpose of evolution. Our soul's mandate is to progressively evolve toward perfection. We arrange for difficult beings and challenging circumstances to appear so that we can develop divine traits like patience, compassion, and forgiveness. In essence, they give us the opportunity to develop the highest traits of our true nature.

The divine spirit within us is inherently perfect but our human ego is intrinsically imperfect. We can and do identify with both our spiritual nature and our human ego. Our divine spirit fills us with the radiant light of our true self and breathes life into our being. Our human ego gives us a form and an identity that allows us to interact with the world around us. We are spiritual beings having a physical experience. The purpose of incarnating is simply to give us the unique experiences we need for our progressive evolution toward perfection. Within each of our earthly experiences, there are important lessons that we've been sent here to learn. Fortunately, we receive guidance from our higher self and our spiritual guides who know what lessons we need to learn. Because we have a strong connection to our higher self, as an aspect of it, we intuitively know what we have come here to learn as well. On a subconscious level, we are attracting the people and experiences that will teach us these lessons. When we become more enlightened and aware of our life lessons, we can consciously create the experiences that are necessary for us to learn and grow.

With this mindset, we can begin to reflect on our life knowing that all of our experiences have served a divine purpose: the progressive evolution of our soul. This will help us approach these reflections with a broader and more enlightened perspective. I want you to have fun with this process and although it may be difficult at times, it is a very effective way of embracing the precious moments forever and letting go of the more painful ones for good!

Self-Exploration

You are about to embark on a cathartic and introspective examination of your life. For this 10-day workshop, we will be focusing on the memories from your past that stand out as transformational or transitional. For the purposes of this book, I am focused primarily on adulthood however this is your reflective experience to consciously create in the way that is most beneficial for you. If you feel you would like to begin your experience with events or turning points in your childhood, I encourage you to do so. I recommend that you stay focused on specific experiences within which you can identify a cause and effect relationship — that is, vivid turning points that influenced the choices you have made in your adult life.

As an example, let's take a story from my mother's life that she has openly shared. When she was growing up and going to school, she was one of the tougher girls brave enough to stand up to the bullies. She would always defend the girls who were afraid of them, especially against the most aggressive males who would constantly tease them. In her adult life, she became very dedicated to defending women's rights in the workplace. This is an obvious cause-and-effect pattern for her in this lifetime.

To begin your reflection each day, you will be asked to close your eyes and scan the memories that mark different time periods in your life. As you do this, related personality characteristics may stand out. There may also be significant events or periods in your life that have left a strong impression on you and influenced the decisions you have made or the path you have chosen. It is important to identify these in order so that you can reveal your authentic nature and identify patterns within your life experiences. There may be some childhood memories that require a greater understanding of yourself before you can reconcile them with your adult experience. Therefore, it may be more beneficial for you to begin your reflection within the parameters of your adult experience and then as you do so, the developmental years of your childhood may make more sense to you. Once it does, this opportunity to harmonize your childhood with your adult life will reveal the synchronicity of events and allow you to see more clearly why they had to happen just as they did. This will open the door to forgiving yourself and others for things you might regret or still resent. It will also help you recognize the heroes and angels that you have been blessed with along the way.

The main focus of this workshop is to identify the major transformational stages of your life and find the lessons hidden within them. You will also have the opportunity to take a closer look at your relationships and uncover the significance they have had for you on your evolutionary path. Important choices you have made regarding education, career choices and personal relationships will be examined to see if they align with your authentic nature and true calling.

It will also be necessary for you to think deeply about the mistakes you have made and any regrets you may have so you can reconcile them and forgive yourself. Maybe you have deep–seated resentment or anger toward others in your life that you need to resolve. By taking a closer look at the true nature of these conflicts, you can determine what their underlying purposes might be. Often times, the more challenging people and circumstances are the best teachers of all and that's why it's so important to identify the lessons they are teaching you. I know for myself, that this process has allowed me to transform resentment into gratitude as I realize the valuable lessons I learned from each experience. This transformative process of identifying patterns and reconciling experiences with their true cause and effect nature is liberating and empowering. It will give you a whole new perspective on your life and you will welcome challenges and embrace opportunities in a much more enlightened way!

If you participate fully and consciously commit to the interactive nature of this workshop, I am confident that your perceptions of reality and your place within it will be dramatically enhanced. The level of consciousness within which you view your reality will be significantly elevated! In this higher state of consciousness, the deeper meaning and greater purpose of your existence will become crystal clear. From this higher perspective, you will be better equipped to see the exquisite synchronicity of the symphony of your life. Once you see that even the most difficult experiences were necessary to balance karma, and therefore help you progress on your evolutionary path, you will see them in a whole new way. You will find that the easy experiences and the neutral people didn't help you to progress and build character nearly as much as the difficult and more challenging ones.

After I began to recognize the divinity within the experiences of my life, I developed a strong faith that everything happens just as it should and for a good reason. Trusting in the divine plan has made me feel much more at peace with the events that unfold around me. I know that I have projected these experiences in order to learn the lessons I need for my soul's evolution and refinement. Also, now that I am more capable of taming my mind and controlling the emotions of fear, anger and resentment, I am not experiencing those emotions reflected back to me. As a result, I naturally create more harmony and encounter less difficulty. This perspective has made my life so much smoother and more enjoyable. I've also become acutely aware that, as I project compassion and kindness, these divine traits are reflected back to me. This is true across the board and rarely does it fail me. When it does, I am able to see the symbolic nature of the experience and then identify my own personal emotions that, left unguarded, created conflict. Negative feelings, or trapped emotions, that still need my attention and repair are exposed. From this perspective, I am then grateful for the conflict because it revealed lessons I still need to learn. I can commit to learning those important life-lessons right then and there and avoid re-creating another experience just like it! It's really that easy. All you have to do is be introspective about the things that take place in your life, contemplate their meanings and apply it to a greater understanding of yourself. Once you know yourself better through this process of self-exploration, it will get much easier and come more naturally.

My spiritual journey has exposed many personal truths and revealed even more human truths about the nature of creation and evolution itself. My sincere intention is that this adventure through *reflection, exploration, and realization* will bring you much closer to your own personal truths as well. I am confident that they will be revealed to you as you reflect upon the synchronistic nature of your experiences. Along the way, you will see how they parallel with the collective experience of life. As you begin to appreciate the harmonious rhythm of all of creation, you can tune in to the true symphony of life and bring more peace, happiness, abundance and joy into it!

Let's get started by taking a quick look at the workshop format:

Life Experiences

I will be your trail guide for this part of the adventure and as such, I will lead you down my path first by sharing personal stories that will move and inspire you. My joys and sorrows will become your own as you find echoes of those things that parallel your experiences or trigger important memories. As I climb out of distressful times and rejoice in better ones, I hope you will do the same. I want to go on this adventure together and that's why I have made it interactive. We are having much more of a collective experience on this planet, through the shared field of consciousness, than we are an individual one. As I uncover my own strengths and weaknesses, successes and failures, you will find yours reflected in them.

Cause & Effect / Lesson Analysis

By applying the "cause and effect" analysis to our mutual reflection, we can identify the lessons we have come here to learn. This brings us one step closer to actually mastering them and then we can move on to more advanced ones. This is how we create with purpose and evolve with intention! While we do not want to dwell on the past, and we most certainly want to live in the present moment and look toward a brighter future, the past may hold the keys to our greater happiness here and now. Sometimes it's better to open up an old wound if it was never fully healed. We can treat it with the proper cleansing so that it can heal perfectly. Then we can just forget about it and move forward unscarred by the past. We can consciously evolve and that's what we're here to do – evolve toward a higher consciousness where we can unleash our highest potential!

Choices

So let's head out and explore where we've been, see the choices we've made in the past and discover our true calling in the present. By the time we reach the end of the workshop, we will be much more capable of making conscious choices that will benefit our lives now and in the future. Using our free will wisely will contribute to our spiritual evolution and we will find ourselves walking on the ascension path – the one that leads to the top of the mountain where we can have a much broader perspective!

A Personal Note on Reflection

It is my strong desire that by reading and interactively experiencing this book, through my own personal reflections, you will become determined to seek and discover your own revelations. By reflecting honestly and with introspection upon your life experiences, you will discover their symbolic cause and effect nature. This will allow you to see your life more clearly as a series of learning experiences designed to further your spiritual evolution. In this way, you can reflect upon your experiences as teachings that have had to be repeated time and again until finally they are completely understood and applied. Also, this deep reflection on your most transformative life experiences will reveal your true nature and divine purpose. The experiences you recall from the past which you feel guilt or shame about can be dealt with honestly, not with justification but with pure compassion.

You will develop an understanding that, as a human being, you are only capable of performing actions in accordance with where your consciousness is, or was, at the time. This level of sincere compassion for thoughts, actions or words that were less favorable to your own pure nature can be forgiven-truly and with finality. This allows for personal advancement and spiritual progression. A leap in one's spiritual evolution takes place when one is able to forgive him or herself completely. It may be helpful with those words or acts that may have caused harm to admit them aloud while looking in the mirror. This mirror ritual becomes very significant as you admit, confess and then forgive yourself for past wrong doings. You can express compassion for yourself as a human being by saying for instance, "I forgive you for all past mistakes and wrong doings. I recognize that you are a fallible human being and were doing the best you could at the time with where you were at in your mind. I have sincere compassion for you and I love you. You are forgiven completely. I forgive you and I love you."

Engaging in this reflection will also uncover the many altruistic words and actions that you have said and done. Embracing these positive memories of the past are just as important as letting go of the negative ones. Make sure to write these down in detail and recognize in them your true nature as a thoughtful, compassionate and generous person. I recommend you do a mirror ritual to reinforce these positive attributes, saying for example, "You have chosen many compassionate thoughts and words and acted in many kind, considerate, and loving ways. You have revealed your true nature as a pure being with the highest intentions of love and purity." This is your authentic nature and it is always available to you. Accessing this highest part of your self is always possible through the practice of sincere mindfulness in every moment of every day and in every thought, word and action. You will be rewarded greatly for your efforts as these intentions will be returned to you in many profound and beautiful ways. You will increase the level of joy, happiness, gratitude and love that you experience every day by being mindful and wise about your choices. You will be inspired to do this out of pure love for yourself and others and learn to apply mindfulness and wisdom to your life every moment of every day from now on.

I have found this type of self-reflection to be extremely beneficial to my spiritual growth in many ways. Self-realization is a process that requires uncovering personal truths about yourself and those around you. Your experiences in this lifetime are the clearest pictures that you have of your own personal evolution and recalling them in detail, good or bad, will help you paint that picture so you can know yourself more deeply. Once these experiences have been recalled, you can let go of the negative ones and cherish the positive ones. You are moving forward with the positive attributes which reflect your true nature and discarding the negative ones which are false and untrue, making them unreal in reality. Love is the only reality. Everything else is man-made and false. The purpose of this workshop is to embrace pure love and let go of guilt, shame, fear and all of the negative emotions of hatred, anger and resentment. You will learn to replace them with love, compassion and forgiveness and this will allow you to move on to a higher place living from a more enlightened mind.

Through the cathartic process of transforming energy from negative to positive, you will make significant progress on your spiritual path. You will become more 'self-realized'. To enhance this process, I encourage you to dig up old photos and memorabilia as you move through your reflections. This will increase the healing power of the workshop and make it more interactive. This may also inspire you to reach out to friends or loved ones you have not spoken to in a while. You may want to share fond memories with them or repair broken fences. You may find yourself laughing or crying, expressing gratitude or apologizing. Before reaching out, however, make sure that whatever you want to share is beneficial for you both. Sometimes bringing up the past is not conducive to your well-being (or the well-being of others). In some cases, sending a greeting or apology through intentional thought may be best.

The most important thing to remember is that you are on an adventurous journey of self-discovery. "To know thyself" on a deeper level can be a profound and life-changing experience if you remain open to it. Along the way, you will discover your own distinct 'uniqueness' by highlighting the activities that have always given you the most enjoyment and recognizing those that do not. By looking for those aspects of your nature that have revealed themselves repeatedly over the course of your lifetime, you will be able to make a distinction between those that have rewarded you with positive emotions and those that have caused you to suffer. Your true calling is aligned with those activities and pursuits that generate enthusiasm and excitement. Your highest self is revealed in those which ignite your passion and reflect your true nature. This is the path that you want to follow and base your current pursuit of happiness on. The things that you have engaged in that did not give you pleasure, fulfillment or joy are just as important to highlight. Use these to construct the path you do not wish to follow. If some of these reflect the path that you are on now, you can make a determination to take the next detour and get back on the higher path as soon as you can. You are painting a clear and colorful picture of your highest self. To find a deeper meaning and greater purpose in your life, by following the direction of your higher consciousness, is the ultimate goal of your life's journey.

Recognizing that the pure being that lies within you is a gracious, compassionate and loving soul, and making the effort to stay mindful of this, will bring you inner peace and great joy. As you express your inherent nature of love, kindness and compassion toward others, you will find it reflected back to you. Life will become more fulfilling and pleasurable as you attract like-minded people into your space who are also full of grace and kindness. You will be highly rewarded for every minute that you devote to this attainment. You will find that the quality of your life is enhanced in many ways and on many levels when you make a sincere effort to express your true nature and live from your highest self!

WORKSHOP FORMAT

Karma Consciousness

Guidelines for the "Cause & Effect" Reflection Process

Before engaging in the process of applying a karmic cause-and-effect analysis to our experiences, it is important to understand how this will help us evolve into a more enlightened state of being. At first, this whole practice of reflecting appears to be a trip into the past which some may feel is opening up old wounds or digging through old storage that has already been boxed up. By looking through old storage, often times, people find real gems that they wish to save and cherish realizing that it has significant benefit for them now and in the future. So instead of being a rehashing of past events, it is both a healing and a treasure hunt. It allows us to move forward free of scars and, at the same time, discover the precious gems that were hidden in storage all along!

By bringing our consciousness into these past events, we are bringing them into the light and out of the darkness. In Eckhart Tolle's book *The Power of Now*, he quotes St. Paul as saying, "Everything is shown by being exposed to the light, and whatever is exposed to the light itself becomes light." From this, we can see that just shining a light on important events in our past, in essence "reflecting" upon them, we are one step closer to enlightenment as we learn to transmute the energy of our "past-consciousness." The gems within these reflections are the lessons and that's what we are really in search of.

By understanding the cause-and-effect relationships within these experiences from the past, we can identify the lessons we have come here to learn. We can stand outside of ourselves and witness the events in a more objective way by applying a contemplative analysis to them. This is an excellent way to develop our ability to be a witness to our behavior in the present as well. By witnessing our thoughts, words and actions, we can monitor them more closely and thereby separate virtuous from non-virtuous ones. Now we are getting somewhere! This is how we become more enlightened in the present by highlighting the past! If we can uncover the motivation behind our actions in the past, distinguishing virtuous from non-virtuous intention and attaching these to positive and/or negative outcomes, we can attain the highest benefit from this karmic cause-and-effect practice.

Karma has been described as a Sanskrit term meaning "action." Through the actions that we perform, we produce effects which bring us either happiness or suffering. The effects of positive actions bring us happiness and the effects of negative actions cause us suffering. So what we are seeking to identify here is the relationship between our actions, or causes, and the resulting positive or negative outcomes, or effects. Then we can apply this "cause and effect" understanding to the habitual patterns of our life today, thereby mastering the lessons we have learned! As a divine and creative being, we have the ability to manifest our experiences,

and direct and control them, with the power of our thoughts and intentions. This becomes especially important when, through cause-and-effect, we identify our lessons based on the outcomes of our actions. Our perception of actions as either virtuous or non-virtuous are often based upon the conditions of our programming. What we believe is right or wrong, considerate or rude, helpful or harmful, and so on... stem from the consciousness we have developed during this and past lifetimes. Even during this lifetime, we go through phases where at one stage, we think and act one way and then later, we have a completely different perspective about what is right and wrong and may think and act altogether differently! Either way, we can always transform our consciousness by bringing it into the light and reflecting upon it. We can intentionally purify it and start to 'mold it' by defining it with established moral and ethical values that will benefit our "karma" in this lifetime and the next.

Let's take a look at Robert Thurman's book *Jewel Tree of Tibet*, and see what he has to say about "The Practice of Mind Reform" because that's what we're really talking about here. By reforming our mind, we are demonstrating an effort to consciously evolve. This evolution of consciousness motivates us to create only the best experiences by using our highest thoughts and applying our best behaviors. Under the chapter, "Mind Reform," Robert gives us the following advice):

- Be consistent, carefully mindful, and impartial
- Use force (of intention) to abandon addictions and develop virtues
- Overcome excuses for self-preoccupation
- Consciously prepare for difficulties
- Don't rely on extraneous coincidences
- Change your attitude but remain natural in behavior
- Don't criticize the faults of others
- Don't meddle in others business
- Don't expect rewards
- Avoid toxic food
- Don't spoil practices with selfish motivations
- Be critical of yourself, and don't stubbornly hold grudges
- Don't tease people maliciously
- Don't wait in ambush
- Don't go for the jugular
- Don't overload or jeopardize others

- Don't always try to get ahead, and don't exploit the Dharma teachings
- Don't turn God into a demon by being spiritually preoccupied
- And finally: Don't seek happiness through others suffering

It becomes increasingly apparent that we must take full advantage of this precious lifetime by applying mindfulness and practicing virtue in all of our thoughts, words and actions. We can start by understanding our tendencies, personality characteristics and motivations better through this process of "Reflection." Getting to know ourselves in this way will help us avoid those behaviors that do not represent the highest virtues and develop those that do. Now that we have outlined some of the virtuous and non-virtuous mindsets and behaviors, let's take a closer look at some of them. Most of us can probably identify our behavior in the past (and maybe even in the present) with some of the non-virtues even if it is to a small degree. When I began to study Buddhism, one of the things that appealed to me was that your bad behavior wasn't seen as punishable by a judgmental deity. Instead, it just became your 'karma' - something you have to live with and either benefit from or suffer from as a result. My mother told me that growing up she was always afraid of the big man in the sky who was judging everything she did and said, which would make her feel guilty about even the slightest things. Of course, this would lead to the fear of being punished. I prefer this concept of being 'accountable' for our own lives with the understanding that we are only benefiting or harming ourselves. There are however similarities when it comes to the value of confession. I am not familiar with the Christian view of repentance or redemption so I will not discuss it. I am somewhat familiar however with the Buddhist concept of confession so let's take a look at that.

My sister gave me a little book called *The Bodhisattva's Confession of Moral Downfalls*. When she first gave it to me, I thought, "Wow, she must really think I need to confess some stuff!! I wonder what she thinks I've done wrong!" Then I admitted to myself, "Ya, I have some stuff to confess. As painful as it might be, I'm sure it will do me some good." And so I did. And it was painful. But it definitely was good for me. The most amazing benefit was that I stopped dwelling on bad things from the past that made me feel guilty and ashamed. Even bad dreams that would bring up past people and events started to dissipate! It worked! Then when I started to understand more about karmic cause-and-effect and was able to reconcile these relationships, I came to the understanding that it all had a greater purpose: To teach me the lessons that I needed to learn so that I could evolve, learn and grow. These are the things that motivate me to write this book! As a witness to the value of spending time in contemplative thought (and even in confession), I know that these practices lead to a more enlightened mind - one that harbors less suffering and experiences more pure joy, love and happiness. That is my most sincere desire for you, the reader.

So there you have it. I believe this will be a good start. We can see how the cause and effect analysis shines a light upon the past, bringing it out of the darkness, and how that alone begins to transmute its energy from negative to positive. We also understand that lying hidden amongst our experiences are precious gems. These jewels are the valuable lessons that upon being learned, lead to our souls evolution. With that being our highest purpose in this lifetime, we can see that it is well worth the time and effort to engage in reflection to find them.

Note: I have provided lined pages for you to use as a journal however, I recommend that you also have one of your own handy in case there isn't enough room for all of your thoughts and feelings. I do not want you to feel limited in your expression by the lack of space available. Please take advantage of those times when your thoughts are flowing to write as much as you can. Journaling is very cathartic and reflecting in this way, embraces the whole spirit of the workshop!

I admire you for seeking to live your life in a more enlightened way and am proud of you for participating in this process of reflection. I know that it may be difficult at times but be courageous and know that it is serving your highest purpose.

The Spiritual Essence

I am blessed to have many friends who share my "desire to inspire." The message we wish to convey is simply that each and every one of us is an aspect of the One Great Self and, as spiritual beings, we can all access the pure love and ecstatic joy that flows from this infinite source. Our common goal is to help others bring these divine aspects of themselves into their everyday experience of life by providing clear and simple guidance that can be easily applied. To help guide us through the lessons we are learning in this workshop, I have reached out to one very special friend who has made a profound impact on my life. Her name is Janet Myatt and she is a spiritual counselor and a divine healer. With a Master's degree in Educational Psychology, she combines her academic knowledge with her psychic intuition to develop a comprehensive understanding of the human spirit. For many years, she has been studying and discovering the truth behind the interplay of the divine spirit and the human ego.

I met Janet a few years ago when I decided to seek out a psychic intuitive who could help me progress on my spiritual path. I wanted to connect with my higher self and with the divine beings who were guiding me. I wanted to increase the quality of my meditations so that they would be more revealing. I went on the internet to search for an intuitive in my area and that's when her website popped up. When I pulled up her site, I found a picture of her which I enlarged and left on my screen for a while. It was more important to me that I felt a strong connection to her energy than it was to research her credentials (which were impressive). With long golden hair and bright blue eyes, I thought she looked like an angel. She actually looked etheric as the light of her spirit radiated on the screen. I knew that she was the one that could help me progress on my path. When I called her, she didn't pick up and so I left a voicemail. Shortly thereafter, I felt inspired to take a walk out in nature where my connection to spirit is always greater. I took my phone along in case she called back. While I was walking, I was visualizing her face and trying to connect with her energy on a spiritual level. At high noon, just as I had sat down in the soft grass to meditate, the phone rang. I instinctively knew that it was her. The first thing she said was, "I heard you calling me. The light on my voicemail was flashing but, even without listening, I knew that the message was from the spirit who was beckoning me." From that moment on, I knew we had made a strong connection both physically and spiritually. That was the beginning of what would become a powerful friendship.

Janet showed me how to enhance the power of my meditations. Her techniques gave me access to the spiritual realm I was seeking. The spiritual energy between us was strong and during our sessions, we would connect with divine beings in higher realms who would guide us both on our ascension path. I was making significant progress and becoming more radiant every day. As the light of my spirit began to shine brightly, those around me took notice. My demeanor also improved as I walked in the light of spirit. I began to radiate love and light everywhere I went and I expressed compassion, patience and understanding toward everyone I encountered. Those around me wanted to know more about the spiritual path I was on. They too wanted to experience the joy and peace that I had found and I knew that I wanted to share it.

I began to refer people to my friend, Janet, and she inspired each and every one of them. I knew in my heart, however, that spirit had something much more collaborative in mind for us. As I listened to my higher guidance, it became clear that we would work together on an inspired project that would enhance the lives of many. During this time, I had a powerful epiphany in which a divine message was revealed to me that the meaning of life was simply to create and the purpose was to evolve. The day after this revelation, I was compelled to sit down in front of my computer and begin typing. I became aware that I was being guided by spirit and as such, was engaged in an automatic writing experience. What I 'downloaded' on that day was a workshop designed to help others realize their full potential by intentionally creating and consciously evolving. I knew that I was meant to co-create this workshop with my friend, Janet. Together, we designed a powerful program to enhance the physical, mental and spiritual well-being of the participants. The workshop modules included clean-eating and purification for the body, thought awareness for the mind, and guided meditation for the spirit. Developing and presenting this workshop ignited my own passion to intentionally create and my inherent desire to consciously evolve. I knew that I had found my true calling! I knew in my heart that I would dedicate the rest of my life to helping others create and evolve. I would unite those who shared the same passion and together, we would enhance the well-being of many others. I knew that the key to reaching one's highest potential was to integrate the power of the body, mind and spirit.

Since then, I have presented many workshops and written three books. The testimonials from my workshops were so inspiring that it motivated me to expand my reach by writing "The Up Trilogy" with one book dedicated to the body, one to the mind, and one to spirit. I can honestly say that, without Janet's guidance and friendship, I may not have awakened to spirit with such a passionate calling. By deepening my connection to spirit, she helped me access my higher self and the divine beings who are guiding me. This is the source of my inspiration. Whenever I teach or write, I am always being guided by this higher intelligence and their guidance is always based on the highest intentions of pure unconditional love for all beings. All of the divine beings in the spiritual realm want to help the souls who have incarnated to flourish and grow. They want us to be happy and joyful. They want us to be peaceful in our hearts and minds. They want to help us realize the power of our creative intelligence and the ability to manifest our experiences. They want to help us learn and master our life lessons so that we can move on to more advanced teachings. They want us to consciously evolve so that we can make progress on our path of self-realization. Most importantly, however, they want us to experience the power of love and the beauty of life in every moment of every day. They want us to adore the creation and each other. They want us to laugh and have fun and spread joy and peace. They want us to unite in our efforts to create a better world full of compassion and understanding. They want us to be patient and kind towards each other. They know that once we begin to apply these highest virtues, we will ascend on our paths. We will walk in the light of spirit and radiate love to all living things and beings.

On the ascension path, life takes on a much deeper meaning as we fulfill our divine purpose. The meaning of life is to create and the purpose is to evolve. That is the divine message I received from my spirit guides on one very magical day. The purpose of this book is to help you create meaningful experiences based on your life lessons so that you can intentionally evolve. Naturally, I have called on my friend Janet for her spiritual guidance and valuable insight. She will help to identify the teachings that come out of the most challenging periods of our life. Over the course of this 10-day workshop, we will be exploring themes that occur throughout our lives. Based on my own experience of life, I have identified 10 different topics that have defined my evolutionary path. Knowing that we share common patterns in our lives and that we all face similar challenges, I have chosen these topics to guide you on your path as well. The topics I have chosen are as follows

1. Transformation
2. Transition
3. Closure
4. New Beginnings
5. Harmony
6. Healing
7. Reawakening
8. Synchronicity
9. Suffering
10. Death and Dying

I have asked Janet to help us reveal the lessons that are hidden within these types of experiences. Every day she will share her insight in "The Spiritual Essence." As you move into the "Realization" phase of the workshop each day, her observations will guide you toward a greater understanding of the meaning and purpose behind your experiences. She will help you to expose the cause-and-effect relationships between the events that have unfolded. This will allow you to see why they happened just as they did. What you will discover is that the purpose is simply to teach you the important life lessons that you came here to learn. I am grateful to Janet for all she has taught me and am very pleased that you have the opportunity to learn from her as well. I have told her many times, and I mean it from my heart, that she is a blessing to all.

I would like to share the following excerpt from an interview that we recently did together:

SUZANNE: I would just like to take a moment to share how you and I came together. I shared this in the introduction to my book as well. I write about how my desire to progress on my path and to have more profound meditations led me to search for a spiritual teacher on the Internet. When I found your website, I instinctively knew that you were meant to have a powerful impact on my life and you have. Doing one-on-one sessions with you and collaborating on wellness workshops has been very illuminating. You have taught me, and many others, how to walk in the light of spirit and I am very grateful for that.

JANET: Well, I'm glad to hear that but it's also been a two-way street because you have had a tremendous impact on my life as well and that's the nature of divine work. As we give, we receive and as we receive, we give. It's very balanced, I believe, in that way. It's the nature of the divine work and the divine connections, you know. I'm grateful that I have had the opportunity to work with you and to be of service at the same time. You coming into my life has likewise, been a blessing.

Self-Realization

Before we can begin the journey of self-realization, we have to ask some important questions like: "Who is my true Self?" and "How do I come to know my Self?" Essentially, the "Self" or soul is who we are at the deepest level, beyond our ego identity. I like to think of the Self as an aspect of my eternal soul, and the source of life within my being. It is who we are without our body or name or labels like, "mom, sister, lawyer, athlete,…" This isn't always easy to accept. We may accept that our true Self is not defined by the name we were given at birth or the labels that describe our different roles, but understanding that this Self is separate from our physical being isn't quite so simple. To fully grasp that our true Self has little to do with our physical body is difficult in a society that puts so much emphasis on it. On top of that, we are just very attached to our physical body and it identifies us as "who we are" in many ways.

In Buddhism, there is a simple practice of visualizing each body part being taken away one at a time to show that, even without these parts, you are still essentially "you." I saw a very disturbing movie once called, "Boxing Helena," about a model who was kidnapped and tied to a chair and one limb at a time was removed until she looked like a box. I couldn't help thinking of this image while I was performing this Buddhist visualization. Disturbing as it was, this vision really helped me get the point of the practice! I mean, here she was a beautiful model, right? Her entire identity was attached to her physical beauty and this is how others related to her as well. She would have spent most of her time focusing on, and tending to, the beauty of her physical being. Every day, posing in front of a camera and walking down the runway, the entire focus would be on her appearance. It would be the primary definition of who she was and she would be very attached to her physical being. She might think, "My silky hair, my lovely face, my shapely body – this is who I am. I am a beautiful person and others see me that way." Now suddenly she has no arms and no legs and is no longer beautiful in the physical sense. What remains? Well, she still responds to the name "Helena" and she recognizes her thoughts as her own. She still has the same memories and personality that she developed throughout the course of her lifetime. With the exception of her altered physicality, she is still the same "person" inside. She is still essentially who she was before - even without the body she was so identified with. I realize this is a disturbing example but it almost has to be this dramatic in order to really drive home the point that "you are not your body." Believe me, as a Personal Trainer for the last 20 years, this was not an easy concept for me to grasp either! I still work in a large health club full of people whose identity is closely tied to their physical appearance. It's how we see ourselves and how others see us, or even recognize us, after all!

Even though our appearance is a form of self-expression, you can't necessarily tell how someone is on the inside just by their outer appearance. In fact, many times the physical body masks the person's true identity as they try to fit into society's standards by wearing the latest fashions and copying the most recent trends even if they don't match their personality. Remove all that, however, and you still have the true essence of the person underneath it all. It's like when people ask their mate, "Will you still love me if I get fat?" The sad truth is that some can't answer honestly and when and if their mate does get fat, maybe they don't love them as much and might even leave them! They are still the same person, fat or not, for goodness sakes, and need love and support now more than ever, but it just shows how much society identifies with the physical form. If you and I are going to proceed down this path of self-realization, we have to start by detaching ourselves to some degree from identifying so much with our outer being in order to get more in touch with our inner one.

Eckhart Tolle refers to pure consciousness as being the "self beyond the form." He instructs us to try and accept the "I am" identity of ourselves instead of identifying with our form (or forms in general for that matter). Once we understand that all things and beings are living spirit expressing itself, we can start to move beyond the identity with form and begin appreciating the soul essence of ourselves and others. We can do this but it does require effort to move beyond the habitual perception of form that has been so ingrained since birth.

When we first come into this world, we are still very connected to our spiritual essence and the veil between the spiritual and physical realms is still very thin. Many young children still remember who they were in a past life and can easily communicate with the spirit world. This veil has been called the "veil of forgetting" and it enshrouds us like a shield against past-life memories so that we can fully embrace our identity in this one. As soon as we open our eyes and absorb the light of our surroundings, our identification with form begins. Upon seeing the faces of other beings and observing material things, the veil between worlds begins to thicken. As we become an infant and then a toddler, the veil gradually shields us from spirit so that we can focus our attention on our ego identity and the lessons of this lifetime. By the age of six or seven, for most children, the veil has become thick enough to prevent them from seeing and communicating with spirit directly and their consciousness is projected solely in the physical realm. This is when the spirit realm becomes unreal and the physical realm becomes their only reality.

Spirit is the true essence of our being. Once it becomes housed within the physical body, however, our identification with form becomes very strong. It becomes who we are – an individual who is separate and distinct from all others. This identification with our form as a separate being can be defined as our "ego identity." Our senses keep us very attached to our physical form and our body becomes the focus of our identity. In the course of our busy lives, we have a tendency to forget about the spiritual essence of our being. Our ego-identity and sense of "separateness" strengthens our individuality and weakens our connection to spirit and to the spiritual essence of all other beings. If our spirit is who we truly are (separate from our ego) we must make a conscious effort to know our true spiritual Self. This will allow us to fulfill our divine purpose by creating a life that aligns with our true Self. This is what will bring us the most joy and create harmony in every aspect of our lives.

To start down the path of self-realization, we have to begin detaching from our ego-identity, learning to focus off our physical form and see who we are beyond that. We have to transcend our body and our labels and realize that what is left is our spiritual essence. In quiet contemplation, we can be alone with our thoughts. At first, our thoughts are mostly focused on our ego-identity and all of its attachments to the physical world along with all of the relationships and responsibilities we have in it. The first goal then becomes quieting our mind enough so we can let some of these thoughts go.

I so often hear, "There's no way I can meditate" (with emphasis on the I) implying that meditation is for other people whose minds aren't as busy as theirs or that they have some special condition that prevents them from engaging in such a practice. Besides, they're too busy anyways. They are too focused on their attachments in the physical realm, is what it comes down to, and drawn in by all of the sense attractions to it. There is always down time that could be spent in other more meaningful ways. A good test I use is to engage them in a casual conversation and then, at some point, ask about their favorite shows on T.V. I watch them light up as they go into a full-blown animated description of the latest reality T.V. show and I just nod my head knowingly. This is not a "gotcha," it's a simple nudge that they really do have a little free time that they could be spending in a much more useful way. Let's see, "reality T.V. or fulfilling my divine purpose to consciously evolve in this lifetime," hmmm....

Well, congratulations! Here you are! You have already evolved in this lifetime! You have come to the realization that to grow and learn and progress is our divine purpose. The Buddha reminds us that we have to make the most of this precious lifetime as a conscious human being in a physical incarnation! This type of incarnation gives our soul a special opportunity to progress along the evolutionary path. As I understand it, not all souls get to have a physical experience and when other souls ascend from theirs, they can't wait to hear all about it! In Buddhism, they also emphasize the immediacy of death and the transient nature of all things. What it comes down to is that, if we are going to make the most of this precious life, we better take advantage of every opportunity to grow and flourish because "times a wastin'!" On that note....

Let's start by connecting to spirit. You can begin by just focusing on the simple act of breathing. Seated comfortably in a quiet place, free of distractions from the outside world, just close your eyes and begin the practice of breathing: consciously inhaling and exhaling through the nostrils. As distracting thoughts arise, visualize placing them on a cloud and sending them away so that your mind is like a clear blue sky. To prevent such distractions from arising, make a sincere effort to direct all of your attention to your breathing. The act of counting may help to narrow your focus: start by counting to five on the inhalation, holding for five, and then exhaling for five. This also promotes rhythmic breathing. Repeat this until you become relaxed, and then you can increase each count to seven. Seven is a significant and powerful number that will strengthen your connection to spirit. Feel the air caressing your upper lip as it moves in and out of your nostrils. Connect to this sensation and begin to visualize the air flowing into your nostrils as bright white light. Upon inhaling, the light fills your head and consumes any darkness lurking in the shadows. As you exhale, you release any dark shadows in the form of grey smoke. The darkness represents the distracting thoughts of ego. Do not attach a negative connotation to this darkness. It is just the presence of ego-energy that is distracting you from connecting to spirit. Inhaling the white light and exhaling the darkness fills you with the pure consciousness of spirit and releases the distorted consciousness of ego. The positive emotions of love, gratitude, compassion, and forgiveness are pure, and the negative emotions of stress, fear, anger and resentment are distorted. The more pure energy you breathe in, thereby releasing the convoluted energy, the more relaxed and peaceful you will become. At this point, you can start identifying with your pure spirit by simply asking yourself, "Who am I?" Think deeply about who is having this experience.

You can deepen the experience by imagining two columns of light — one extending from the crown of your head ascending into the heavens above, and one leaving the base of your spine and descending into the earth below. This will help you, as your "middle self," connect with your "higher self," or Divine Spirit, (your origin and destination) all the while sustaining your connection to your "lower self" - the spirit of Mother Earth (your foundation). Start by imagining a bright white light descending from the heavens and spiraling into the crown of your head. You can imagine a violet disc spinning clockwise at the top of your head which acts like a portal through which this light can enter your being. As the white light enters, it swirls through your forehead clearing away any distracting thoughts and any negative stress or emotions. As the white light replaces the darkness of these emotions, imagine it literally pushing the darkness down as the light descends into your neck, shoulders, chest and abdomen. As the light descends and replaces the darkness, all of your muscles relax and any pain or discomfort simply dissipates. Imagine the light now swirling through your pelvic region and down into your thighs, moving into your knees and calves and down into your ankles and feet. All the while, the dark energy is exiting your body through the soles of your feet where it dissipates. You can imagine your entire being sparkling with pure white light. You are now vibrating at a higher frequency. Light vibrates at the highest frequency and, as a being of light, you will sense this higher vibration. This is the pure energy of your spirit expressing itself. When you connect with the feeling of this higher frequency, you are connecting with the spiritual energy that is the essence of your being. You will feel a sense of total well-being consume you. Your breathing will be rhythmic and soft. You will experience a deep inner peace as you resonate with this frequency. You may also feel connected to the spiritual essence of your surroundings as you realize the vibrational nature of all things and beings.

This is the beginning of self-realization as you become aware that the true nature of all forms in reality is simply vibrational light. This light vibrates at different frequencies giving forms their color and density. This light is the way in which the spirit expresses its 'self' as it paints the colorful picture of reality in all of its forms of energy and matter. You are this creative spirit! All things and beings are an expression of the creative spirit and this spirit is within you and all around you. You are a creator and as such, you are painting the picture of your reality with the power of your thoughts. That's how you, the creative spirit, creates – by intentionally directing your thoughts into the vast field of consciousness just waiting for your instructions! The power of your emotions is the fuel that ignites your creation.

To enhance your belief in the power of your spirit, repeat the following verse out loud or in your mind. Make a sincere effort to connect deeply with the meaning behind the words as you say them.

I have the infinite power of the Great Spirit within me.

Divine love is working through me here and now to create this.

The Spirit within me is creating miracles in my life.

I am one with the Great Spirit.

My higher self is guiding me in everything that I do.

The Spirit lives within me and manifests in the world through me.

I give thanks to Mother Earth for nurturing me and sustaining me.

The Light of the Spirit surrounds me. The Love of the Spirit enfolds me.

The power of the Spirit flows through me

where ever I am.

The Spirit Is and

All is Well!

— Shakti Gawain [1]

Enjoy harmonizing with this higher frequency until you feel yourself reconnecting with the physical realm. You will know when it is time to reconnect with your ego identity and the physical world around you. When it is time, direct your attention to your feet as they become physically dense once again. Imagine this density returning to your being as it ascends into your ankles, calves, knees, thighs and pelvis. Continue to imagine your body returning to its physical form as the density of your body returns to your abdomen, chest and shoulders, extending down your arms and back and up into your neck, chin, face and forehead. Open your eyes and take in your surroundings. With a deep inhalation, absorb the smell of your environment. Listen for any sounds that you can hear. Move your tongue around and lick your lips. Place the palms of your hands firmly on the floor to feel the ground beneath you as you reconnect to your foundation. With your senses re-engaged, your attachments to the physical realm, and to your ego identity, have been reestablished.

Although you have returned to the physical realm, you have deepened your connection to the spiritual one. Once this bond has been consciously made, you will remain connected to it and you can access it at any time just by drawing upon it. You have made a strong connection to spirit and opened your conscious self to receiving guidance from your higher self. Your higher self will use your emotions to guide you and in a higher state of awareness, you will be able to follow this guidance as necessary. Positive emotions which excite and inspire you are a sign from your higher self that you are expressing the highest thoughts, words and actions. These are the passionate emotions that help you to progress along your path of self-realization.

Whenever your emotions become disturbing and negative emotions arise, this is your higher-self letting you know that your ego is in the driver's seat now. All you have to do is take a deep breath and redirect your thoughts. Close your eyes and visualize your higher self in the passenger seat tapping your ego on the shoulder and saying, "Excuse me, but I will be taking the driver's seat now. You are welcome to sit beside me. I respect your place in my life as a protector and survivor and I respect the identity of my physical being. However, I will now receive guidance from my higher self which allows me to replace negative emotions with positive thoughts." Breathe in the white light of these positive emotions and allow them to enter your being as you exhale the darkness of the negative ones. Restored by this new sense of self, you can move forward in a higher state of consciousness. The more that you apply this practice and bring your higher self into your daily life, the stronger your connection to spirit will become. You will begin to radiate light and literally feel a lightness of being. You will feel more connected to the living things and beings around you and develop a deeper appreciation for their spiritual beauty. Your sense of awe, wonder and curiosity about the world around you will increase and your senses will become amplified as sights, sounds and textures become more vivid. Everything will seem more alive and vibrant as you harmonize with the world around you. You will naturally begin to resonate at a higher frequency in this state of increased awareness. You will begin to have a knowing about the true nature of reality as an illusion of light swirling and vibrating in a symphony of color like a mosaic of images constantly moving and changing.

Walking meditation is another great way of increasing the awareness of your senses and deepening your connection to spirit. While walking through nature, make a point to consciously engage your senses by noticing the bright colors and distinct smells of everything around you. Feel the wind caressing your skin and reach out and touch the leaves and flowers. Kneel down, pick up a rock and hold it in your hand. Try and feel the energy emanating from it. Run your hand along the surface of the earth feeling the texture of the dirt or grass. As you do this, you will feel love and gratitude toward Mother Earth and develop a sense that she is a conscious being providing sustenance and beauty for the benefit of all of her children. On this walking meditation, send loving thoughts to any creatures that you see. You might be surprised by their reaction. I have had birds follow me, butterflies land on me and even bugs stop and look right up at me! I know then that my spirit has made a direct connection to theirs. I know I am connected to the creative spirit within me and all around me.

As you are moving forward on your walk, try and imagine that you are actually standing still and that the scene around you is moving past you. This is a powerful practice that will give you a greater sense of the true nature of the illusion we call reality. This will give you the sense that reality is more like a moving picture that is being absorbed by your senses allowing you to "experience" it. Your senses enable you to interact with this reality by heightening your awareness of it. This keeps you attached to the reality around you making it seem so "real" but when you become the observer, you are able to detach from it and see it for what it actually is: colorful light vibrating at higher and lower frequencies, giving form its definition and density.

Eventually the illusion of reality becomes more like a movie with colorful lights moving and changing and forms swirling and dancing around you. As we progress along our path of self-realization throughout this journey, you will begin to realize that you are directing this show and that, with the power of your intentions, you are creating the moving pictures that define the experiences of your life. By learning how to do this effectively, and with pure intentions, you will be empowered to become the creative spirit that you truly are. Just like Shakti Gawain says, you are "One with the Great Spirit." The power of it flows through you and the light of it surrounds you. The essence of this spirit is pure love. Connecting with it will bring you more happiness and joy than you ever thought possible and that's what we will do on this journey. As we apply breathing techniques and use basic meditation in our daily practices, our goal will not only be to "connect" with spirit but also to "direct" spirit by creating a reality aligned with our true self.

Creating a Sacred Sanctuary

We all need a place, free from distraction, where we can just sit and be quiet. I have led many people through meditation who've shared with me that they don't have a place like this. For many, their car has become a sanctuary of sorts. Far from being undistracted, it is still a place where they can be solitary and listen to spiritual audio CDs or just enjoy the silence. Some will drive to a quiet spot, even a remote parking lot, so they can sit in their car and meditate. This is especially useful for those who wish to engage in meditation prior to going into work or before returning home. Obviously, this is not ideal but it does serve the purpose and gives those who live in busy households an escape. I recommend that, if they use their car as a sanctuary, that they bring along sacred objects like pictures, beads, crystals or a cross. Obviously this isn't an ideal location for lighting candles!

Realizing that some of my students could only find refuge in their vehicles, I began to suspect a larger issue; Many were hiding their spiritual pursuit from their family members. I have no judgment about this and realize that, for some, sharing their desire to become more spiritual may have to be a gradual process. I intuitively feel, however, that the act of hiding entails some deceit which cannot be conducive to one's path. Openness and honesty are crucial to spiritual growth and must define one's existence if they are to progress. Those who love you will support you if they have a clear understanding of your intentions. For most people, simply saying, "I want to be a better person and I feel drawn to a path that includes a healthier lifestyle and quiet time to reflect." It can be just as simple as that. Emphasizing that this choice will benefit the quality of your relationship with family members will help them understand and support you as well. It helps to clear the pathway of understanding and harbor the support you will need. This is a good time to establish a quiet time and place in which those who love you will give you some space. You just have to be strong in your determination and stand firmly in your conviction. Negotiating to support a personal interest of theirs might be helpful. Of course, you never know, they might take an interest in what you are doing and want to know more. Please understand the concept of "allowing" however, which encourages you not to judge the way others choose to live their life or impress your spiritual beliefs upon them unless they inquire. The best that you can do is to live by example. Gandhi said, "My life is my example." When your loved ones start to observe the positive changes in you, they will develop more appreciation for the path you have chosen. When they see that your practice is benefiting your life and theirs in many beautiful ways, they will encourage you to continue whatever it is that is making you more peaceful and patient, joyful and happy, loving and compassionate.

Once you have established a quiet place and time where you can reflect and restore, you will need to create a sacred sanctuary. Even if it is something that you set up and take down every time, it is well worth the effort, I promise. I recommend that you set a goal of spending at least 20 minutes a day in your sacred sanctuary. This is a case where more is better but I want to be realistic for those who are just beginning or have very busy lives. The first and most important aspect of your sacred space is that it is clean and free of too much clutter. You may want to have a special rug that you sit on, or a pillow to prop up your behind. If sitting on the floor is too uncomfortable, a chair will do just fine. Just make sure your chair is not a recliner. It is important to sit up straight and yes, to stay awake! Sitting up straight will not only keep you more alert, it is conducive to the flow of energy in your spine. Choosing the objects that you will place in your sanctuary is purely intuitive. I suggest that you sit quietly and think about what objects inspire you the most. I have chosen pictures of the spirit guides and archangels who I feel most connected to. I also have a picture of Jesus and a statue of Buddha. I have included objects from nature that have significant meaning for me. I believe that crystals are a form of "crystallized consciousness" that promote and enhance the flow of spiritual energy. Whenever possible, I light a candle in recognition of our primal connection to this fundamental element. I have red rocks from Sedona, Arizona where the spiritual energy swirls in powerful vortexes and pinecones from Lake Tahoe where the mountains radiate with divine energy. I have also framed a couple of special prayers which help set the tone for my practice and when I sing or chant them, it raises the vibration of the energy in the room. Increasing the vibrational energy in your space can be very powerful and you can do this simply by singing or humming. Of course, using a bell or gong, or even a Tibetan singing bowl, is effective but it can be disturbing to other household members. The purpose of raising the vibration is to raise your level of consciousness. You are seeking to bring the light of spirituality into your presence. Light resonates at the highest frequency and so does spiritual energy. Raising the vibration will benefit your spiritual practice. There are other techniques of visualization and meditation that we will explore in the next chapter which will also produce this effect.

I wrote a poem about my shrine that I would like to share with you:

My Shrine

The sacred shrine I have created

In the Deities presence I am elated

My picture of Jesus, the Holy One

My candle whose flame is just like the Sun

My rock represents sweet Mother Earth

I honor your creation, the place of my birth

The mirror which I can see myself in

My eyes reflecting God that's within

The clear water inside a virgin chalice

The Bible, the word, fills me with bliss

My idol, the Buddha of compassion

Pure love and peace his only mission

Archangel Michael always protecting me

Against any lurking lower energy

And finally my crystal whose prism of light

Always fills my heart with pure delight

In the presence of all these beautiful things

I am so inspired that my heart, it sings

A prayer of hope for unity and pure love

Please radiate peace from your home above

I honor and bless all the loving beings

Truly grateful for the joy their presence brings

I thank you God and each day I pray

That all your children will find their way

Back to their home, the divine origin

Reunited with love - the God that's within

—Suzanne Ross

WORKSHOP FORMAT

By using your intuition to create your shrine and opening your heart and mind to the process, your space will become sacred. The pictures and objects that you place there will enhance the divine energy and every time you practice there, this energy will intensify. This private space will become more sacred the more you use it. This space will literally become a sanctuary for your soul. In this space, your spirit will have the freedom to express itself and to explore its divine nature. Spiritual guides will assist you in deepening your connection; Some may make themselves known to you by entering into your consciousness. Depending on how open you are to receiving this guidance, you may become aware of their identity. You may even wish to call upon certain guides or deities whom you feel an intimate connection with. I suggest that you always visualize loving angels in every corner of the room as a way of inviting positive energy and loving support during your meditation.

You are accessing spirit and opening a portal through which it can flow, so I suggest that you protect yourself from any lower energy by calling upon these angels and asking them to remain present at all times. Archangel Michael will gladly protect you from any lower energy if you simply ask him to. Since I practice my own personal philosophy of "Eternalism," which merges belief systems, I believe that I receive guidance from Buddha, Jesus, and the Ascended Masters. I have developed my practice to the point where I am aware of who is present and when. I can tell by their distinct energy and personality and also by the guidance I am receiving. Your practice will be a very personal and intimate activity and your faith and intuition will guide you.

Just close your eyes, quiet your mind, take deep rhythmic breaths and remain open to whatever comes into your consciousness. Once you learn to let go of the distracting thoughts of your ego self, your higher self will emerge in all its glory. Your spirit guides will rejoice in your decision to call upon them. The creative spirit within and around you will radiate with vibrant energy in a celebratory fashion as you embark upon and progress along your spiritual path. The creative spirit, as the Divine Mother, wants all of her children to enjoy an abundance of health, wealth and happiness. As you begin to draw from this creative spirit more and more, your creative potential will expand wildly in all directions. Your life will unfold in miraculous ways as you harmonize with the creative spirit in and around you. You will recognize divine synchronicities falling into place in your higher state of awareness. In this state, you will be open to seizing these as opportunities to create and expand into your most authentic self. These are like signposts on your path pointing you in the right direction. Your passionate response to these doorways, which are opening and inviting you, is your higher self applauding your progress. All you have to do is open to spirit by engaging in the practices of breathing and meditation in a sacred space of your own. Once you unleash your creative spirit, anything is possible and dreams that before were only fantasy, begin to emerge right before your eyes. In my live workshops, I use a visualization called, "The Golden Dream" to help people realize that their dreams can become their reality and that the only thing limiting them is their own beliefs. I have included it here, along with the "Great Spirit of Light" meditation as a way for you to develop faith in the power of spirit and belief in your infinite potential.

What is the Golden Dream?

The Golden dream is your fantasy reality. In this fantasy, you can have anything you've ever wanted. You can be anything you've ever hoped for. You can go anywhere you've ever dreamed of and you can experience anything you've ever fantasized about. Just close your eyes for a moment and picture your fantasy reality. What do you see? Do you picture wealth and riches? Are you thinking, well, if I had lots of money, I could have anything, be anything and go anywhere. Then I'd really be happy! I am going to challenge you to go deeper. How about the Golden dream of you? What does the fantasy you look like? Do you picture yourself taller, thinner, richer, more attractive, more successful, more well-liked and accepted? Why don't you have everything you ever wanted? In a world where anything is possible, why aren't you living your fantasy reality as your dream self?

Ask yourself: Why am I limiting myself and experiencing a narrow reality in which I believe I am only capable of achieving a certain level of success, having a certain level of abundance, and looking and feeling only moderately well? Are you ready to shatter these limited beliefs about yourself and the reality within which you live? The universe you live in is infinitely abundant and you can have access to as much of it as you desire. You have unlimited potential to be, to do and to have everything you have ever dreamed of. You just have to learn how to tap into that potential and become the creator of a new reality in which the possibilities are endless.

By following the evolutionary path, you will not only believe that you can create this reality, you will begin to know it and experience it. Once you discover your creative powers of manifestation along with your inherent desire to experience joy, inner peace and pure love, you will begin to experience the Golden dream. Are you ready to create your fantasy reality? Of course you are! Let's get started down the evolutionary path of creation! To get started on this path, begin by creating your sanctuary. Once your sacred space is created, you can initiate it by engaging in the practices of "The VIS-MED Method." This method includes a series of special techniques I've designed to help you receive spiritual guidance as you reflect upon your life experiences. This guidance will enable you to uncover the lessons hidden within your experiences and reveal the true essence of your "self." Connecting with your higher self, and the higher consciousness of your spirit guides, will greatly enhance your ability to clearly see the deeper meaning and greater purpose behind all of your experiences.

Remember my divine revelation:

MEANING: TO CREATE
PURPOSE: TO EVOLVE

Reference

1. Shakti Gawain, *Creative Visualization*, Nataraj Publishing, a division of New World Library, Novato, California, 2002,1995,1978, Part One: Basics of Creative Visualization

The VIS-MED Method

Dynamic Movement, Inspirational Breathing & Visualization/Meditation

I designed "The VIS-MED Method" as a creative way to help you connect with the greater field of consciousness, be it your higher self, the collective consciousness or universal mind. Starting with "Dynamic Movement Therapy," you will stretch, bend and reach to open and expand your body. This will help you open and expand your mind as well. Next you will perform "Inspirational Breathing" techniques that will help increase the flow of oxygen to your whole body, including your brain. This will help to clear your mind and increase your ability to focus. Then, you will find a quiet place to sit where you can focus your attention without too many distractions. The guided visualization will help you transcend your current reality so that you can project your mind into the past where your memories are stored. This is sometimes referred to as the universal mind and within it, your personal memories can be accessed by calling upon your higher self. Through visual and vibratory practices, you will be connected to your higher self and the true meaning and greater purpose behind your experiences will be illuminated. Enlightened by this guidance, you will be ready to engage in contemplative meditation so that you can explore your reflection more deeply.

In a colorful and imaginative way, you will engage your five senses to re-create your reflection. You will imagine yourself actually present during the time of the experience and picture yourself interacting with others. You will be able to see the meaning behind the experience more clearly and discover the lessons it was meant to teach you. You can go one step further and re-create your role in the experience. If you feel that you could have said or done anything different that would have been more favorable and virtuous, re-create the experience to reflect that. You can even re-create the reactions of others to put them in a more favorable light as well. This is a way of clearing the negative energy from the experience and shedding a positive light on it. You will find that this enhances your ability to forgive yourself and others by remembering only the positive aspects of the entire experience. Once you have clearly identified the lessons within and balanced the karmic entanglements, you can return to the physical realm and journal your experience more enlightened and empowered than before!

If you remain focused and make a sincere effort, the truth behind your life experiences will be revealed. Your love and compassion toward yourself and others will increase as you release the entanglements of the past. We are all entangled in this web together and if the threads are strengthened by the power of love and forgiveness, our bond will remain strong. We will find ourselves united by the gravitational force that binds the web which is, of course, pure unconditional love. Be prepared to have spectacular experiences and awe-inspiring revelations!

Make sure to have your journal handy in case the pages provided here cannot contain the depth of your experiences. Every day of your reflection will bring you one step closer to the realization of who you are, why you are here and where you are going. This is the divine purpose of the 10-day workshop. I encourage you to fully engage in each and every magical moment of this adventure with your heart and mind wide open.

The following segments: "Dynamic Movement Therapy," "Inspirational Breathing" and all of the daily meditations are available as an audio download from my website *www.suzannerosstranscendence.com* as this is a much more conducive way to follow along.

Dynamic Movement Therapy

These therapeutic movements will open and expand your body to prepare you for opening your mind and expanding your consciousness during the visualization. They will also help to reduce the distractions of the ego as you free-flow through the movements using your own creative expression. You will begin to feel as if you are connecting with your expansive spirit as you add your own unique flair to the moving therapy.

1. Start by standing with your feet slightly apart and your arms down by your side. In a sweeping motion, bring your arms out to the side, inhale, and bring your palms together overhead. Now exhale as you bring your palms down into your chest in a prayer position. Inhale and extend your arms directly overhead, then separate your palms as you exhale and lower your arms back down to your sides. Repeat this movement three more times.

2. With your feet spread wide and your arms extended straight overhead, inhale and reach both arms over to the left, bending at your hips as you exhale. Now inhale and return to the center with your arms directly overhead. Exhale and drop over to the right now, extending both arms over and bending at the waist. Inhale and return to the center. Repeat this movement — exhaling and dropping over to the left, inhaling and returning to the center and then exhaling as

you drop over to the right — three more times. Then lower your arms down by your side and breathe normally.

3. With your feet just hip -width apart and your arms down by your side, inhale and sweep your arms overhead and then exhale as you fall forward and reach for your toes. Now inhale as you slowly roll up, one vertebrae at a time, sweeping your arms overhead and then exhale as you lower them down by your side. Repeat this movement three more times.

4. Stand with your feet slightly apart and your arms down by your side. Inhale and sweep your arms up, palms together, and then exhale and bring your arms down by your side as you lower your body to the floor and take a cross-legged, seated position. Place your palms facing up on your knees with your thumb and index finger touching.

5. Inhale and sweep your arms up, palms together, and on the exhalation, bring your arms down as you exhale and twist to the left. Place your left hand behind you and your right hand on your left leg. Look over your shoulder and inhale. Return to the center and exhale. Repeat this torso rotation on the right side and then return to the center. Repeat this movement three more times.

6. Now extend your legs directly in front of you. Inhale and extend your arms directly overhead and lengthening your waist, exhale and fall forward reaching for your toes. Inhale and roll up, as you spread your legs wide and keep your arms extended overhead. Exhale and fall over to the right reaching for your right foot. Inhale and rotate your body so that your chest faces your thigh, exhale and reach for your toes. Staying bent at the waist, inhale and sweep over to the left. With your chest facing the left thigh now, exhale and reach for your left foot. Inhale and return to the center bringing your feet together and your arms down by your sides.

7. Now pull your knees into your chest and wrap your arms around them, interlocking your fingers just under your knees. Inhale and drop your head down. Exhale and fall back, rounding your spine. Inhale and pull your chest toward your knees looking up and then exhale, drop your head and fall back, rounding your spine. Repeat this movement three more times.

8. Now place your hands on the floor to support you as you gently lie back. Lying flat on the floor with your legs extended and your arms down by your side, take several deep breaths. Now hug your knees into your chest and gently rock right and left, massaging your lower back. Take slow rhythmic breaths as you rock back and forth. When you are ready, release your knees, drop them both over to the right and extend your arms out to the side. Hold this position and breathe rhythmically. Now drop your knees over to the left and hold that position as you take several breaths. Return to the center and extend your legs straight out. Bring your arms down by your side with your palms facing up.

9. Now close your eyes and just focus on your breaths. Perform nostril-belly breathing: as you inhale through your nose, distend your belly to the count of five and then exhale and draw your belly in to the count of five. Repeat this several times until you feel tranquil and relaxed.

10. When you are ready, circle your feet outward and then reverse and circle them inward. Point your toes and contract your calf muscles holding the contraction. Now release it. Press your knees into the floor, contracting your thighs. Hold the contraction briefly and then release it. Now press your pelvis into the floor, contracting your abdomen, and then release it. Press your shoulders into the floor, contracting your chest muscles. Hold the contraction and then release it. Lift your arms slightly up off the ground and spread your fingers apart, contracting all of the muscles in your arms. Hold the contraction and then let your arms drop to the floor. Tighten all of the muscles in your face, pursing your lips and squeezing your eyes shut. Now relax all of the muscles in your face, letting your tongue relax and your eyes fall back. Relax your cheeks and your forehead. Reach up and massage your head, stimulating your scalp briefly, and then return your arms down by your side. Take a deep inhalation and on the exhalation, feel your entire body completely relax into the floor beneath you. Focus on your breathing as you softly inhale and exhale. When you are ready, come to a seated position. You are now ready to engage in the "Inspirational Breathing" practices.

Inspirational Breathing

To inspire not only means to illuminate and enlighten; it can simply mean "to breathe." Inspiration and expiration are terms that are sometimes used to describe inhaling and exhaling. Dr. Justin O'Brien pointed this out during a wellness retreat I attended. He has graciously given me permission to use the following excerpts and instructions from his book, *"The Wellness Tree."* In his book, Dr. Justin O'Brien describes the many benefits of various breathing techniques and the ways in which our breathing reflects and influences our state of mind. He says that *Breath is the thermometer of life* [1] and offers this insight:

> *Learning to voluntarily manipulate the energy of your breath means that you can consciously influence your thinking and govern your emotions. Mood always yields to the behest of breathing. When you change your breathing, you change your mental outlook. Your breath always mirrors your mind.* [2]

During his retreat, Dr. O'Brien offered four different types of breathing techniques. I've incorporated two of these into my pre-meditation practice. He recommends that we begin with "diaphragmatic" breathing (I call it nostril/belly breathing). You will be inhaling and exhaling through your nostrils only during this exercise. He suggests that you place one hand on your belly and the other one on your chest during this breathing exercise. This will help to ensure that you are performing it properly. On the inhalation, it is important to distend your belly, and you should feel it rise. On the exhalation, you should feel your belly fall. If you feel your chest rise and fall instead, you are not performing this belly-breathing technique properly.

Once you have established a rhythmic pattern of belly breathing, you can move into the "Cleansing Breath." This technique involves a forceful exhalation followed by a normal inhalation in which your belly rises. Dr. O'Brien teaches that you should hear a rushing sound through your nostrils as you perform a quick "expulsion" (as if blowing your nose). On the inhalation, make sure your belly rises. You will repeat these cleansing breaths five times in quick succession and then just take five normal breaths. Repeat this one more time performing five cleansing breaths followed by five normal breaths.

"Inspirational Breathing" (pre-meditation) includesdiaphragmatic or **"Nostril/ Belly breathing"** and the **"Cleansing Breaths."** Upon completion of these two breathing cycles, five long breaths will transition you back into soft, natural breathing.

Dr. O'Brien offers a clever acronym to describe the benefits of breathing:

B - balances metabolism
R - relaxes muscular tension
E - energizes cell life
A - alleviates psychological stress
T - toxicity declines
H - heals body and mind [3]

I offer my sincere gratitude to Dr. Justin O'Brien for these therapeutic breathing practices. He is a fascinating gentleman and known as a pioneer in the exploration of wellness and consciousness. He has written several books in the area of consciousness and personal development.

References
Justin O'Brien, PhD, *The Wellness Tree*, Yes International Publishers, St. Paul, MN, 1990, 1993, 2000, 2008
1. pg. 55   2. pg. 54-5   3. pg. 65

Now you are ready for the "VIS-MED"!

The following **"Great Spirit of Light" VIS-MED** has been offered to demonstrate how guided visualization can be used to illuminate past experiences and how contemplative meditation can be used to balance and purify the karmic energy associated with the past. The reflection at the end helps you bring your creative self into the journaling experience. You can also be guided through this meditation by downloading the audio version of it from my website at ***www.suzannerosstranscendence.com/Up!Trilogy/ WakeUp!Meditations.***

Seated in a comfortable posture, close your eyes and follow your breath: breathing in through your nose while distending your belly and exhaling through your nose by pulling your belly in. Continue to repeat this style of nostril-belly breathing. Feel the coolness of the breath on your upper lip as it flows in, filling your lungs, and then flows out, emptying them. Breathe in and out at least 10 times like this or until you feel tranquil and relaxed. Call upon your spiritual guides, angels and archangels to guide you and protect you through the process of connecting to spirit.

Now imagine a line of spiraling energy being released from the base of your spine and traveling through the earth until it reaches the very center of the planet. Imagine a crystal heart at the center of Mother Earth and connect with it. Then bring that line of spiraling energy back up from the center of the earth through the fire and lava, breaking through the crystallized rock and gold-flecked dirt until it penetrates the ground beneath you and connects with the base of your spine.

Imagine the power of this energy spinning a bright red disc at the base of your spine. This disc is your root chakra and it represents the consciousness of survival and free will. As it spins, you are filled with a strong sense that you are a survivor and have the ability to create at will. Now visualize two electric blue cords ascending from your root chakra, braiding your vertebrae, and connecting with a second disc, your sacral chakra, located behind your sexual organs. The power of the electric blue cords spin this vibrant orange wheel which represents the consciousness of desire and creation. The power of this wheel fills you with the desire to create a bounty of abundance for yourself and others. The spiraling blue cords continue up your spine to your third chakra which is a bright yellow disc spinning behind your navel. This wheel represents the consciousness of power and control and spinning it gives you a strong sense of empowerment. You feel as if you can and will use your creative power to manifest whatever you desire with the highest intentions.

Now imagine the blue cords traveling up your spine to the fourth chakra, behind your heart. The power of the electric blue cords spins this fluorescent green wheel, filling you with a sense of unconditional love for all things and beings. The power of this love is so expansive that it includes all living beings on this planet and beyond. Now visualize the blue energy spiraling up toward the base of your throat where your fifth chakra is located. This is your communication chakra and it sparkles with pale blue energy, just like the color of the sky. Spinning this wheel opens the line of communication between you and your higher self. It increases your sense of communion with others and improves your ability to express yourself clearly. The electric blue cords now spiral up the back of your head and spin the sixth chakra behind your forehead. This is your wisdom chakra, and it is a deep indigo-blue energy that ignites your soul. All of your memories from the beginning of time and all of the knowledge stored in the field of consciousness can be accessed by spinning this wheel. You know that this knowledge holds the keys to unlocking the mysteries of the universe and that you will put it to good use. You will use it to reveal your own divine source and uncover the true nature of your existence.

Now the blue energy travels to the crown of your head and spins your violet chakra, opening this portal to divine consciousness and cosmic intelligence. The light that enters your being through this portal is the sacred light of the source. This gives you a direct line of communication with the creative source of the Great Self. Spinning this wheel unites your soul with the omnipresent and omnipotent spirit. You have become one with the Great Spirit and the Divine Source.

Meditation

Now, in this enlightened state, you are ready to reflect upon your transformative experiences with greater insight. Bathed in the light of spirit, you will see the experience more clearly. You will look upon it with the loving compassion of your higher self and with the wisdom and intelligence of your higher mind. In this higher state of consciousness, you will have the opportunity to observe any past experience from above. Looking down upon it as the observer, you can identify the causes leading up to it and the effects that it had on everyone involved. From this higher place, you can send love and forgiveness to both yourself and the others. With a greater understanding of how and why these experiences occurred just as they did, you can balance the karma attached to it by replacing the negative emotions with more positive, loving ones.

You can actually transmute the darker energy attached to any experience by shedding light upon it. Just imagine pulling all of the darker energy from the experience into your heart flame, where it is burned up and then simply dissipates. Inhale and pull any darker energy from the memories of your experience into your heart, feel the intensity of it briefly and then burn it up and feel liberated! Repeat this visualization, inhaling the dark energy of resentment, blame and anger into your heart and then extinguishing it, followed by exhaling the pure white light of love, compassion and understanding. This is a form of spiritual cleansing. Repeat this process of balancing and cleansing until you feel that you have purified and released the experience. Hold the memory of this experience in your mind with clarity while you focus on the lessons, causes and effects.

Reflection

Journaling your experiences from the past can be very cathartic. As your feelings and emotions flow out onto the pages, you are releasing them. You are shining a light on them by bringing them alive on the pages of your journal. This gives you an opportunity to relive them as they were and then to re-create them with a more enlightened perspective. Using your five senses, and your creative imagination, you can reenact every sight and sound, detailing their color and texture, as you walk through these past experiences. Illuminating them in this way will help you peel back the layers of the experience, and allow you to step back and see the cause-and-effect relationships of each event as it unfolds. Once the synchronicity is revealed, the lessons within will become clear. You can see why everything had to unfold just as it did. You will also see the characters within your experiences as teachers, and you will be grateful for their guidance. This is your opportunity to be as creative and colorful as you can. Let your creativity flow from your imagination and let your emotions flow from your heart and mind.

Self-Reflection
Journaling as a Form of Creative Expression

I have found that when I engage in visualization and meditation, my creative potential expands and flourishes. I become inspired to write poetry and express myself creatively in many different ways. I also find that my perception of reality becomes more vibrant and alive. As I look up at the sun, I see it as a symbol of unconditional love shining brightly on everyone without discriminating. I have great reverence for the awesome power of the sun and it inspired me to write this verse.

Ode to the Sun

Oh Sun, the source of light and love
I am so blessed you shine above
You awaken my soul each brand new day
God's pure omnipotence in every ray
Oh Sun, your brilliance is so very grand
Shining across the sea and down upon the land
Thank you for illuminating all living things
You are the source from which all life springs
Within the prism of your brilliant white light
You radiate the image of every colorful sight
Oh Sun, I am grateful for each bright new day
And promise to express it in every possible way
Just like you radiate pure love and light
I will do the same all day and every night
For you inspire the very core of my being
Without your luminosity I wouldn't be seeing
The truth that has enlightened the depth of my soul
In God's omnipresence I am now whole.

— Suzanne Ross

WORKSHOP FORMAT

After meditating, you have a unique opportunity to realize your own creative potential. This is a great time to journal! Share your deepest emotions and express them with the most descriptive words you can find. If you have some negative energy to release, do it. Then reflect upon it and replace fear, anger and resentment with love, compassion and forgiveness. Use your sense of humor as much as possible. Seeing the humorous side of your life helps you to lighten up! That's one of the primary purposes of this workshop — to release toxic thoughts and behaviors and replace them with more enlightened ones — so you can lighten up!

As you move through your experiences, the causes will reveal themselves and the effects will be apparent. This analysis will lead you directly to your life lessons. As the lessons become clear, especially the ones that repeat themselves through multiple experiences, you will begin to create a lesson plan. As you accumulate daily lesson plans, you will begin to see a pattern and a master plan will unfold that contains the major themes of your life. This is what my friend Janet calls your "blueprint."

As I understand it, we come into this world with baggage, just like landing in a new destination with bags full of the stuff you brought from home. The baggage that you come here with carries lessons you still need to learn on your evolutionary path. You have a choice to make; you can allow your ego mind to control your thoughts and govern your desires, or you can intentionally create meaningful experiences in order to express your highest virtues. In this way, you can consciously learn your lessons and move forward on your path. You will move out of the darkness and into the light as you progress along your path of self-realization. You will discover the true nature of your being and realize that your authentic self seeks to express the highest virtues and engage in activities that benefit all of mankind.

Once you step onto this illuminated path, you will never look back. Once you become more enlightened, you will want to share your feelings of joy and harmony with everyone around you. You will want to enlighten everyone as to the true meaning and purpose of their existence by revealing the spiritual essence of life.

It reminds me of what my dear friend Ron told me just before I went into a "Mantra Initiation" with my guru. He said, "Fasten your seatbelt, Suzanne, you will never see reality in the same way again" and he was right! I walked out of the initiation and into the garden. I looked all around me at the brilliant colors of the flowers and plants. I looked up at the sun and felt the wind in my hair. I heard the birds chirping in the trees and the squirrels rustling around in the bushes. I knew, in that moment, that there was one life force that permeated everything. There was one consciousness creating and I was one with it. I stood there and said out loud, "I am" and then I said, "I am that I am" meaning I am the creative source that is! Then I just smiled and said, "All is well."

Tread lightly, my friends, and absorb every magical moment for all that its worth. Bless you for taking this journey with me . You are fulfilling your destiny as a divine being radiating the light of pure love.

Practical Spirituality

Throughout the introduction to this workshop, I have expressed my belief that the meaning of life is to create and the purpose is to evolve. This is based on a divine revelation that came to me a few years ago. I believe that we can intentionally create the experiences that will help us to consciously evolve, but how is that done? By basing these experiences upon the lessons we have come here to learn, I have provided a specific process by which these lessons can be revealed and applied. This involves living in a higher state of awareness in which we are very present with our thoughts, words and actions. Then we can consciously direct them according to the lessons we need to learn. As we uncover our life lessons, it becomes clear that they are centered on a higher way of living and being. This enlightened way of being is reflective of a higher consciousness which we refer to as our "higher self." By making an intentional effort to draw upon our highest self when applying these life lessons, we are expressing our divine nature. When the progressive evolution of our soul has become our highest priority and we are intentionally creating our experiences accordingly, we are fulfilling our divine purpose. This leads to the question:

"How do we intentionally create the experiences that we need to consciously evolve?"

As divine beings, we have the inherent ability to create our experiences according to our desires. We can manifest anything we desire just by visualizing it in our minds and feeling the passion in our hearts. This is how we create with a strong intention. When we envision what we wish to create and express a strong desire to do so, our subconscious mind gets the message loud and clear. Our subconscious mind is sub-ject to the thoughts in our conscious mind. It responds by creating whatever we focus our attention on. In this sense, we can basically "think things into being" and transform our thoughts into reality. If spirit can see that our desires serve a higher purpose, it will set things in motion on a universal level. With the highest intentions in mind, we can co-create the "thought-forms" that are necessary for our soul's evolutionary progress. Based on our passions, we will discover our true calling and with the power of these emotions, we can create everything we need to make our dreams come true. Once we get the hang of it, magical synchronicities will unfold all around us and we will find ourselves successfully fulfilling our true purpose! Wayne Dyer once said, "You have to believe it to see it." This is definitely true when it comes to manifesting with intention. You must have faith!

Faith in your ability as a Creator is essential!

Your ability to concentrate will also be extremely helpful and you will develop this skill during the meditations. By engaging in the visualizations, you will learn how to project your thoughts according to your intentions. You may even begin to see that everything in creation is essentially a thought-form projected from the mind of the Creator. As an aspect of the Creator, you have the same creative potential to manifest form by projecting the thoughts in your mind. To strengthen your faith, I have chosen to share my beliefs about our divine potential.

We are all "thought-forms" in the mind of the ultimate Creator. If we imagine that the entire field of consciousness within which all of creation exists as the "mind" of the Creator, than we can grasp the concept that we are essentially "thought" transformed. He thinks everything into being by projecting his loving thoughts; wherever he wishes to manifest things and beings. Spirit activates these forms by breathing life into them. They become illuminated by the living spirit within them. Living beings are each endowed with an energetic pattern, or personality, that is unique to them. We are all energetic vibrating patterns of light and love. When we learn how to project our consciousness, we are actually directing a beam of vibrating light that contains the patterns of our thoughts and intentions. This light has the power to manifest based on the instructions it contains. Like our Creator, we thus have the power to "transform" thought into form.

It's like fiber optic cables that transmit "data-filled" light between communications systems. This information travels at the speed of light between its origin and destination. We are sending "data-filled" light when we project our consciousness with a strong intention. Just like the Creator, we can manifest thought into form by projecting the light of our consciousness. But it's best to consult with a higher source before creating. We have to remember that the omnipresent spirit has a much broader perspective than we do. It knows what's best in the big picture of interconnectivity. That's why it's wise to call upon our higher self rather than relying on our ego. Here's where faith comes in again. Sometimes, we may not understand why things are happening the way they are. We may get frustrated and think, "Why isn't that person responding?" or "Why didn't I get that promotion?" If we are co-creating with spirit, we must have faith that there is a good reason for what happens, and that there is something much greater in store for us. With faith in spirit, we know in our hearts and mind that:

Everything is as it should be.

This doesn't mean that we just "Let go and let God." We still have to actively pursue our goals and diligently apply ourselves. If our aspirations are based on the highest intentions, however, spirit will always lend a helping hand. The divine purpose of being is to co-create on the path of self-realization. The whole purpose of creation is based upon the Creator's desire to "know thyself" through experiences in both the physical and spiritual realms. Therefore, he devised a divine plan to create worlds that would expand into eternity and evolutionary beings to inhabit and experience them. The Creator increases his "knowledge of self" through our experiences in these worlds. He is the One Great Self - the One Infinite Source of creation – and we are all aspects of his personality. We are each a "point of view" from which he can observe the eternally expanding experience. As a unique point of view, we can provide the Creator with the best experience possible by accessing our highest self. As beings in the physical realm, we are projections of our higher self which exists in a spiritual realm. Our higher self projects many aspects of its self throughout the various realms of creation. In this sense, we are one of many selves existing at the same time. Our higher self "ensouls" all aspects of its projected selves just like the Creator "ensouls" all of his creation. We have a direct connection to our higher self and to the One Great Self. This is because they are one and the same. I want to emphasize this point because I want you to know that you have the same ability as the Creator to create at will. You are a creator and you have the divine potential to do, be and have anything you truly desire.

To help you access your divine potential, I have created a series of daily practices to help you learn to create from spirit rather than from ego. Spiritual fulfillment will bring you everlasting happiness while ego will only bring you temporary happiness. That's why we want to create based on the spiritual guidance we receive during meditation and reflection. I have included this section on "Practical Spirituality" to help you merge your divine being with your ego identity. This will help you transform your intentions into the realization of your true self. You will begin to create meaningful experiences based on your life lessons that will bring you more joy, peace and happiness than you ever thought possible.

There is no great secret to manifesting. It's simply a matter of directing your thoughts with the highest intentions. If your desire is to create something to benefit yourself and others, you will receive plenty of assistance from spirit. This is an endlessly abundant source of health, wealth and prosperity! The Creator wants all of his children to enjoy the abundance of his infinite creation. Ask and you shall receive my friends. Just remember that the key to manifesting spirit into form is the purity of your intentions. If you have unconditional love in your heart, spirit will be on your side and you will become love in action! The people that you need to fulfill your divine purpose will be attracted to your light and together you will co-create your shared intentions. This exponentially increases your creative power!

One last thought: Be grateful every day for all of the blessings in your life. Be grateful for your health, your home and your loved ones. Be grateful for the unconditional love of the spirit that surrounds you. By recognizing the abundance you already have, you will attract more into your life. When you express infinite love and eternal gratitude for all that is, you are blessed with unlimited access to your creative potential.

Bless you on this journey into the light.

"It is now time to completely heal the past and embrace a brand new paradigm of Love, Limitlessness and unprecedented Grace for your life and for the planet." [1]

— Adama, The Seven Sacred Flames

Reference

1. Aurelia Louise Jones, *The Seven Sacred Flames,* Mt. Shasta Light Publishing, Mt. Shasta, CA, 2007

Awakening through Reflection

DAY ONE

TRANSFORMATION

WORKSHOP MODULES:

1. Life Experience & Analysis: "Awakening from Suffering"

2. The Spiritual Essence of Transformation

3. Self-Exploration #1: Revealing a Transformative Experience

4. Self-Realization #1: Meditation on Transformation

5. Self-Reflection #1: Uncovering Life Lessons

6. Practical Spirituality: Balancing Ego & Spirit

LIFE EXPERIENCE

DAY ONE

Awakening from Suffering

WHENEVER I have gone into meditation and asked for guidance about the most effective way to reach people with my message of hope and inspiration, I always hear loud and clear: "Share your journey! How did you get from there to here? Share what you know and what has worked for you along the way. That's what will inspire others!" And so I have. For the purposes of this book, my reflection starts with the moment I first began to awaken almost twenty years ago.

My Revelation in the Desert

I grew up in San Diego but had never spent any time in the nearby desert. I had the chance to discover the majesty of this landscape when my sister moved there for healing and respite. She had just returned from the War in the Gulf where she had been leading firefighters into the oil fires that had erupted there. As a result of all the black smoke she inhaled, she developed an acute respiratory condition. Her doctor told her she should rehabilitate in a place that was warm, dry, and unpolluted. His recommendation inspired my parents to set her up in a home out in the desert where she could breathe in the pure, clean air. This environment turned out to be an oasis for her recovery.

Even though I was from San Diego, I had actually been living on the East Coast for the previous seven years. When I heard my sister had returned from the war and was recovering in the desert, I knew I wanted to be by her side. We hadn't seen each other in years and I wanted to do whatever I could to welcome her home and help her rehabilitate. The prospect of spending time in the sunny desert together sounded wonderful. At the time, I desperately needed a break from the extreme weather back east and the stress of my unhappy life. I had begun to feel as if the harsh weather conditions were a reflection of my own inner turmoil and misery. I had been depressed, anxious, and generally stressed-out for several months as a result of my cold and chaotic existence on the East Coast. I knew that I was totally misaligned with my true calling because everything lacked meaning and nothing gave me the fulfillment I desperately longed for.

As a California native, I'd felt like a fish out of water back east. I was working in the corporate world at the time and found the politics to be very mean-spirited. I also felt that the demands of the job were unreasonable and unfair. To add to my distress, my husband traveled around the globe and was rarely home. I had great difficulty merging with the culture and attitude of the East Coast which, from the perspective of a Southern Californian, seemed foreign and abrasive. As a result, I didn't have any real friends. I had left my family and childhood friends on the West Coast and missed them terribly. I didn't respond well to the extreme cold weather either, and had acute eczema which often resulted in open wounds. My hair had been falling out in clumps and I didn't know if it was the weather or the stress. I had been taken to the emergency room with panic attacks on two different occasions and was given medication to calm my nerves. The meds made me feel lethargic and detached so I stopped taking them. I was badly in need of a break from it all.

The moment I arrived in the desert, I fell in love with the landscape; I actually felt ecstatic, joyful and free there. I recognized these feelings but hadn't experienced them for a very long time. I was so thrilled to be warm and happy again. I adored the bright sunshine and clear blue sky; the violet mountains that surrounded the desert valley were majestic and inviting. I felt like I was living in a fantasy world full of vivid colors and natural beauty.

Then one morning I woke up consumed with dread and desperation. I realized that my time in paradise would soon be over, and I started to shake and cry. I threw on my clothes and ran out the front door, headed for the mountains with tears flowing down my face. I ran and ran, thinking maybe I could escape my fate if I just kept running away from it. The sun was coming up over the mountain in a glorious blaze of fiery orange and fuchsia. I was heading for the base of the mountain as if being pulled toward it, and I wanted to run straight to the top (although I wasn't quite sure why). Despite the burning in my lungs and the pain in my legs, I sprinted up the mountain, leaping over rocks and bushes along the way. When I got to the top, I threw up my arms, looked up into the heavens and cried out: "Please help me! I need some answers! I am unhappy in the extreme but see no way out. I am so conflicted and confused. I feel desperate and lost and need to find my way. Please help me! Please!"

And then suddenly, a total sense of calm washed over me. I dropped my arms and began smiling, inhaling this feeling of pure contentment. It was as if the air around me had enveloped me in a warm and loving embrace. Then I heard a voice saying loud and clear as I looked out over the desert landscape: "Can't you see you have come home? You will stay here and you will heal yourself and many others. Don't worry about the details. You will be guided every step of the way. You are loved more than you can possibly imagine and always will be."

47

I just stood there in awe. I had an unprecedented sense of total serenity, coming from deep inside the very core of my being. Then gradually the feeling of deep inner peace transformed into one of pure joy as the significance of this divine revelation began to unfold. I felt the anticipation and excitement well up inside as I considered what I had just heard: A new home here in this magnificent desert? A new life? A new beginning? I will heal myself and others? The voice was so powerful and all-knowing, I never even questioned it for one minute. I took off running down the mountain and I never looked back.

From that moment on, there was not a shred of doubt or fear about what I needed to do. Finally I had a genuine purpose. I was being powerfully guided and felt like I was just along for the ride. It was almost as if I had stepped outside of my former self but was not fully inside of the new one either. I felt like I was observing this transformation from above myself and at times, felt like I was just going through the motions as if being led around by an invisible force. I was, however, deeply in touch with the feelings and emotions running through me. They were fueled by pure joy and excitement. I had a fearless self-confidence and a deep knowing that everything that was happening, every interaction and every experience, was just as it should be. And so it was. I went from being terribly depressed and overly anxious to feeling joyful and exuberant. I actually felt as if I had emerged from the void of a desolate darkness and was now floating through a brilliant world full of colorful lights and glorious sounds. Everything that I had been searching for: meaning, purpose, love and happiness — started to emerge and expand. My fears and doubts were replaced by inner peace and sheer confidence in myself and the world around me. It was as if everything that was wrong in my life was now being righted and I had finally come home to my true calling.

THE TRAIL TO MY SALVATION

Self-Reflection
Time Period: December 1995
Topic: Transformation

Memories, Thoughts & Feelings:

For six years, leading up to my "revelation in the desert," I had been in a great deal of suffering because I was totally misaligned with my authentic self. I had been raised in a society centered on the belief that the true meaning and purpose of life was to follow the "American Dream." Doing this, I was told, would bring me happiness and fulfillment and I would have everything I ever wanted. Success and money were the two highest achievements; Marrying "well" also played into the fulfillment of this dream of happiness. For me, creating a life that didn't reflect my true nature turned the dream into a nightmare.

Suspected Causes: Related past history

1. Instead of marrying for true love, I married someone who I admired for being successful in business, and who fit into society's image of a "suitable" husband. In essence, I "married well."

2. Believing the "American Dream" was *my* dream. This included pursuing a degree in business because in the 80's the economy was booming and that was what was expected of you. Although I had little or no interest in economics, finance or management, I followed that path in pursuit of "the dream" and spent ten painful years in the corporate world.

3. I fell into the trap of acquiring the material possessions - nice car, house, and clothes - I thought I needed to look prosperous and successful as well.

Effects:
Occurring as a result of the causes identified

Primary effect: total disharmony within the very heart and soul of my being. The disharmony showed up as physical and mental distress in many different manifestations ranging from chronic bladder and kidney dysfunction to recurring anxiety attacks. I had such severe eczema on my shins that open wounds erupted. Clumps of my hair were just falling out. I developed a chronic respiratory condition. I was walking around in a constant state of sleep deprived agitation which made me bitchy and demanding. Other times, I just felt defeated and depressed and didn't want to get out of bed. I resented my job, my husband, and the world around me.

Lessons Hidden Within:

When you are not aligned with your authentic self, your physical and mental health will decline until you wake up and get realigned. You must be true to your heart.

Do not pretend you are someone you are not. Do not pretend to love someone you are truly not in love with. Do not pretend to crave money and corporate success when those things do not make your heart happy.

Do not separate yourself from your family. You must cherish that connection and stay in close contact.

Lesson Plan:

I will never again pretend that I want something just to please somebody else or just to fit into society's idea of success.

I will take good care of my health by listening to my body. I will seek balance in my life by setting boundaries.

I will create harmony in my life by following my heart and cherishing my loved ones.

I will not be controlled by a schedule of commitments that does not allow for "me" time.

I will take time getting to know myself better so I can align with my true nature.

I will always be kind to others and strive to be of service in selfless ways.

I will focus on developing love, forgiveness and compassion for myself and others.

DAY ONE

The Spiritual Essence of Transformation

A Conversation with Spiritual Counselor & Minister Janet Myatt

SUZANNE: Good afternoon Janet, and thank you so much for joining me today as we explore the meaning and purpose behind the important life lessons we have come here to learn. We are looking for the lessons that are hidden within our most memorable experiences. Once we identify these, we can make a lesson plan that will help us apply them to our life today. By participating in this workshop, we have chosen to consciously evolve by creating meaningful experiences that incorporate these lessons. As a spiritual counselor and psychic intuitive, your insight will help us see the deeper spiritual truths within our experiences of life.

JANET: Good afternoon. I am delighted to have this opportunity to help readers see the deeper meaning and greater purpose behind their most powerful experiences. With this insight, it will become clear how and why their life unfolded just as it did.

SUZANNE: The personal story I've shared is a transformational experience that changed my life dramatically. I explained how, in a moment of desperation, I threw up my arms, looked to the sky and asked for guidance from a higher power. In response to my request, and willingness to surrender, I was suddenly surrounded by a warm feeling of pure love and inner peace. Moments later, I heard a voice within me and all around me that delivered an important message of hope and inspiration. I was given clear instructions about the nature of my true calling and reassurance that I was deeply loved. I knew, from that moment on, that there was a higher power and it would always be there for me. Janet, I know that you have a powerful story about an awakening that transformed your life as well. Can you share with us how your spiritual journey began?

JANET: I was a pretty psychic kid even though I didn't know what that meant at the time. I had a sensitivity and an awareness that no one really had an explanation for. Later, I wanted to figure out why I could see things that other people couldn't see and sense things other people couldn't sense. As a young adult, I started experiencing strange little ailments. By the time I was 26, I had chronic laryngitis and things just weren't working for me. I wanted to figure out why and how to make things better. So, I started reading a lot of new age books.

At one point, I had a deeply mystical experience. I was reading Richard Bach's book *One* while my boyfriend and his sister were playing tennis. I was sitting on the sidelines when all of a sudden, everything shifted and became full of the most extraordinary light. I was full of light, the tennis courts and people on them were bathed in light. The trees, fence, everything became filled with this amazing, beautiful, compelling light. A huge, pure white light ran from me up into the heavens and connected with this vast loving Presence that I now know of as God. Suddenly, I just knew that God truly existed. God became real rather than just a concept. And, I realized that I was part of this God Presence, that everyone was a part of it, and that it existed in everything. And that even though life was hard at times, somehow there was a greater truth behind everything and I felt totally at peace. I also felt that now this connection was established in my mind, it could never be taken away from me.

That experience launched me on a very long journey with lots of ups and downs. A journey I am still on today. And, it's been full of both positive and negative experiences, wonderful and heartbreakingly painful experiences. In other words, this moment of awakening wasn't a promise that seeking the light would be easy, but it was a powerful connection that never would leave me again. It was too real, too strong and too deep to be denied.

SUZANNE: At that point in your life, after reconnecting with the divine, it sounds like you began actively seeking a deeper understanding of yourself and your life's true purpose. Can you tell us a little more about this transformational journey?

JANET: One of the first things that came out of this transformational experience was a twofold process of healing my body and getting my life in stronger alignment with my true path. I spent over a year healing my laryngitis through the power of positive affirmations, and changing my work life. I learned that the emotional issue underlying my laryngitis was the belief that it was not safe or okay for me to speak my truth or ask for what I really wanted from others and from life in general. In essence, I was bottling up my creativity, my light, and my passion in an effort to fit in. I was trying to be what I believed I needed to be in order to be loved and accepted. I was following a rulebook handed down to me from the outside world rather than living authentically from the directives of my inner being. And because I really didn't know how to do that, I was still very identified with a distorted sense of my "self", which I now call the ego, rather than with my spirit.

In short, the ego is a fearful "self" sitting in opposition to the indwelling spirit. It's the body-identified, mortal self and its sole focus is to physically survive in the externalized world. One of the most basic instinctive drives of the ego is to be accepted by the group to ensure our survival. There are other drives as well, but this is a powerful one. As we grow up, we develop all kinds of ideas about how to survive. We come up with what I call core beliefs or core adaptations that serve as our compass. They become our personal truths.

SUZANNE: And then our lives unfold and experiences arise that compel us to question those truths.

JANET: Yes, powerful experiences unfold that create suffering, disappointment, lack of fulfillment, a strong desire for something better, and a willingness to change. These are the things that drive us to finally question our truths. When our coping strategies and our formulas for living fall short of the promised results, we have a choice: stubbornly cling to our current beliefs and continue to do the same things over and over again always hoping for a different result, or start to question our status quo and work towards a new understanding. Einstein describes the former strategy as the definition of insanity. The latter strategy catalyzes the evolution of our consciousness and the fulfillment of our greater universal purpose.

SUZANNE: So doing the same thing over and over again and expecting different results is insane, and questioning everything and reinventing ourselves is our true purpose?

JANET: Yes! Let's take a moment to define transformation a bit.

Any experience that affects us in a deeply emotional, intuitive and/or inspirational way has the power to be transformative. When it captures our attention in a way that connects us with the greater field of life, we are in a transformational moment. The veil between us and our higher potential becomes thin and may even drop away. Our ability to rise up to a higher expression of ourselves becomes possible and we feel it. We intuitively know it.

These powerful experiences can be positive or negative. They can hit us suddenly in a moment or creep up on us slowly. The positive experiences are fun, like when you were on the mountaintop. A powerful, ecstatic expansion of consciousness takes place and there's no denying it. We feel it throughout our entire being. Powerful, negative experiences are not fun but also have the potential to awaken us. For instance, a cancer diagnosis, coming face-to-face with a substance abuse problem, a divorce or devastating loss, or just a chronic dissatisfaction with life, can move us to a place where we become willing to seek a new way of being. My laryngitis story is an example of a negative experience that led to a positive transformation. I suffered from laryngitis for over seven years before I took any concrete steps to address the problem. That's a long time! But it wasn't until after I met with an ENT specialist who told me I would probably have to give up singing altogether and possibly teaching as well — (two things that were vitally important to me at the time) — that I became catalyzed to do the deeper soul work. And, it was out the ashes of that experience that the transformational moment on the tennis court arose.

Suzanne: Yes, I have had powerful negative experiences as well as a direct personal experience with many of the ones you just mentioned and I can honestly say that I am incredibly grateful for every single one of them. Each of these challenges lead to a powerful transformation in the way I viewed myself, others and the world around me. Each time that I emerged victorious, I had a much deeper sense of gratitude for all of the blessings in my life and each time, I felt more and more empowered!

JANET: Our opportunity to transform ourselves and our lives can easily elude us, however, if we don't stop and take stock in our inner knowing. We really have to learn to take the time to listen deeply and then seek out ways to act upon what we discover. There have been times in my life where I had a little intuitive indication: "Oh Janet you should do something" - this or that - but then I haven't acted on it. And, it's not like the world comes to an end, but it becomes a missed opportunity that has to come back around. If it's important to our evolution though, chances are that the lesson will come around again and again, with increasing intensity and with larger consequences each time we ignore these nudges, until suddenly were shoved into a situation that forces us to pay attention. That's been my experience anyway.

SUZANNE: That is such an important point. I have also been slow on the uptake sometimes and it has literally taken an act of God to wake me up! Sometimes we have to get to a point of desperation before we are willing to surrender and ask for guidance. If we live in a higher state of awareness and take the time to sit and reflect upon our lives, we should be able to transform them before we get to that crisis point.

JANET: The subject of transformation is so important because we are all transformers. We are all transformers of energy and transformers of consciousness. One way to look at it is to envision that we as a whole, as the human race, are collectively the incarnation of a mighty cosmic being of light and love, and we are here to transform matter through merging our consciousness with it. As we clothe ourselves in matter, we have the opportunity each time we incarnate to take that substance we embody and infuse it with light until it's so perfected we can reveal ourselves fully in an objective form. We have the opportunity to move our consciousness from a state of contraction, separation, and fear and return it to a state of expansion, connection, and love. Together, we each are charged with bringing more light and more order into what has fallen into chaos, fear and separation. Those transformational moments, those big moments, are when we get to tap into the divine order of things and see it clearly. But, every single day of our lives we are making choices. We are choosing to invest in fear or invest in love, to invest in limitation or to invest in freedom, to invest in connecting or disconnecting. Every moment of every day, we are being given opportunities to take our creative essence and use it in a particular way. We all have free will about how we're going to do that, but in the process of making these creative choices, we are actively transforming ourselves and the world around us.

I believe the time has come when many of us are in the process of awakeningm a deeper divine purpose. And, there are things we can do to help facilitate this process and develop our conscious evolution. One of the most important things we can do is learn how to go within and connect with our inner wisdom. This involves quite a bit of work because we have to learn how to tell the difference between the fearful voice of our mortal, ego-based personality and the divine voice of our indwelling spirit. We have to figure out how to stop acting out of fear and falling for our standard knee-jerk reactions. These fearful reactions usually emerge with an arsenal of great rationalizations that we use to justify our behavior and we remain stuck in our own limiting viewpoint. So, there's this huge process of learning how to live honestly with ourselves and developing a tolerance for facing what is not so pretty within us. All the while, we need to diligently find ways to connect with what is beautiful, loving, kind, forgiving, uplifting, and divinely true.

SUZANNE: What a lovely message. Thank you for sharing your tremendous insight on transformation, Janet. The truths you have shared about how and why it is so important will be very useful to the readers as they begin their own personal reflection.

Now it's your turn!

SELF-EXPLORATION #1 -
REVEALING A TRANSFORMATIVE EXPERIENCE
Theme: Transformation

Think about a time when you made a significant shift in your life circumstances. This could be a job change, relationship change, or simply a move to a new location. It might even be an event that rocked your world enough to shake up the status quo. Close your eyes and focus on this singular experience. Use any photos and memorabilia you can gather to help determine what experience you will choose to write about. Once you have decided on the transformational experience you wish to explore, the following Q & A exercise will help you to unravel the meaning and purpose of it. This exercise is designed to expose the cause-and-effect relationships among between the details of the experience. The insight you gain from exploring your heart and mind will help you understand how and why the synchronistic events unfolded just as they did. In the final analysis, you will clearly see the lessons that were hidden within the experience so you can learn them once and for all!

Explore Your Heart and Mind

Name the experience (ie. Move, Job/Relationship Change,...):

_____

Time Period: _____

Now share your memories, thoughts and feelings:

What triggered the sudden shift in the way I experienced the world around me?

_____

_____

_____

_____

Did this shift lead to more positive experiences, or did it trigger a negative series of events?

_____

_____

_____

_____

Who were the key players at the time and what roles did they play in my life?

_____

_____

_____

Now identify the causes:

In retrospect, can I see the synchronicity of events and how each choice lead to the unfolding of the next series of events? Align the choices with the subsequent series of events that followed:

_____

_____

_____

_____

_____

_____

Can I see the reasons behind the choices I made at the time?

_____

_____

_____

_____

Were there outside influences that lead to the paths I followed? If so, who or what were they? List the influence followed by the path it lead to:

_____

_____

_____

_____

Now focus on the effects:

How did these choices affect my life and what were the changes I made as a result?

_____

_____

_____

_____

How did these changes affect my life going forward?

_____

_____

_____

Looking back, can I see the deeper meaning or greater purpose behind the shift?

_____

_____

_____

_____

_____

Did I see myself resisting or surrendering to the changes that unfolded around me?

_____

_____

_____

_____

In retrospect, would I have done anything differently or can I see why everything had to happen just as it did in order to be shown my life lessons?

_____

_____

_____

_____

_____

Identify Lessons and Shifts

Do I recognize these lessons as ones that I've have been shown before in other circumstances or at different stages in my life?

_____

_____

_____

_____

Am I learning from these lessons and applying them to the choices I am making here and now?

_____

_____

_____

_____

In the big picture, what are the most important ways in which this shift changed my life?

_____

_____

_____

_____

_____

_____

_____

Were there times when I felt like I was being guided by an invisible force? If so, what guidance did I receive and what choices did it cause me to make?

_____

_____

_____

_____

_____

Now that I have a clearer picture of the transformational shift, do I need to forgive myself or anyone else?

_____

_____

_____

_____

_____

Do I need to thank anyone else and/or express gratitude for my own strength and courage?

_____

_____

_____

_____

_____

_____

Start a lesson plan:

After reflecting upon the lessons you have identified, think about ways in which you can apply them to both your personal and professional life today. Focus on your life choices and your relationships. Are you reflecting the divine virtues of your higher self? In light of the lessons this experience has taught you, what will you do differently?

_____

_____

_____

_____

_____

_____

Make a promise to yourself that you will continue to work on mastering these lessons and increasing your awareness about the synchronicity of events that are continually unfolding in your life. If you have identified spirit guides or living angels in your life, thank them and have faith they will always be there for you. Trust in the guidance. Believe in the love that surrounds you. Believe in yourself.

SELF-REALIZATION #1
Meditation on Transformation

It's time to progress on your path of self-realization.

Before journaling your experience, please engage in "Dynamic Movement Therapy" to open and expand your body. Then be seated comfortably and perform the "Inspirational Breathing Practices" to oxygenate your body and clear your mind of distractions. You can find instructions for the movement and breathing practices by referring back to the written guidelines in the introduction, or you can access the audio download for free at *www. suzannerosstranscendence.com/Up!Trilogy/WakeUp!Meditations.*

Now you are ready to go within by performing the guided visualization and contemplative meditation. Performing this meditation prior to reflecting gives you a much clearer perspective. Your recollection will be illuminated by the light of love and wisdom rather than clouded by the attachment to past feelings and emotions. As you write, you will begin to see the past in a much brighter light that reflects its true purpose and you will be grateful for the lessons within.

Before engaging in a reflection upon past life events, it's important to quiet your mind so that you can release the thoughts that are attached to the present moment. Find a quiet place where you will not be distracted. If you were able to create a sacred sanctuary, that is ideal. Preparing for contemplative meditation requires a series of activities that are conducive to opening to spirit. Start by cleaning the environment where you will be meditating. Chaos is not only distracting to yourself; but you are also making the room presentable for the spirit guides who may be joining you during the meditation. It's also important to wash your face and hands as a sign of purification.

Arrange a special shrine that includes objects of affection and objects from creation. Pictures of Deities, Angels, and spiritual guides are especially conducive to your meditation. Objects from creation may include crystals, rocks, shells, and maybe even a living plant or flowers. To represent the elements of fire and water, include a candle and a bowl of fresh water. These objects can also be seen as offerings to the guides. This is a way of honoring them and inviting them into your meditation. Once you have cleaned the room, purified your body, and displayed your shrine, you are ready to begin the **VIS-MED for Transformation.**

You can download an audio version of this guided meditation by going to my website at *www.suzannerosstranscendence.com.* On the Up!Trilogy menu, select **Wake Up! Meditations** and go to the **VIS-MED for Transformation**

DAY ONE
Self-Reflection

Name of the Experience (ie. Move, Job/Relationship Change,…):

_____

Time Period: _____

Topic: Transformation

Memories, Thoughts & Feelings:

_____

_____

_____

_____

_____

Suspected Causes:
Related past history

_____

_____

_____

_____

_____

_____

Effects:
Occurring as a result of the causes identified

_____

_____

_____

_____

_____

_____

Lessons Hidden Within:

_____

_____

_____

_____

_____

Lesson Plan:

_____

_____

_____

_____

_____

DAY ONE
PRACTICAL SPIRITUALITY

Transformation: Balancing Ego and Spirit

"My religiosity consists in a humble admiration of the infinitely superior spirit that reveals itself in the little that we can comprehend of reality"

— Einstein

I believe the reason I was led to a spiritual path rather than a religious denomination is that spirituality has allowed me to open my heart to all belief systems without boundaries. I am able to see the divine essence of all traditions and therefore, the divinity within all seekers. I used to think that religions were judgmental and hypocritical. Upon closer examination, I realized it wasn't the religions at all. They too had a divine origin and nature and it was just the ego's interpretation of it. The human ego casts shadows on the beauty and truth of spiritual messages like clouds that block the sun or borderlines that divide countries. The light of pure spirit becomes filtered and fragmented. In the true nature of being, all is one and every living being is united by spirit. It is the ego that keeps us fragmented, not religions, cultures or borders.

Ego is threatened by spirit. When we die, ego dies. That's why we are so afraid of death. But even in life, our spirit can overcome our ego. Just as our soul is liberated at the time of our death, when it merges with the light of spirit, we can make a sincere attempt to free ourselves from our ego in this lifetime by connecting with the living spirit now. We can start just by having a higher level of awareness about the qualities of ego and spirit. This will allow us to distinguish between the two and therefore identify which kind of consciousness we are bringing forth and to what extent.

It's very helpful to say "spirit, spirit, spirit" whenever you feel ego is over-stepping its boundaries. Anything other than pure unconditional love is ego, of course, so we have to be very cautious with our words and behaviors. We must notice when ego is rearing its ugly head and clouding our judgment. Then we can stop and redirect the thoughts in our mind. So this becomes a daily practice: Just say to yourself, "Is this ego or spirit talking?" If its ego, we can ask ourselves, "How can I redirect my thoughts towards spirit?" If its spirit, we simply smile and express gratitude for the guidance we've been given.

Staying in spirit allows your divine purpose to unfold in many beautiful and mysterious ways. A sweet harmony of synchronicities takes over and you move effortlessly through life as you allow them to flow freely. If you stay open to spirit and surrender to the will, your heart will overflow with an abundance of joy and brilliant rays of light will emanate from your being. Those who recognize the light will be drawn toward it and you will know that you were destined to walk together. As your circle of light expands, you will begin to see more and more of your own true self in the reflections of others. The other light beings are simply reflections of your own spirit expanding just like you are. In the truest sense, we are all reflections of the One Great Self experiencing - God portraying being-ness, if you will.

Remember, you are a child of the Creator, his spirit is within you and, as such, you are an expression of pure spirit – a divine aspect of his personality. Your physical being is a vehicle within which you can realize your true self through experiences in this realm. As long as you stay in spirit and strive for the highest expression of yourself, by exemplifying your best traits, your path will unfold effortlessly. An insatiable curiosity will lead you to the truth and an open heart will help you find it. Ask and you shall receive all the guidance you need. Always remember: all is one.

You are one with the Great Self who is guiding you.

Recently, while struggling to balance my own ego-identity with the divine spirit within, I asked for guidance. I simply said, "I am struggling to balance my ego with my spirit. I am finding it difficult to bring my spiritual aspirations in alignment with my ego identity." I asked, "How do I bring the light and love of spirit into my mundane existence as a physically incarnated being? How do I inject spirit into daily tasks like going to the DMV or paying bills? How do I transition from bathing in the light to sitting in congested traffic?"

There is a strong pull in the direction of spirit which makes me want to hibernate somewhere remote so I can be isolated from the distractions of the world. On the other hand, my ego identity has obligations in the physical realm. There are many things to be done that seem like distractions from my true purpose of writing, teaching and learning. I know, however, that when I am out and about, I have many opportunities to radiate the light of my spirit, and that this too fulfills my divine purpose. I just need to learn how to embrace every moment of my life as an opportunity to express my spiritual self. I need to learn how to set aside my ego so that my spirit can shine through my thoughts, words and actions.

I have to remember that the spirit resides within me like a brilliant light radiating outward from my heart and mind in all directions. When I am focused on my spiritual practices, out in nature or with spiritually minded friends, my inner light glows brightly and strong feelings of unconditional love, pure joy and inner peace consume me. I feel deeply connected to spirit and my body feels like it's shimmering with light. At other times, the light of my spirit grows dim as my ego consumes me. I feel a sort of heaviness set in as thoughts of resentment and frustration arise, and my patience and compassion towards others diminishes. At these times, I feel separate from others and from spirit. I feel overwhelmed by the mundane tasks and personal obligations of my ego identity as Suzanne. I begin to view these as distractions from spirit and begin to resent them. I want to flee from the ego demands of my physical world and retreat into my true nature as a spiritual being.

This is the biggest challenge of our lives: to balance ego and spirit.

I was facing this challenge head-on one afternoon when the frustrations of trying to resolve a property tax issue boiled up inside of me and started turning to anger. Darkened by the shadows that were dimming my light, I decided to run a nice hot bath. With my string of mala beads in hand, I began to call on spirit. For each mala bead, I simply repeated the phrase: "The power of the infinite spirit is within me." Halfway through the beads, my shoulders dropped and I began to relax. I pictured a sky full of clouds and each cloud had a name – *taxes, mortgage, work,...*, and, one by one, I sent these clouds away.

Finally, all that was left was a clear blue sky with a golden disk in the center. The brilliant rays of the sun consumed me and I felt drawn into the light. Embraced by its warmth, a sense of deep inner peace overwhelmed me and I knew that everything would be fine. Then one by one, simple, easy solutions to the issues that had been gnawing at me just flowed forth. I had called on spirit to ease my mind and now it was flowing through me. Once I removed the dark clouds of my ego mind, the bright light of my spirit could shine through once again. This is the message that came through loud and clear: "Ask and you shall receive. Surrender to the light and it will guide you." And so I asked, "How do I bring my spiritual essence into my physical experience? How do I bring the spiritual realm into the physical world? How do I challenge my ego to step aside so that my spiritual light can shine brightly at all times?" This is the answer I received:

"Each and every task is an opportunity to serve and should be cherished as such. Shine your light upon each and every person you encounter and, in this way, you can overcome the darkness and bring peace, joy and happiness into the world while performing daily tasks. These errands are simply an opportunity for you to interact with spirit in the physical realm and, if you are mindful, you can transform this realm into a spiritual experience. Remember, you are a spiritual being having a physical experience in order to learn the unique lessons it has to offer. Beyond that, you can transform what appears to be a physical experience into a spiritual one by seeing the divine light of love in each transaction and in every living being. This is how you bring spirit into the world of ego, my dear. Go out and shine your light and radiate your spirit. You are never separate from it for it is omnipresent — just like my love."

Upon receiving this guidance, I expressed my eternal gratitude and promised to shine my radiant light throughout the remainder of the day. I made an oath to bring spirit into my every thought, word and action as I tended to my tasks with joy in my heart and peace in my soul.

Before heading out into your day, take the time to sit and connect with spirit. This way, you will walk in the light and it will not allow the darkness to pervade your space. If you ask for guidance, spirit will help to clear the clouds of ego away so the sun can shine brightly through. If you listen carefully, you will be guided through the tasks and what seemed difficult, will suddenly seem so simple. It is a matter of surrendering and going with the flow. Once you drop all resistance and judgment, you can move into your day with an open heart and mind. Then, everything around you will fall into place beautifully. You will be in the divine flow and as you shine your light upon the world, others will respond with joy and kindness. Your day will unfold magically and you will become aware of a divine synchronicity as mysterious and unexpected people, places and things show you special messages with hidden meanings. If you engage in these experiences with a reflective mind, these meanings will be revealed.

This is spirit guiding you, and if you can remain in a state of expanded awareness by being fully engaged in the moment, you can follow its guidance and progress along your path. Following the path of spirit will fill your heart with so much joy that you will begin to attract an abundance of opportunities. If you make your wishes clear and your intention is pure, you can attract the opportunities that will bring you the most happiness and fulfillment. With your mind focused on spreading the light and love of spirit, you will be presented with many glorious people and things to help you do just that. The Creator wants all of his children to enjoy the abundance of the universe. All you have to do is ask, surrender and then just open your heart to receive.

Awakening through Reflection

DAY TWO

TRANSITION

WORKSHOP MODULES:

1. Life Experience & Analysis: "The Desert Dream Comes True"

2. The Spiritual Essence of Transition

3. Self-Exploration #2: Exploring a Transitional Phase

4. Self-Realization #2: Meditation on Transition

5. Self-Reflection #2: Uncovering Life Lessons

6. Practical Spirituality: Self-Love & Empowerment

LIFE EXPERIENCE

DAY TWO

The Desert Dream Comes True!

In the movie "We Bought a Zoo!", a father tells his son that sometimes it just takes twenty seconds of insane courage to go after what you really want. After my revelation on the mountaintop, it was more like twenty days of insane courage! I knew exactly what I needed to do however. If I was going to fulfill my dream and honor my new revelation, I would need to remain open to the guidance I was being given. I knew now that I was being guided by some kind of force greater than myself and I felt it. As I walked down the mountain, I became convinced that I was a fully qualified fitness instructor and that my first step was to get a job as one in this desert resort town — my new home. I thought, "O.K., I can do that. I've taken hundreds of fitness classes over the years!" I had often thought it would be great fun to teach as I watched with envy and admiration while aerobics instructors led their students in a frenzy of sweat and creative expression.

So I jumped in the shower, put on my best clothes, and drove out to the most beautiful four-star resort in town, where I knew they held fitness classes for local residents and hotel guests. I walked right up to the front desk and asked who I could talk to about employment opportunities. The gal at the desk was friendly and warm, and she actually seemed excited for me as she directed me to the administration offices. I thanked her and as I turned and waved, she shouted out, "Good luck!" I had such butterflies that I actually felt weak in my knees. It was as if I were floating through this surreal experience. While my actions seemed irrational and spontaneous, I didn't care. I was in the mood to throw caution to the wind and go with my instincts. How could something that was filling me with so much excitement and enthusiasm — a stark contrast to what I had been feeling for years — be wrong or misguided? It felt so totally right.

I also had a strong premonition about how things would go each step of the way, which may have accounted for my overly confident attitude. It was as if I had already seen this movie before, and it was playing out in front of me just as I knew it would.

I walked into the personnel office and the receptionist greeted me warmly.

When I inquired about employment opportunities, she smiled and replied, "Oh sure, have a seat. I'll call the Human Resources Manager." As soon as the manager introduced herself, we made an immediate connection and she treated me like an old friend. I told her I was interested in providing fitness services. She assumed I was responding to the ad she had just placed for a fitness instructor and was thrilled. Apparently, theirs had just resigned! "What ad?" I thought.

She told me all about the job and seemed genuinely excited that someone interested in fitness had come to town. They didn't want to have to recruit someone from out of town and then pay for them to move here and provide them with employee housing. She informed me, however, that they would need me to start in two weeks if I was interested. She didn't even ask me about my specific qualifications or experience. It seemed to be enough that she just liked me. We really hit it off and she couldn't wait for me to meet the general manager. As she left me sitting alone in the conference room, I sat there saying to myself, "It's happening, it's happening!" Then the G.M. walked in with a big smile on her face and extended both hands warmly. As she took my hands in hers, she expressed how fortunate they were that I was interested in the fitness position.

To add to the dreamlike quality of the experience, I still felt like I was observing it from above, even though I was fully engaged with the characters in my movie. They were so approachable — not what you would expect in an office. They didn't wear stuffy suits or pantyhose and heels, and their hair wasn't all neat and tidy with perfect makeup to match. The H.R. manager had crazy red hair and seemed more interested in becoming friends and talking about life in the desert than the job interview itself. I thought for sure we'd make plans to meet later for a drink. We were laughing and joking around and I felt more like we were sitting in her living room than in an office.

The G.M. actually seemed angelic to me. She had golden blonde hair swept back and she was wearing a flowing coral silk pantsuit with bulky turquoise jewelry. She seemed to float in, welcome me with genuine sincerity and float out. It became clear that the job was mine if I wanted it and if I did, I needed to be ready to start in two weeks! The H.R. manager said something to the effect of, "So what will it be my friend? Do we have reason to celebrate?!" Without hesitation, I jumped up and said, "Yes! Why not?" and gave her a hug, which didn't seem at all inappropriate. She was thrilled and we rejoiced as she handed me the necessary paperwork almost as an after-thought. She said, "Just leave those with the receptionist whenever they're completed." Then she waved me off and said, "See you in a couple weeks! Welcome to the family!"

Family? Hugs? Joy and excitement? This was the opposite of anything I'd ever experienced in the stiff and judgmental scrutiny of the corporate interviews I had gotten used to. They always left me feeling unworthy, as if I should be grateful they were even taking time out of their busy day for the likes of me. Even though I usually got the job it seemed to be offered begrudgingly with skepticism like, "We'll see if you can cut it, but I doubt it!"

As I left the resort, walking to my car through the luscious landscape and gorgeous architecture, I could barely contain my excitement. I wanted to break into skipping and I actually thought about jumping up and clicking my heels together. But I didn't want to draw attention to myself since I had driven there in an old farmer's truck I had borrowed. In fact, I had parked in a remote lot and planned to drive out a side exit. I had been getting around mostly on an old scooter my father had recently purchased but couldn't see myself riding through town in a skirt and heels with my purse strapped to the handlebars.

I loved riding the scooter all over town. If I needed anything from town, I could just hop on and take the back trails that went behind the businesses. I would pick up anything I needed as long as it could fit in a bag that I could roll up and strap to the back. I felt like such a free spirit! I didn't need to be properly dressed, fix my hair or apply makeup and then make sure I had gas, find parking and wait in line while planning all the other boring errands I needed to run. I just threw on a tank top, shorts and flip-flops. I couldn't stand wearing pantyhose and uncomfortable suits that seem to bind and choke me, and heels that I could barely balance on.

A few weeks before, I'd been living in a big house (empty and lonely), driving a Porsche (too fast), picking up dry cleaning and buying expensive Scotch and gourmet food for my executive husband who rarely showed up for dinner anyhow. Now I was living in a trailer park, borrowing a beat-up old truck, wearing cutoff jean shorts and strapping my dinner to the handlebars of my scooter. And I was absolutely loving every single minute of it. It didn't seem as if I had lost my mind. Actually, I felt like I had finally found it.

MY NEW RIDE...

...FREEDOM AT LAST!

THE PEACEFUL SERENITY OF THE DESERT LANDSCAPE

THE SIMPLE LIFE, AT LAST

My Reflection
Time Period: January 1996
Topic: Transition

Memories, Thoughts & Feelings:

Following my divine revelation, I found myself being guided by an invisible force as I started to carve out a new life for myself in the desert. With faith in the guidance, I proceeded to apply for a job for which I had few qualifications. I had a new-found confidence in myself and I was offered the job. In the meantime, I discovered that fancy things (extravagant house, cars and clothes) were really not my style and the freedom from it all made me much happier.

Suspected Causes:

Primary cause: Awakening from suffering

The cause of the pure joy, freedom and faith, as well as my ecstatic exuberance and confidence, was all the result of a sudden awakening that sprang out of intense suffering.

Secondary cause: Surrendering to the universe

The cause of the divine intervention was total surrender on my part — Giving up control to a higher source and asking for help. This demonstrates the truth behind the biblical statement, "Ask and you shall receive."

Effects:

Primary effect: Faith in a higher source of pure love and divine guidance.

A sense of total liberation from the expectations and false images of myself
Knowing that once I broke free from the confines of my ego and allowed my higher self to emerge, true happiness and pure joy would pervade my consciousness. Realizing that, when you believe in yourself, others naturally will as well.

Happiness and joy are contagious and when expressed openly, like-minded people are attracted to you.

Lessons Hidden Within:

The ego is a tough customer and it can be stubborn and demanding. Sometimes you just have to stand up to it and allow your higher Self to take the driver's seat.

When you are in the right place at the right time and open to the synchronicity of events unfolding, everything will fall into place beautifully.

When you allow life to unfold and "go with the flow" (instead of resisting and trying to control everything) things tend to go your way in a more harmonious fashion.

When you feel happy, peaceful and joyful all at once, you are aligned with your true nature. When you feel sad, chaotic and angry, you are not!

Lesson Plan:

I will listen to my inner guidance, which provides joy, harmony and smooth sailing when I am on the right track, and confusion, anxiety and distress when I am not.

I will think, do and say those things that represent my higher Self and authentic nature, knowing that this will allow synchronistic events to unfold harmoniously.

When I am feeling uncomfortable — angry, resentful, agitated or fearful — I will go within to discover the source so that I can realign my thoughts and redirect my emotions.

If I am directing any unpleasant emotions toward others, I will reevaluate the nature of the situation and take full accountability for my role in it. I will make a sincere attempt to replace my negative thoughts with positive ones, highlighting the other's best traits, helping me to see things from their standpoint.

I will always do my best to align with my highest Self and make a sincere attempt to control the distractions of my ego-based mind.

DAY TWO

The Spiritual Essence of Transition

A Conversation with Spiritual Counselor & Minister, Janet Myatt

SUZANNE: Once a transformation has taken place in our lives, we have to transition into a new way of being. But how do we do that? How do we adjust to this new light shining on our lives? How do we make the necessary changes?

JANET: In the ascended master teachings and in Theosophy, they talk about how spirit can reach us through inspiration, illumination, and intuition. Each of these divine qualities affect us somewhat differently, but they all mean connecting one-to-one with spirit.

Let's start with inspiration. We all have those moments when we are deeply inspired. It can be when we're cooking, gardening, painting or making music. Or it can be going on a bike ride and just connecting with nature. These moments are transformational when they move our point of view out of the negative or limited self into the soul. Creativity and movement foster inspiration and inspiration fosters creativity and movement. And, inspiration creates an alchemical change within us as we shift our consciousness out of our limitations. For instance, we may have awoken in a grumpy mood. But as soon as we begin to be active and creative, our mood slowly transforms from grumpiness to contentment and even enthusiasm as we move into the experience of what we're doing or creating. Experientially, we move into the present moment as we think about what herb is going to go best with that chicken or what we want to plant in the garden. It's a moment of present-time communion with the creative indwelling soul. These experiences teach us how to live in present time. And why is this important? Because we can only ever create in present time. We cannot create in the past and we cannot create in the future. Inspiration brings us into the present moment and activates our creative power.

SUZANNE: Anyone who has a passion knows that when you're involved in doing what you love, you lose all track of time. You forget about your worries or aches and pains. Instead of feeling limited, you feel liberated because you are "in-spirit."

JANET: Then there is illumination, which Theosophy calls the "Christ-mind" or the "Buddha-mind." Suddenly we are able to see something in a whole new light. If we've been boxed into a particular emotional or mental pattern, even a physical condition, ina moment of illumination the blinders comeoff and limitations disappear. Weenter into a state of mind that lifts the veil of distortion off of our consciousness and we are suddenly able to see the deeper truths underlying whatever we've been grappling with. We are able to recognize a greater pattern and see where we need to shift our thinking, behavior, or understanding of the situation. Within our relationships, for example, we might suddenly find ourselves able to move out of the need to justify ourselves or point the finger at the other person. We shift from being a victim into interconnectivity, love, and forgiveness for ourselves and others. The higher point of view gives us the ability to stop taking everything personally and provides us with the insight we need to make necessary changes, establish healthy boundaries, and get out of repeating negative patterns. We hold ourselves accountable for our part and we learn how to establish healthy rhythms and interactions with others. This grows our capacity and our ability to give and receive love intelligently.

SUZANNE: Sometimes I call these illuminations "epiphanies," and they often come to me when I am out in nature. My mind feels expansive and I can see things in a new light. My spirit flows freely and I naturally feel lighter, as the lingering shadows of frustration, resentment, blame or fear dissipate. In these moments of illumination, I will suddenly gain a much deeper realization about the true nature of being — like an Oprah "A-ha" moment!

JANET: The third divine quality is intuition, or "pure thought" — a clear one-to-one connection where we simply *know* something without distortion. Our consciousness moves into the Divine point of view and expands. Intuition is a state of knowing that comes to us from an internal source rather than external. It's very different from learned knowledge like we experience in school. If that's sudden clear, strong, unshakable knowing that requires no external proof or validation. Like the moment I experienced on the tennis court in my twenties. I suddenly knew without a doubt that God existed within me and within all things and I didn't need anyone outside of myself to tell me I was right. I just knew it. This then became a guiding force in my life that nothing and no one could undo. Our intuition helps us in times of transition because we must move from an old way of being into uncharted territory. We don't yet know how to do it. Our intuition shows us the way.

Like all new habits, these changes take a little doing. How do we make our epiphanies real, and change all our old ways of thinking and being? First, we have to commit to the new vision or understanding that has bubbled up. And, then we have to act on it. We have to think about what we need to change, heal, or develop in ourselves and evaluate the choices we make. We have to move out of the habit of trying to control or change others to meet our needs. Instead, we have to ask: "How can I change this? What is required of me? What can I do? What part of me is wounded? What part of me is looking for something from others that I actually need to give to myself?" As we pursue this soul searching and look for direction and guidance from the divine within, we begin to unfold and reveal a new way of being.

SUZANNE: This is such a critical time, this transition between illumination and inspired action. Once we realize the potential we have to elevate our lives by thinking and seeing in this new light, we have to act on it before the "wounded ego" intervenes and tries to distract us from our true purpose. In the Aramaic version of the Lord's Prayer, there is a line that says: "Do not let me be seduced by that which would divert me from my true purpose, but illuminate the opportunities of the present moment."

JANET: The key is to approach each change with enthusiasm rather than self-criticism. Sometimes it can be helpful to imagine that we are on a huge adventure finding all of the things that stand between us and happiness. It's a very active way of living our life *in the moment* versus continually reacting from the subconscious, what I call "habitual living." If a habit is causing us pain, it's going to continue to cause us pain.

A simple example would be that if I need certain types of foods and exercise every day in order to have internal balance, and I don't honor that, I'll continue to be out of balance; my body will be in a state of chaos or dis-ease. So, I must make those changes a priority and stick with it until it becomes habitual.

Transitional periods are about breaking apart dysfunctional energetic patterns and allowing functional patterns to emerge. We start by identifying the dysfunctional energetic thought or feeling pattern from a place of neutrality and curiosity, *then* we are able to take the necessary steps to break up that old pattern. Simultaneously, we allow the divine, loving, intelligent pattern to emerge from within us and take its place. No one can do this work for us. We have to do it for ourselves, and the best answer is always going to come from within, from that divine part of us.

SUZANNE: Every day and at all times, especially through a transitional period, we have to check in with ourselves that our thoughts, words and actions align with our new way of being. We can't lose the opportunity to transform our lives once we've had a life-changing experience, or even a simple epiphany. Once we become inspired, we need to rejoice and embrace this "re-birthing" process. We have to take action.

JANET: Yes because sometimes you can get the memo, but then not act on it!

Now it's your turn!

SELF-EXPLORATION #2 – EXPLORING A TRANSITIONAL PHASE
Theme: Transition

Think deeply about the transition that took place following the transformational experience you shared yesterday. Try to recall the necessary changes you had to make in various areas of your life, and how these affected both yourself and others. Close your eyes and get in touch with the emotions you were experiencing as you picked up the pieces of your life and rearranged them to fit your new circumstances. Picture yourself interacting with others and explaining the changes in your life. Remember the courage it took to transition into a new way of life and reflect upon the way you adjusted.

Explore your Heart and Mind

Adjusting to a shift in one's reality can be challenging even if the transformation is a positive one. It can leave you feeling stunned at first. Describe your recollection of how the transformational shift affected you initially and what your first adjustments were:

_____

_____

_____

_____

What was the most significant change in the way you perceived your reality? Did you perceive it as full of new possibilities, or did you feel more limited by your new circumstances?

_____

_____

_____

_____

Did the dynamic between yourself and others change? Did you see people in a different light after the transformation?

_____

_____

_____

_____

_____

Did the transformation bring new people into your life? If so, recall how you felt about these new relationships. Did these people have positive or negative influences on your life?

_____

_____

_____

_____

Looking back, do you feel good about the way you handled the transition? Did you embrace new opportunities or resist the change? In other words, did the transformational experience make you feel more grateful and open, or resentful and closed off?

_____

_____

_____

_____

Identify Lessons and Shifts

Try to recall the causes which led to the transformation so that you can more clearly identify the effects they created. You are looking for a cause-and-effect relationship, focusing on the transitional effects that impacted your life most significantly. Think about why it may have been necessary for these changes to take place in your life. Positive or negative, change always wakes you up to a new reality and forces you to face your fears, weaknesses, passions and strengths.

Can you identify ways in which your fears and weaknesses were shown?

_____

_____

_____

_____

How were your passions and strengths demonstrated?

_____

_____

_____

_____

Did these revelations cause you to feel stronger and more capable, or weaker and more vulnerable?

_____

_____

_____

_____

Did you feel like you did the best you could in light of the changes, or do you feel like you could have handled the transition differently?

_____

_____

_____

_____

See if you can make a list of your strengths and weaknesses. This will help you illuminate those traits you should embrace and highlight those you still need to work on. The strengths represent lessons you have learned and mastered. The weaknesses indicate lessons yet to be learned. This is where your focus should lie as you make a strong determination to master them. This will allow you to turn weaknesses into strengths and start to become the master of your mind.

STRENGTHS REVEALED DURING THE TRANSITION

Lessons mastered

_____

_____

_____

_____

WEAKNESSES SHOWN DURING THE TRANSITION

Lessons to be learned

_____

_____

_____

_____

Time for your Reflection

Now that you have triggered some specific memories about your transition, you are ready to describe it in greater detail. Identifying the causes and effects that define your story will help you avoid causes that led to negative effects, and learn from the causes that created positive ones. See if you can find photos or memorabilia from this transitional phase. It will help to bring the story to life. Once you balance the karma associated with this phase, you can move on. One of the objectives of this process is to help you stop looking back so you can keep moving forward.

SELF-REALIZATION #2
Meditation on Transition

It's time to progress on your path of self-realization.

Before journaling your experience, please engage in Dynamic Movement Therapy to open and expand your body. Then be seated comfortably and perform the Inspirational Breathing Practices to oxygenate your body and clear your mind of distractions. You can engage in the movement and breathing practices by referring back to the written guidelines in the introduction, or go to my website for an audio download that will guide you through the practices at *www.suzannerosstranscendence.com.* Now you are ready to go within by performing the guided visualization and contemplative meditation. Spiritual cleansing is extremely beneficial during a time of transition. It is an opportunity to remove psychic debris from the past that blocks your energy from flowing freely. This debris is attracted to your lower energy centers, where your will to survive triggers deep-rooted fears. This type of survival consciousness is condensed into the root chakra at the base of your spine. This energy is red and fiery and ignites your fight-or-flight response.

The next lower energy center where debris tends to accumulate is the orange desire chakra located behind your sexual organs. This is where your sensual attachments to this earthly existence are condensed. Passionate desires like lust and greed can get trapped here. These strong desires may trigger emotions associated with envy, resentment and blame, directed at whomever or whatever has prevented you from acquiring desired material things, or from connecting with the people you have an attraction toward.

The third lower energy center is located behind your solar plexus, or belly button, and it spins on a bright yellow disc. Just like the sun, it is a powerful energy center and it tends to fuel the need to control and have authority over others. This center becomes blocked when you feel out of control or dominated. The great equalizer is the next energy center, your soothing green heart chakra, which neutralizes the negative emotions that tend to accumulate on the lower energy centers. It radiates the power of unconditional love and has the power to transform fear, resentment, blame and the need to control into forgiveness, compassion, understanding, patience, unity and most of all, love.

This VIS-MED for Transition will focus primarily on cleansing the lower energy centers. Once the debris from the past has been removed from these energy centers, our attention will turn to the heart chakra where the toxic thoughts and emotions related to the past will be neutralized by the power of unconditional love.

This is a powerful practice for clearing any blockages that are preventing you from accessing your higher self and expressing the highest thoughts, words and actions. Your ability to tap into your unlimited potential will be unleashed when harmony prevails within your being. With your energy flowing freely, you will have a much clearer picture of this transitional period and the cause-and-effect relationships within it will be revealed. The lessons that this period taught you will be uncovered and you can begin to learn them and apply them.

You can download an audio version of this guided meditation by going to my website at *www.suzannerosstranscendence.com.* On the Up!Trilogy menu, select **Wake Up! Meditations** and go to the **VIS-MED for Transition.**

DAY TWO
Self-Reflection

Name of the Experience: _____

Time Period: _____

Topic: Transition

Memories, Thoughts & Feelings:

_____

_____

_____

_____

_____

_____

Suspected Causes:
Related past history

_____

_____

_____

_____

_____

_____

_____

Effects:
Occurring as a result of the causes identified

_____

_____

_____

_____

_____

Lessons Hidden Within:

_____

_____

_____

_____

_____

Lesson Plan:

_____

_____

_____

_____

_____

DAY TWO
PRACTICAL SPIRITUALITY

Self-love & Empowerment

"In our false sense of separateness, we have had no desire to interface with the existence of the true I AM, who is the core of our conscious existence. We have unconsciously lived in alienation to our real self, our true identity, because our whole life has been lived in and from our rational mind."

— Sean Calvin

During a transitional phase, it is particularly important to let go of any limiting beliefs you may have about yourself. This will empower you to move forward with the true perceptions of your higher self and leave behind the false perceptions of your ego. We all have the innate capacity for complete happiness and perfect health. The only thing that can possibly prevent us from being totally happy and perfectly well is the limiting beliefs we have about ourselves. This divine potential is *within* each and every one of us; there is nothing outside ourselves that can limit our inherent potential.

So why do we limit ourselves? Why do we see ourselves as separate from the divine source of pure love by not loving ourselves and others unconditionally? Why are we limiting ourselves by being disconnected from the unlimited abundance of the source? How do we reconnect and stay connected to it? These are the questions that we are going to explore. We are going to dig deep within to discover why we don't firmly believe that we are anything less than perfectly divine beings capable of tapping into our highest self at any and all times. To enhance our ability to connect with our highest self and overcome these limiting beliefs, we are going to start by engaging in the following practice. Simply fill in the blanks:

Re-Directing Your Beliefs

False Perceptions of Ego

1. I am not _____ enough.

2. I am not _____ enough.

3. I am not _____ enough.

4. I am not _____ enough.

5. I am not _____ enough.

6. I am not _____ enough.

7. I am not _____ enough.

8. I am not _____ enough.

9. I am not _____ enough.

10. I am not _____ enough.

Now Simpy Redirect These Thoughts

True Perceptions of Your Higher Self

1. I am _____ enough.

2. I am _____ enough.

3. I am _____ enough.

4. I am _____ enough.

5. I am _____ enough.

6. I am _____ enough.

7. I am _____ enough.

8. I am _____ enough.

9. I am _____ enough.

10. I am _____ enough.

Now perform the following "Mirror Practice." This will help liberate you from the false beliefs of your ego and allow you to merge with your highest Self.

The Mirror Practice

Stand in front of a mirror. Look yourself square in the eyes and smile. Realize that the light behind your eyes is the spirit of your highest Self. Know that the source of this light is the pure unconditional love of the infinite spirit, and that it is within you and all around you always. It transcends your ego and you can always draw upon it. Greet your higher Self and say,

"Thank you for loving me unconditionally."

Now recognize your ego-identity and say, "I love my skin and hair. I love my face and neck. I love my mouth, tongue and esophagus. I love my brain. I love my chest and shoulders. I love my heart and lungs. I love my stomach and intestines. I love my back and spine. I love my central nervous system. I love my kidney and liver. I love my bladder. I love my hips and thighs. I love my knees and calves. I love the feet that support me and the hands that feed and care for me. I love every bone, muscle and joint, I love every cell of my being." Now envision every cell of your being illuminated by the light and love of your spirit.

Know that your higher self always resides within you and the love of the infinite spirit is always around you. Make a commitment to honor your spirit at all times.

Awakening through Reflection

DAY THREE

REFLECTION

WORKSHOP MODULES:

1. Life Experience & Analysis: "Goodbye Old Self"

2. The Spiritual Essence of Closure

3. Self-Exploration #3: Creating Closure

4. Self-Realization #3: Meditation on Closure

5. Self-Reflection #3: Uncovering Life Lessons

6. Practical Spirituality: Letting Go

LIFE EXPERIENCE

DAY THREE

Goodbye Old Self!

In my drive home from the resort, still reeling from the warm welcome I had received and the promise of a new opportunity, I began to feel doubts and ask myself questions: *Two weeks?! Are you crazy? Can you really pull this off?* I knew I was on the right path, but now I had to figure out how I could quickly get my life in order to accommodate my new commitment. Then a voice inside me said, "You can do this. Think clearly and stay strong. Those who love you will support you and you will discover there is more love within you and around you than you ever imagined."

During this time, it felt like there was two of me: the previously anxious and depressed corporate manager married to an executive living on the East Coast; and the new confident, relaxed, joyful and independent adventurer who had just been "born" in the desert. I felt as if I were being transported from the body and mind of the old me into the new me. I was just along for the ride, compelled by a force greater than myself that had only my best interests at heart.

The old me kept exclaiming: *Two weeks?! That's insane! You have to fly home to Pennsylvania, tell your husband you're leaving him, file for divorce, pack all of your things, fly back to California and move into the mobile home in the desert (not to mention, learn how to teach aerobics!).*

The old me replied: *The mobile home does belong to your parents. You'll have to tell them this: "Hey mom and dad, I just wanted to let you know that I am leaving my successful husband, my big house, pool, and Porsche and moving into your little mobile home getaway. I don't have a car but a new friend has promised to loan me a truck, so don't worry, I've got it all figured out!"*

Fortunately, the new me was more convincing and just as light overcomes the darkness, she prevailed! With confidence and faith, I broke the news to my parents and told them that I was terribly unhappy on the East Coast, and desperately needed a new start. I told them that I knew in my heart that this would lead to much greater things going forward, and that I was destined to heal myself and many others in this beautiful oasis I wished to call home. Initially, my mother was understandably concerned about my financial stability and security. I knew she believed in me though and, because she loved me dearly, would eventually accept my new way of life.

My older sister was also concerned for my welfare. She simply said, "You know, it sucks to be poor!" I knew she was just looking out for me, but my immediate reaction was strong. *Poor!?* I thought, *Why would I ever be poor?* I had an education and a resume a mile long; I was perfectly healthy, capable, motivated and ambitious. "Poor" just never entered my mind. I was grateful for my sister's reaction though because it made me more determined than ever to prove I was capable of providing for myself and of being successful in whatever I pursued. She knew it would.

My father never really liked my first husband. Even though he worked for the same corporation for fifty years, my father always had a disdain for the corporate climbers who seemed not to care about the people below them. He could clearly see I wasn't happy. So there we were sitting on the front steps of the mobile home the day after my announcement and he said, "You know what sweetie, I just want you to be happy and if you think this will make you happy, then do it and I will support you. I love you and will always be there for you." I was so touched that I cried, and when I looked at him, he had tears in his eyes too. We hugged and then took a long walk in the desert discussing our dreams. He had fulfilled many of his dreams in life and knew that I would as well. As we walked and talked, I knew there would be many times just like this ahead and that, in the magic of the desert, my family and I would experience a new bond and have many incredible adventures.

Then it was time to break the news to my husband. What had originally been a ten-day visit to the desert had turned into a three-month stay. During that time, I had been enjoying my family and my newfound friends so much that I had become distant from our life together. I had ignored several of his calls and when we did speak, we were both well aware of the gap that was growing between us. So when I called to tell him that I was coming home but that we "needed to talk," we both knew that was code for "it's over."

When I arrived at the Philadelphia airport and walked toward the baggage claim, I saw my husband standing there and my knees became weak and my chest felt tight. A lump in my throat began to form and I wasn't sure I could get any words to come out. He was tall and handsome, and had a warm smile on his face. When I approached, he reached out and embraced me. We held each other as if it would be the last time. Then suddenly, the heavy air lifted, and we both felt lighter and joked around, albeit a little awkwardly. We decided to sit and have a drink in the airport lounge. I shared some desert adventures and he told me about his travels and work.

When we got back to the house, we sat down on the couch, no longer delaying the inevitable talk. I explained that I'd been unhappy on the East Coast for a long time, and lonely because he spent much more time on the road than he did at home. I told him I missed the sun and my family, and missed laughing and playing and feeling free. I also told him that I felt misplaced in the corporate world. He said he understood, but still was very sad and wondered if I could be patient until he too could move to California with me. He could tell by the look in my eyes that this was not what I wanted; he actually began to sob, which surprised me. So then of course I began to cry. We needed to cry together and so we did.

After our tears dried up, he got up and made a couple of drinks. We moved to the kitchen table where we calmly and reasonably made plans to go our separate ways. Our divorce was extremely amicable and even as we sat in the attorney's office a few days later, the lawyer looked at us as we were joking around, and said, "Are you guys sure about this?" And we were. Before leaving, I gave him some advice for his next attempt at marriage: "Try to be home sometimes. Either that or wait until you can be." He accepted my advice graciously and we wished each other the best of luck, truly meaning it.

MY

FAMILY

*This is the text of a letter that my sister and parents gave to me
at this time as a sign of their love, support, and encouragement...
along with a little advice!*

Dear Suzy,

*It seems a little redundant to say that I am very proud of your accomplishments.
The fact that you have emerged a beautiful, slender, and intelligent woman with
a mind and body so full of energy and enthusiasm is not only a source of pride but
also a thrill to observe and experience.*

*We have watched you grow from the most beautiful baby we have ever seen to
our favorite adult person. Our only wish is that you have grown independent and
confident and, of course, fulfilled and happy. Our purpose in your life has been
to love and to guide you with whatever knowledge we have accumulated over a
lifetime.*

*You are now ready to experience and learn as we have. It has never been our
intention or desire to impose our values or thoughts on you. However we would
like to share with you some of the experiences and ideas we hold dear and that
have made us successful and happy. We give them to you as a gift and hope that
somewhere along the line they will serve you well and enrich your life.*

1. *Discover where your true chance for greatness lies and let no power
   or persuasion deter you from your task.*

2. *You are possessed of many gifts. Do not compromise. If you use your talents
   and you fulfill your purpose on earth, you will honor yourself. If you don't,
   it is a mockery of your life.*

3. *Face your life with commitment and drive. If your life works well, it is
   because you have taken charge. Placing your life in someone else's hands
   will lead to uncertainty and a sense of loss.*

4. *Be courageous and willing to pursue your goals.*

5. *Pursue excellence with honor and distinction.*

6. *Pursuit of knowledge will bring fulfillment and lasting joy to your life.*

7. *Run with the best and surround yourself only with those whose talents
   and aspirations match your own.*

8. *Respect those around you who have talents that are well recognized.*

9. *Care about things that really matter.*

10. *Have fun, enjoy yourself and those around you. Enjoy nature.*

11. *Be sure music and art are a part of your life. They have power and beauty that nothing else can provide.*

12. *Success requires concentration of force and power. The power to finish the race must come from within.*

13. *Love yourself for what you are. Remember who you are. Stay true to yourself and know they don't come much better.*

14. *Be honest with yourself. Do not confuse your heart with false words from your mind.*

15. *You are an important part of a whole entity. Remember always: Your purposes to yourself are also important purposes to all around you. Therefore, care and take pride in the difference you make in this world.*

16. *The love and respect of your family will always be there in times of need and of great happiness.*

Self-Reflection
Time Period: February 1996
Topic: Closure

Memories, Thoughts & Feelings:

After running around trying to organize a life for myself in my new desert home, it dawned on me that I wasn't the only one in the picture! I had to break my plans to my parents and my sister; I really wanted their support, love and acceptance. I also had to break it to my husband, but I knew he already had a feeling I might be moving on.

Suspected Causes: *Related past history*

In the past, I relied on others to steer me in the right direction. I would ask my parents, sister, and husband for advice. I always felt compelled to meet the expectations that society and others had of me. Intent on fulfilling the roles of "dutiful wife," "successful daughter," and "corporate achiever," I always looked outside myself for models to emulate. I never looked within, not trusting or even recognizing my own inner resources.

The cause of my newfound independence came from the realization that only I and my spiritual guide truly know what's best for me. I had to learn to distinguish between others' loving advice and my own desire to please them.

Effects:
Occurring as a result of the causes identified

My own identity: Emerges as labels and layers of my old self start to peel away.

Self-confidence: An inner knowledge that I am worthy and capable of making my own decisions flourish.

Courage: I know that I will survive, and thrive! I know that the "new me" is strong, smart and talented.

Self-reliance: I am determined to do things my way this time around. I will not accept criticism or judgment. I will politely and gently defer advice and ask others to refrain from using the dreaded word *should*.

Lessons Hidden Within:

Ultimately, those who really love and care about me want me to be happy. If I am gentle but firm about what I truly need and want, they will understand. In a surprising and touching way, they even reach out to do whatever they can to support me, even if my decisions are initially hard to accept.

Family rocks. I know that no matter what, they will always be there to support and encourage me.

Above all, I learned to love and trust myself.

Lesson Plan:

I will be more independent and courageous going forward.

I will trust that my own decision-making capacity is reliable and reflects intelligent choices.

Knowing that the wisdom and experience I have gained over my lifetime are both valuable, I will confidently use my own insight to guide me.

I will recognize that when I am in the right environment with like-minded people, I will be respected and I will flourish.

I will have confidence in my ability to persevere, knowing that there are no odds too great to overcome.

DAY THREE
The Spiritual Essence Of Closure

A Conversation with Spiritual Counselor & Minister, Janet Myatt

SUZANNE: Good afternoon, Janet. Welcome to day three of the workshop. Yesterday we covered the topic of transition and the alchemical changes that take place within a transformational experience. As part of that transition, there is also going to have to be some closure. We will have to end old ways of seeing ourselves and others. We may have to say goodbye to people, places and things that defined our old way of being. So, how do we deal with the loss of the familiar?

JANET: I liken this to moving. In order to move, we have to go through a sorting process because we're going to be packing up all of our belongings and moving from one location to another. As we do this, we come across things that no longer serve us. We're not going to take the time to box them up because there's no place for them in our new home. I remember when I was moving once and I came across my kid's children books. I was sad to see them go, but they no longer served us and I knew that someone else would benefit from them.

This sorting process allows us to honor something that used to be important to us; we recognize that we wouldn't be where we are today if we hadn't had those experiences, for better or for worse. The good influences and the bad, the people we've loved and the people we've hated — all have served their purpose.

SUZANNE: I firmly believe that the most challenging people in our lives are our best teachers. Once we recognize them as such, we can actually be grateful for their influence on our lives. They have been placed in our lives to illuminate who we are and to activate our higher self. They challenge us to rise to the occasion and take the higher road. They often teach us patience and tolerance and force us to consider another point of view we may have been resistant to. Or they may simply be showing us a way *not* to be (which is likely a reflection of some aspect of ourselves). That's why they may have triggered such strong reactions, because they are hitting very close to home and highlighting our own faults. These interactions are a great opportunity to reflect upon our own reactions to the people, places and things we encounter on a daily basis.

So when we are sorting through our old ways of being and trying to create new ones, we can appreciate the challenging people and circumstances along with the more pleasing and enjoyable ones. Both have taught us important lessons that we can apply to our life today. Through this sorting process, we can take precious lessons with us, keep positive memories, and let go of any negative energy that no longer serves us.

JANET: Yes, there's a moment of consciously *allowing* all these things from the past to be complete, to be done. Then we can live in the present moment, without having to recreate the same old things over and over again. Forgiveness is the key to closure, along with a willingness to change our minds about who we really are and what we're here to do. We can be free to create our best life right here and now in the present moment.

Now it's your turn!

SELF-EXPLORATION #3
Creating Closure

Think about a time when a significant relationship or set of circumstances abruptly came to an end, such that you never had the closure you needed to move on in a healthy way. Maybe there are things you wish you could have said or done before the situation was lost. Close your eyes and review the memories that play across the movie screen in your mind. One will stand out above all the rest. This is the one that needs your attention the most at this time. You may want to use photos and memorabilia to help you relive the emotions and enhance these memories. The Q & A will expose the cause-and-effect relationships between the details of the experience. This new insight will help you understand how and why events unfolded just as they did. In the final analysis, you will clearly see the lessons you were meant to learn from this experience and apply them to your life today.

Explore your Heart and Mind

What were the reasons behind the circumstance ending?

_____

_____

_____

_____

Was the ending a result of your desire to move forward or were you forced into moving on?

_____

_____

_____

Do you feel that you had the opportunity to express what was in your heart at the time, or were there things left unsaid?

_____

_____

_____

Are you pleased with the way that you handled the significant ending in your life or do you wish you would have done things differently?

_____

_____

_____

How did you learn and grow from the experience of ending a life circumstance? Did it cause you grief or did you see it as an opportunity for a new beginning? Did you feel both sadness and anticipation?

_____

_____

_____

_____

Identify Lessons and Shifts

In retrospect, can you see how your life benefited from closing one door and opening another?

_____

_____

_____

_____

Even though you may miss some things about the past, are you able to see how you learned from those experiences and why the new "wiser" you had to move forward?

_____

_____

_____

_____

Are you able to look back and embrace the positive aspects of the past and let go of the negative ones?

_____

_____

_____

_____

_____

Now that you realize those experiences were necessary for your personal growth, can you release any blame or resentment you may have placed on yourself or others?

_____

_____

_____

_____

_____

Looking back, can you see how you are now a new and improved version of the person you were before, that it is because of those endings that you were able to fully embrace new beginnings?

_____

_____

_____

_____

Even if you weren't the one to initiate the ending, can you honestly look back and thank those involved for opening a new door that ultimately led to bigger and better opportunities?

_____

_____

_____

_____

_____

Once we realize that each and every one of us are doing the best we can with what we know at the time, we are able to view people, places and things from our past as beneficial learning experiences and free them from any blame or attachment. We realize that everything that unfolds in our lives are steps on our evolutionary path.

_____

_____

_____

_____

Time for your Reflection

Now that you have analyzed this experience more closely, you will be able to pinpoint the causes and effects that define it. Understanding this relationship will help you balance the karma and recognize the life-lessons within. Your lesson plan will allow you to apply your learning to your life. You can open your heart, heal the wounds, forgive and forget. You can fold up the past and put it behind you. This will give you the freedom to focus on the present and visualize the future with an open heart and mind, unmarked by any scars from the past.

Now it's time to explore the deeper meaning and greater purpose of this experience by going within during meditation. During this process of connecting with the emotions and feelings attached to this experience, the spiritual essence of it will be revealed and the lessons you were meant to learn from it will become much clearer.

SELF-REALIZATION #3
Meditation on Closure

It's time to progress on your path of self-realization.

Before journaling your experience, please engage in Dynamic Movement Therapy to open and expand your body. You can engage in the movement and breathing practices by referring back to the written guidelines in the introduction, or you can access the audio download for free at ***www. suzannerosstranscendence.com/Up!Trilogy/WakeUp!Meditations.***

Now you are ready to go within. Exploring your deepest feelings and emotions at this time is very beneficial in helping you move forward with a clear mind. It's important to be sure that you are connecting with your authentic feelings, and not justifying your actions solely based on your material or financial well-being. Having a sense of closure after an important chapter in your life has ended is critical to the process of moving on. Without it, you will be plagued with the nagging sense that you should have said or done things differently and these scenarios will play over and over in your mind until you do find closure.

Whether the ending was a conscious decision or out of your control, it still requires that you wrap up any unfinished business and reconcile your relationships with the people involved. There is a spiritual aspect to closure as well. If unfinished business still nags at you, you can use the VIS-MED to remove the debris that has been left behind. This debris causes toxic thought patterns to repeat themselves and may even create toxic behaviors that affect your life today. We will eliminate this toxicity by removing the negative energy and replacing it with positive reinforcements.

Once you have cleansed your energy centers and your spirit is flowing freely, we can examine the events more clearly. We can also look at the relationships more closely and see what purpose they served. We can apply a cause-and-effect analysis to the experience as a whole and in this way reveal the meaning and purpose.

Let's move into this powerful VIS-MED for Closure. We will envision reconciling the relationships with people, places and things that you left behind. These practices will help you move beyond any unfinished business and allow you to move forward with a clear mind. The spiritual and emotional energy that has been blocked will be liberated to flow freely and you will experience higher levels of physical, mental and spiritual well-being.

You can download an audio version of this guided meditation by going to my website at ***www.suzannerosstranscendence.com.*** On the Up!Trilogy menu, select **Wake Up! Meditations** and go to the **VIS-MED for Closure.**

DAY THREE
Self-Reflection

Name of the Experience: _____

Time Period: _____

Topic: Reflection

Memories, Thoughts & Feelings:

_____

_____

_____

_____

_____

_____

Suspected Causes:
Related past history

_____

_____

_____

_____

_____

_____

_____

Effects:
Occurring as a result of the causes identified

_____

_____

_____

_____

_____

Lessons Hidden Within:

_____

_____

_____

_____

_____

Lesson Plan:

_____

_____

_____

_____

_____

DAY THREE
PRACTICAL SPIRITUALITY

Closure: Letting Go

"As you adjust to letting go, your knowledge, faculties, desires as well as your thoughts, intentions and actions will progressively become more positive, constructive, patient and loving. You will perceive a higher calling to life's purposes and experiences."

— Lonnie C. Edwards. M.D.

Adults tend to resist change. Even if we know that our circumstances need to evolve, change makes us uneasy. A simple fear of the unknown keeps many people in situations that are undesirable. Since the meaning of life is to create, however, we must keep creating new experiences that allow us to learn and grow. If we find ourselves in a situation where we are not being creative, and we don't consciously choose to make a change, conditions may begin to deteriorate anyway. One of Janet's teacher once said, "If spirit isn't creating, it's destroying."

Whether we find the courage to make a change or spirit does it for us, it is still difficult to leave our old life behind and move on to new adventures. It feels like we always leave a piece of ourselves behind in the old life, especially at first. We feel fragmented and our mind seems to spend time in both the old and new lives. Our mind may spend time romanticizing the old life and replaying past events. It may also replay scenes that it regrets. Or we may reimagine better versions of these past scenes in which things were said or done differently.

Although we may miss our old surroundings, it is usually the daily interactions with others that are most difficult to let go of. We get used to seeing the same faces and even when we don't like all of them, we still miss seeing them every day. We wonder if they miss us, or whether they are thinking and talking about us. Sometimes it even bothers us that they can get on fine without us, when we thought we were such an important part of their lives.

All this prevents us from embracing our new life fully. As time goes on, our mind will spend less time revisiting the past, but here are some effective practices for consciously moving forward. This practice of letting go involves three stages of detachment.

The first stage involves letting go of the people you left behind. You have two choices when it comes to people with whom you may have never said a proper goodbye to or may have unfinished business with. It may be appropriate to set up a meeting, live or over the phone, or to send a letter or email. On the other hand, depending on the way in which you left, it may be best to leave things lie. In this case, an effective practice is to write a letter anyway and keep it to yourself. Writing a letter that expresses your feelings about leaving a relationship behind is a very cathartic practice.

The second stage of detachment involves compartmentalization. In your mind, put all of the people, places and things from your old way of life in a box. You are no longer creating new memories and experiences there and so it will remain just as it is, frozen in time. It will have a beginning and an end. You will review the contents of this box like a movie streaming in fast forward from the beginning to the end. When you reach the end, imagine the words "The End." Then this box will remain closed and you will only open it when you make a conscious choice to do so. Simply ask yourself if opening the box will serve you, or whether it will be a distraction from your new life. This is a way of consciously controlling the thoughts in your mind rather than just letting them wander around aimlessly. Mastery of the mind is a very powerful practice.

The third stage of detachment is simply repeating the phrase, *"Have faith. Trust spirit. Let it go."* Any time you feel doubts about your new adventure creeping into your mind, repeat this phrase. Whenever you find yourself either romanticizing or regretting your old life, repeat this phrase. If you long for the familiarity of prior circumstances, remind yourself why you made a change and repeat this phrase.

We have been focusing on transitions and closure that have affected your life in major ways. Sometimes during the course of a single day, we can find ourselves transitioning in and out of interactions that need closure. We may have interactions that didn't sit right with us, and will endlessly replay them in our mind. At times, this can be helpful if we find constructive ways to resolve the problem, or make ourselves feel better about what was said or done. Most of the time, however, we just have to let it go. We have to make a conscious choice to release things that are no longer serving us. We have to tell ourselves that we were doing the best we could at the time, and let it go. This is another good time to repeat the phrase: *"Have faith. Trust spirit. Let it go."*

Awakening through Reflection

DAY FOUR

NEW BEGINNINGS

WORKSHOP MODULES:

1. Life Experience & Analysis: "The Desert Blossom Blooms"

2. The Spiritual Essence of New Beginnings

3. Self-Exploration #4: Navigating a New Beginning

4. Self-Realization #4: Meditation on New Beginnings

5. Self-Reflection #4: Uncovering Life Lessons

6. Practical Spirituality: Surrendering to Spirit

LIFE EXPERIENCE

DAY FOUR

The Desert Blossom Blooms

The dawn of my new life greeted me as I got off the plane in San Diego, when I spied a giant bouquet of roses with two legs awaiting me. I had met my new desert friend one night while out with my father dancing at a local lounge. I became aware that he was staring at me from across the room with a big smile on his face.

When we locked eyes, the whole room fell silent and it truly felt like it was just him and I in the world, just the two of us, at that moment.

After that, I felt giddy and shy, which is not my nature at all. My father and I decided to dance to a lively country song and moments after we began to dance, I noticed that the staring guy was dancing right beside us with some friends. He kept eyeing me as he danced closer, laughing and obviously enjoying this opportunity to flirt. We were all having such a great time that night. Everyone was so relaxed and comfortable in this easy environment where no one cared about anything other than just letting their hair down and sharing some laughs.

It wasn't long before the staring guy came over and introduced himself. He introduced himself as Scott, and then requested my father's permission before asking me to dance. My father approved and so we danced alongside his other friends and I instantly felt like I was one of the gang. I was having so much fun with my new friends that I didn't want the night to end. I learned that they were all going to another bar when this band stopped playing and I thought it would be fun to go along. Scott asked my father if it would be okay and reassured him that he would get me home safely. My father liked him instantly and knew I was having fun, so he agreed.

After that night, Scott and I saw each other regularly, hiking and biking all over the desert. I even joined him and his friends to go off-roading in Mexico which I had never done before. I had more fun "roughing it" on this trip than I could remember having in a long time. I realized that I had become quite a princess during my seven-year marriage. Because my husband was successful in business and enjoyed fine restaurants and fancy hotels, I had become used to that lifestyle, even though it never held much charm for me. I grew up on the beach and preferred just being casual and having fun outdoors with my easy-going friends.

I knew I was falling hard for my new friend in the desert. He was sweet, romantic and fun-loving. There was always a twinkle in his eye that suggested some type of innocent mischief but I trusted him implicitly; I just knew when I was with him, I would be well taken care of. This has become the overriding theme of our relationship ever since. We fell madly in love over the course of the next year, got married and here we are, almost twenty years later, still more in love than ever. We have been through rocky roads and smooth sailing, but every morning when we wake up, still together, we know how lucky we are.

Now, back to my new career path - my true calling in health and fitness! While still living in New Jersey, I had briefly worked for a large fitness organization. I truly enjoyed the environment, working in a health club, but spent most of my time in an upstairs office as the Director of Operations. I used to watch the personal trainers with their clients and think, "What a great job that must be! How gratifying it must feel to help someone realize their goals and improve their health!"

Although short-lived because of my husband's transfer to Pennsylvania, the exposure to this environment left an indelible impression on me. And so here was my long dreamed-of opportunity to express the fitness instructor inside me that had been dying to come out and play! Before returning to the desert, I had spent much of the ten days back east memorizing the steps, moves and instructions from every exercise videotape I owned. I practiced and practiced for hours each day and as I did, I became more and more confident that the path I had chosen was perfect for me, and that I was going to have more fun and get more fit than I had ever been before. And so I did.

Working at the resort turned out to be a truly wonderful experience. Everyone I met was so warm and friendly and in a short period of time, I had made many new friends. We would all get together after hours at the resort and listen to music under the stars. During the day, I would teach my aerobics classes, including water aerobics in a huge Olympic-size pool surrounded with palm trees and gorgeous flowers. Some guests would participate and others would just relax in the lounge chairs around tables with colorful umbrellas. The guests of the hotel were always in a great mood because they were enjoying the desert sun and fun as much as I was. Locals were welcomed to join the classes as well, many of whom became my friends. In seven years on the East Coast, I had never made one single friend. In less than one month in the desert, I had made at least twenty. This is how I knew I had truly come home.

I soon became interested in expanding my services and decided to become a Certified Personal Trainer. I obtained all of the study materials and became intensely focused on my goal. At the same time, my sister had left active duty, joined the Reserves, and decided to go to law school. So while I studied anatomy, physiology and biomechanics, she sat beside me at the pool and studied law. Within a few months, I was certified as a personal trainer and decided to put an ad in the local newspaper. I would need a name for my business and so I thought long and hard about it. One night while my family was gathered around, I proudly announced the name I had settled on: "Get Serious!" My dad looked at me, rolled his eyes and said, "Lighten Up!" We all just stared at him and together said, "That's it! Lighten-Up!" I had been so intense for so many years and it was only when I finally decided to let go and lighten up that things seemed to fall into place beautifully.

I thought I might have to travel to San Diego to get a job as a personal trainer in a large club, since there were no real fitness centers in the desert at that time. I was shocked one day when my phone rang and the woman caller wanted to know about my personal training services advertised in the newspaper. I was speechless and about dropped the phone; it was that unexpected.

Fortunately I gathered myself and acted professional. We met the next day and decided that we would work out together in her home. Her husband would join us and I would train the both of them. Little did I know that this woman and her husband were popular at the local country club and it wasn't long before my business began to grow. Soon I was driving from house to house, training one client after the next. It became obvious that I needed a place to train clients; I had met a girlfriend who owned a coffee book store in one of the strip malls and she knew of a studio that was available. It was a scary proposition to make the investment and take on the overhead but once again I had no doubt in my mind that it was exactly the right thing to do. And so I did.

Eventually my business outgrew that space, then another, and finally an old warehouse space in the plaza was renovated per my specifications. It turned out beautifully and I was able to include a large space for classes as well as a massage room and nutrition counter. My business was an incredible success not just because I was making a nice profit, but because I had made my dream come true. I had healed myself and was healing many others — just like the voice on the mountaintop said! Most of my clients were older and suffered from a myriad of diseases and conditions. Over the years, I obtained advanced certifications to help them recover from strokes, diabetes and heart disease as well as knee and hip replacements. I remember one gentleman in particular who I had helped recover from paralysis following a stroke. He arrived in a wheelchair barely able to move his right side, and after six months of dedicated effort, he left with just a walking cane. He was so grateful, he insisted on giving me his R.V.! My favorite client, Betty, swore to her friends and family that I had saved her life, and became a walking sandwich board for my business. I loved all of my clients; I felt like I had fifty sets of grandparents. I had been truly blessed and I knew it. I never took one moment for granted. I was living the life of my dreams, both personally and professionally, and I never worried much about the details or the future. I still felt like I was being guided by this incredibly benevolent force who had told me that I was loved more than I could possibly imagine… and I finally believed it.

SCOTT AND I PLAYING IN THE DESERT

A CELEBRATION OF TRUE LOVE

THE GRAND OPENING

OF LIGHTEN-UP!

Self-Reflection
Time Period: 1996 - 2008
Topic: New Beginnings

Memories, Thoughts & Feelings:

My new life in the desert falls into place beautifully. I fall in love with a man who I'm still married to twenty years later. I am truly enjoying every minute of my new job as an instructor at the resort. I love meeting all the guests and making friends with the locals. I have had the time of my life, but want to keep expanding and progressing so I get certified as a personal trainer. I opened a fitness studio which grows into a large wellness center. I "heal myself and many others" just like the voice on the mountaintop said I would.

Suspected Causes:

Related past history

I opened my heart and opened my mind to new possibilities.

I set aside ego and judgment, and let others in. As a result, they let me in. We learned to accept each other despite our outward differences.

I embraced every opportunity and expressed gratitude for every gift I was given. Whether it was a new client or a new friend, I knew each person was a gift that had come into my life for a divine purpose.

I was determined to be successful in this new venture. I wanted to become the best fitness instructor and most qualified personal trainer I possibly could.

Effects:

Occurring as a result of the causes identified

The effects of opening my heart: I met and married the love of my life. I made many new friends who became very close to my heart, and still are today. I attracted many wonderful clients who became like family to me. I created precious memories with my own dear family.

The effects of opening my mind: I set aside preconceived ideas about what it meant to be truly successful, and didn't allow barriers or limits to enter my mind. I firmly believed that I could do, be, and have anything I desired. And so I did.

Lessons Hidden Within:

Do not allow society's definition of success to prevent me from following my heart and pursuing my dreams.

Do not allow my own preconceived notions about people, places, and things to prevent me from finding profound and positive influences.

Do not allow doubts and judgments about myself to prevent me from reaching for the stars.

See through the barriers that are thrown at me, viewing them as challenges to be overcome and opportunities to grow. Learn to be a victor rather than a victim.

Never set limits on myself, my pursuits, or the people around me. There are no limits in this infinitely abundant universe and you can do, have, and be anything you truly desire if you just keep the faith.

Lesson Plan:

I will never put labels on anything. I will keep an open mind about people and allow them to define themselves. Then they will be free to express and reveal their own true nature.

I will never doubt my ability to expand in all directions without limitation.

I will welcome any barriers that present themselves and view them as opportunities to learn and grow. In this way, they will increase my self-confidence and faith in my own strength and courage.

I will remain open to any and all people and opportunities that come my way, with pure gratitude for each and every one.

DAY FOUR
The Spiritual Essence of New Beginnings
A Conversation with Spiritual Counselor & Minister, Janet Myatt

SUZANNE: Good afternoon, Janet. Thank you so much for joining us today. We had such a wonderful flow going from transformation to transition, and then closure. What we are exploring here is new beginnings: How do we open our hearts to the new opportunities that are presenting themselves without doubting whether we have made the right choice? How do we prevent ourselves from having regrets and thinking that maybe we shouldn't have left our old way of life behind? How do we move forward with faith in our new plan?

JANET: Like any birth process, a new beginning involves some labor! While there is a certain joy of anticipation about new possibilities, they also entail some struggle. We are talking about transformation in a linear manner because that's the nature of language, but actually the stages of change overlap and interpenetrate one another. While we are opening up to the new, we are still letting go of the old. After all, we know our old way of doing things, but we can't possibly know this new way yet. So there will be a learning curve, and a process of adapting to the new. This can be overwhelming if we don't give ourselves time to grieve, to let go, and to discover new things.

SUZANNE: Yes, I see what you mean. In this workshop, we are trying to separate out themes and address them individually, but life is actually "holistic" and we are constantly transforming, transitioning and starting new things while ending others.

JANET: I have found that establishing a daily practice of checking in with myself makes this process more manageable. I have gotten into the habit of asking my inner divine Self, "What do I need to do today that's going to serve the highest good?" In any situation where I'm looking to create a new beginning, I take a moment to go within and ask, "What needs to happen here? What should I do, or not do, in this moment or in this situation?" Most importantly, I have to take another *longer* moment, to listen and discern the answer coming from my soul. In this way, I learn to respond from a new level of intelligent love, rather than reacting from within my old knee-jerk patterns.

We have to get savvy to the difference between the voice of fear coming from our ego, and the voice of intelligent love coming from our spirit. We have to work at sharpening our intuition so that we can notice and respond to those synchronistic experiences where just the right book falls in our lap, or just the right person calls on the phone, or we have just the right conversation with the clerk in the grocery store. We have to learn to recognize when Spirit is responding to our query.

SUZANNE: This means accepting that there are no random events, and that all of our experiences and interactions are symbolic. We have to take the time to reflect upon the greater significance of whatever is unfolding, recognizing how each event relates to the whole. Every moment becomes a precious gift — an opportunity to listen to our higher guidance. We have to allow spirit to flow without the interference of our skeptical and overly judgmental ego.

JANET: We also have to understand our fear responses. The ego will resist change, anything that makes us feel vulnerable. This fear slowly boxes us in until we can no longer grow. Once that happens, there's no room for new beginnings. We have to develop our courage and invest faithfully in the growth that our spirit is leading us toward.

SUZANNE: Esther Hicks, who channeled Group Abraham in the book *Law of Attraction* teaches that we can use our "Emotional Guidance System" to help us determine what thoughts, words and actions will serve the highest good. She says that we instinctively know in our hearts what is best so when we think, say, and do those things that reflect our highest self, we will be rewarded with positive feelings and emotions. When we choose to think and behave in ways that don't align with the highest good, we feel bad. We may even feel guilty or ashamed or even worse, resentful or angry at others. We always know we have gone wrong when we feel victimized, right? This will not help us as we move into a new way of living or being.

JANET: With every new beginning, we are venturing into uncharted territory. Yes, we are bringing our life experience, talents, and skills with us, but we are also venturing into a new aspect of our life. We must be willing to be vulnerable to the process of learning. This requires a tolerance for trial and error without self-punishment and guilt. We have to be patient with ourselves while we go through the process of finding out what works and what doesn't. So there has to be some grace and forgiveness, some amusement and enthusiasm for not always knowing what we're doing.

For a transformational shift to complete itself, we must be willing to:

1. Get in the habit of regularly checking in with our inner wisdom through meditation, prayer, and/or quiet reflection.

2. Get really good at discerning the difference between the voice of spirit(our loving intelligence) and the voice of ego (our fearful resistance and defensiveness.)

3. Be willing to do things differently, be a beginner, make mistakes, and be willing to learn.

SUZANNE: Thanks so much for making these important points so clear, Janet. This guidance will be very helpful as we move forward into any new aspect of our lives.

Now it's your turn!

SELF-EXPLORATION #4 – NAVIGATING A NEW BEGINNING
Theme: New Beginnings

Close your eyes and think about a time when you made a fresh start. Think about the new circumstances, people, and places that you were introduced to. Picture yourself in this environment and remember how it felt to be embarking upon this new experience or phase of your life. Whether it was a positive, voluntary change or a difficult challenge that felt enforced upon you, try to see the big picture of how and why it happened, and what changed in your life as a result of this beginning.

Explore your Heart and Mind

Think about a time when you were entering the first day of a new school year. You may havefelt shy and self-conscious about meeting new people, orfelt vulnerable to scrutiny and judgment. On the other hand, you may have been enthusiastic about the opportunity to make new friends. You may have made an effort to be outgoing and gregarious. Reflecting upon the way you have approached new beginnings in your life, describe the feelings and emotions that have accompanied them over the years.

Were you shy or outgoing?

_____

_____

_____

Were you self-conscious or self-assured?

_____

_____

Did you make new friends easily or were you introverted?

_____

_____

_____

Now think of the ways in which you have evolved over the years by recalling experiences as a young adult, when you may have entered college or started a new job. Looking at the more recent past, compare how you approach new experiences as an adult, versus how you did as a youth.

Do you still see remnants of the feelings and emotions you had when you were younger, or has your ability to adjust to new experiences developed over the years?

_____

_____

_____

_____

In regards to new relationships, think back on those that have affected your life most significantly. Try to recall your first best friend or first love. Do you remember being shy and coy, or were you outgoing and receptive?

_____

_____

_____

_____

Were you the pursuer or were you pursued?

_____

_____

_____

_____

Identify Lessons and Shifts

Have you made a conscious effort to intentionally improve upon your personal skills and ability to meet new people or face new challenges?

_____

_____

_____

Have you ever had to face new environments or challenges for work? Have you ever received special training in this regard? If so, in what ways did it help you embrace new experiences?

_____

_____

_____

_____

Try to recognize a pattern that characterizes your feelings and emotions around relationships. Do you see yourself as the one who pursues new friendships or romances, or are you typically the one being pursued?

_____

_____

_____

Now explore your receptivity to new experiences. Focus on the kind of environment in which you feel at ease and are able to openly engage with others. Now focus on those environments that make you feel uneasy, or less comfortable approaching and interacting with others. Try to recall the specifics about people and places you are comfortable with, and those you are intimidated by:

_____

_____

_____

_____

_____

_____

Recognizing the types of new people and places that you can approach comfortably allows you to appreciate them more. Identifying challenging and difficult circumstances gives you the opportunity to examine and improve upon your perspective so you can welcome all new opportunities.

Time for your Reflection

New beginnings are typically marked by a confusing and contradictory mix of emotions. The following reflection will help to shed light on the true meaning and purpose you may discover in a new circumstance. You will see how new people were meant to come into your life for a greater purpose, and you will understand how the new place is important for your personal growth. As the details unfold, significant synchronicities will be revealed. The cause and effects will uncover the lessons and you can add them to your master plan. You are consciously evolving, my friend, and making significant progress on your ascension path. Now we are ready to move into movement and meditation so we can uncover the deeper truths that lie within.

SELF-REALIZATION #4
Meditation on New Beginnings

It's time to progress on your path of self-realization.

Before journaling your experience, please engage in Dynamic Movement Therapy to open and expand your body. Then be seated comfortably and perform the Inspirational Breathing Practices to oxygenate your body and clear your mind of distractions. You can engage in the movement and breathing practices by referring back to the written guidelines in the introduction, or you can access the audio download for free at *www.suzannerosstranscendence.com/Up!Trilogy/WakeUp!Meditations.*

Now you are ready to go within by doing your visualization/meditation. New challenges can be exhilarating, but they can also trigger anxiety and fear as you release your attachment to the way things were and embark upon an unfamiliar path. You may feel a little melancholy about detaching from the past, and this leads to romanticizing it. You may have a tendency to focus on the things you will miss, and overlook the reasons you moved on. You may also struggle with feelings of self-worth and uncertainty about your capacity to conquer the novel challenges ahead. Before you can fully embrace your new beginnings, it's important to detach from the past somewhat. This doesn't mean that you lose contact with old friends or places, it simply means that you focus your energy on looking ahead instead of looking behind.

We will spin your chakras to be sure that you have cleared away any remaining emotional debris, and then we will use positive reinforcement to help you see your new circumstances more clearly. This will also give you a clearer picture of the events that led up to it. The key to reconciling any emotions still attached to this period will be to identify the lessons within. Once your energy is flowing freely and you have connected to your higher self, you will receive the insight you are seeking.

You can download an audio version of this guided meditation by going to my website at *www.suzannerosstranscendence.com.* On the Up!Trilogy menu, select **Wake Up! Meditations** and go to the **VIS-MED for New Beginnings.**

DAY FOUR
Self-Reflection

Name of the Experience: _____

Time Period: _____

Topic: New Beginnings

Memories, Thoughts & Feelings:

_____

_____

_____

_____

_____

_____

Suspected Causes:
Related past history

_____

_____

_____

_____

_____

_____

_____

Effects:
Occurring as a result of the causes identified

_____

_____

_____

_____

_____

_____

Lessons Hidden Within:

_____

_____

_____

_____

_____

Lesson Plan:

_____

_____

_____

_____

_____

DAY FOUR
PRACTICAL SPIRITUALITY

New Beginnings: Surrendering to Spirit

"When you surrender, it is the human ego, also known as the altered ego, that gradually transforms back into the original consciousness of your divine nature."

— Aurelia Louise Jones

It's your reality that you are creating, and no matter how much you might think that others are interfering with your manifestation, you have intentionally brought them into your life. Their role is to teach you the important lessons that are necessary for your soul's evolution. Remembering that they are essentially your teachers allows you to fully appreciate their presence. You are always being challenged by the lessons you have come here to learn. The only thing that you are being tested on in this "school" called life is the quality of your reaction to, and interaction with, those people, places and things you are constantly presented with. If you remember nothing else, remember this! It comes down to simply asking yourself: *Were those the best words I could have used in this situation, or could I do better next time? Were those the best actions I could've taken or should I try again? Do I need to change the way I'm thinking about things?*

You can make a checklist of qualifying values. Were your thoughts, words, and actions loving, compassionate, supportive, understanding, nonjudgmental, respectful, considerate, appropriate, sympathetic, empathetic, helpful and kind? Following is a personal "progression of thought awareness" that led me to a profound revelation, profoundly accelerating the evolutionary transformation of my soul.

1. I become aware of the cause-and-effect relationship between my thoughts, words and actions.

2. This leads to a greater motivation to attain the highest level of consciousness in creating my experiences.

3. As I become aware that my positive emotions correlate with the best thoughts, words, and acts and conversely, that my negative emotions seem to correlatewith the worst choices, I can use this to direct and redirect my mind, speech and behavior accordingly.z

4. I begin to recognize that my "self" and other "selves" are unified, because we are each other's mutual projections. What I think, they sense. What I feel, they respond to. What I say, they react to accordingly and how I act affects them as much as it does myself. We are collectively sharing consciousness and we are connected as a unified whole in an infinite mind.

5. Now I begin to comprehend that there is only one great field of consciousness, and that my energetic movement within it affects the whole. Realizing that even my thoughts are expressed as energy, as well as my words and actions, I become simultaneously aware of both the vulnerability and invincibility of my circumstances.

6. I realize the profound effect of my free will, meaning I can choose between these states of being:
   · unconscious or conscientious
   · unaware or aware
   · negative or positive
   · neutral and unchanging, or actively evolving
   · victimization or responsibility

7. At this point, the reality of my existence as an energetic vibrational "wave" of individual consciousness within an undulating sea of "other-consciousness" starts to wash over me. Instead of being ONE, I am ALL. Then the concept of ALL-IN-ONE illuminates my soul and I'm elated by this feeling of unity.

8. This ultimate revelation fills me with pure ecstasy, soon transforming into serenity as I recognize the primordial "I AM". I finally realize "I AM THAT I AM." This inspires my creative expression.

As I live and breathe, I AM, when I die and cease, I AM.

For all of eternity, I AM.

I AM! I AM! I AM!

In the fabric of time and space, I am a single thread

Interwoven into the divine plan upon which I am being led

In the light of all consciousness, I am pure radiance

Illuminating the path that leads to Omniscience

In the spiritual realm, I am a white dove

Ascending and descending in search of true love

In my transcendence, I will be reunited with his holiness

I am a swirling spiral of ecstasy in a realm of divine infinity

For all eternity, I AM! I AM! I AM!

I AM THAT I AM!

— Suzanne Ross

I encourage you to read the progressive realizations (1-8) over and again until you feel you have fully grasped the profundity of their implications. The goal is to become acutely aware of your interconnectivity with the world around you and ultimately, with the infinite "I AM."

Awakening through Reflection

DAY FIVE

HARMONY

WORKSHOP MODULES:

1. Life Experience & Analysis: "Glory Days"

2. The Spiritual Essence of Harmony

3. Self-Exploration #5: Living in Harmony

4. Self-Realization #5: Meditation on Harmony

5. Self-Reflection #5: Uncovering Life Lessons

6. Practical Spirituality: Harmony & Equilibrium

LIFE EXPERIENCE

DAY FIVE

Glory Days

The desert turned out to be a true blessing for our entire family. We had been separated by distance for so many years and this remote getaway turned out to be the perfect place for us to reconnect. I love my parents dearly and one of the toughest challenges about living back East had been the 'great divide' between us. Whenever I would have to get on a plane to go back after visiting them, I would have an overwhelming sadness and always felt like I was going against my deepest instincts leaving them. Now that I was living so close by, we were spending a great deal of time together in the desert.

Part One: Desert Days with Dad

The time I spent with my dad in the desert created many beautiful memories. My sister often joined us and the three of us would set out on daylong adventures hiking mountain ranges, exploring caves, and watching wildlife. One day while hiking with our dog Joey, my dad grabbed my hand and gave me the "shush" sign as he pointed at a herd of bighorn sheep scattered across the side of the mountain. We just stood there and stared in awe, knowing we'd been given a special gift. Although there are many bighorn sheep in the desert, it's not very common to actually see them, especially an entire herd!

On another occasion, we were biking through a desert wash and stopped to take a break. I excused myself to go behind a bush. I walked toward what looked like a small cave and squatted down. All of a sudden I heard a loud growling sound just above my head. Going against everything I had been told about running away like prey from mountain lions, I ran like hell with my pants around my ankles, trying to pull them up as I went. When I reached my dad, my eyes were wild and all I could say as I grabbed my bike was, "Go! Go! Go!" We high-tailed it out of there and never looked back.

Every time we set out, there was a new adventure. We would usually end up at this old biker bar, full of interesting characters who were always good for stories of their own. Many of the stool warmers at this bar were old-timers who looked like they had spent many years under the hot sun. Even though they were weathered and worn, they seemed content and always had a great sense of humor about it all. My dad retired a few years after I moved to the desert. We all loved it so much that my parents decided to buy a retirement home there. By this time, my husband and I had purchased a beautiful home that we had renovated and turned into our own little paradise. I was so thrilled that my parents would retire in the desert and be so close by! The thought of being able to see them whenever I pleased was wonderful especially since we had been separated for so long.

My father adored the desert and wanted to stay there year-round. My mother wasn't as crazy about it because the temperature can climb to 120° in the summer. So they bought a home in Canada as well, but my father still spent most of the year in the desert. He helped me with my business by keeping all my books and even worked out at my club every day. My mother got a job working at a local resort and became involved with the Chamber of Commerce, the Art Guild and the Performing Arts Center. Everyone in town knew her and loved her; people naturally want to be around her. This brings me to the second part of today's reflection.

Part Two: Magical Moments with Mom

Once I was asked if I could recall my very first memory. What I came up with was a vision of myself in a high chair, looking out from the corner of the kitchen at a woman who was preparing food for me. In that moment, I had my first awareness of myself as "being." I realized I was in the body of a baby seated in a high chair and I even recalled looking down to check out my fingers and toes as I wiggled them.

The second recognition was that this woman who was preparing my food was my mother. I was very pleased with the whole situation: a jolt of self-awareness as I recognized my "beingness," followed by the reassurance that I was safe and I was loved.

When I was just a toddler, my first thought every morning was, "I want my mommy!" I have reflected on this many times as I try to grasp the true meaning of love. I have come to the realization that this inclination as a toddler was in response to a gravitational pull attracting me into her energy field. As I thought about this, I realized the parallel with Mother Earth, how she is attracting her children and all living things toward her heart center with this same gravitational pull. It's an expression of love; all love is that way. That is what attraction is — a gravitational force pulling us towards each other's heart center, or energy field.

So as a toddler, as soon as my eyes popped open, the first thing I would do was to seek out my mother's heart. I remember quietly sitting on a rug at her bedside and staring at her until she opened her eyes. She later told me that she always knew I was there, but would squeeze her eyes shut and try not to smile so that she could just embrace that peaceful moment together, bathed in the pure love that only a mother and child can truly know and share. As I got older and she started being the first one to wake up, she would respond to the gravitational pull of love in just the same way. She'd come in my room every morning, sit on my bed and stroke my hair. Looking at me lovingly she would say, "You are the most beautiful, smartest and sweetest child in the whole world!" Then she would tell me that she loved me dearly. Every morning we would start the day this way, from my toddlers into my teens, with this pure expression of tender love.

Another thing my mother used to tell me and my sister every morning was, "Today is the first day of the rest of your life!" She was reminding us that each and every day is a fresh new start — another chance to shine our light, be the best that we can be and make the most of every moment. In fact, she called me "Sunshine" because she said I was always radiating love and light everywhere I went. It's no wonder, after all the love and light she poured out! Her infinite love and daily inspiration came straight from her heart and I am eternally grateful for it. I have benefited tremendously from this perspective of optimism and confidence backed by love and trust.

Interestingly enough, this was in stark contrast to the way she was raised by her mother, who harbored anger and resentment for most of her life. Whatever the cause, the effect was an outward expression of bitterness toward her children and the world at large. Granted, times were much tougher back then. Living through the harsh Canadian winters out on the farm, always struggling to survive and keeping nine children clothed and fed must have been incredibly challenging. So my heart goes out to her. Fortunately, my mother had a very close relationship with her father who adored her, and I am sure this fueled her motherly love and adoration toward her own children later on.

Along with inspiring my sister and I with her support and encouragement, our mother also inspired us as a role model. Growing up as she did on a farm out in the middle of nowhere, it is remarkable that she became a highly educated and successful female executive, especially during the 1960s when women were more repressed. She struggled to get her master's degree while raising two young children; we have a photo of her balancing my sister on her knee, surrounded by piles of books and typing furiously on an old-fashioned typewriter. During that time, she also worked at a bank and then later at a publishing company. After she got her degree, she began moving up through the ranks and was recruited by Ohio Bell. She was also very involved with the women's rights movement. She became president of Zonta, a professional women's organization, and traveled around the world to promote women's rights in the workplace.

In the late 1970s, she became the Director of Sales and Marketing for a large pharmaceutical company. She truly enjoyed her job and thrived in the world of sales and public relations. She was beautiful, smart and very charming, but did have to tolerate a lot of sexual harassment and unwelcome advances. This is where growing up on the farm with eight brothers and sisters came in handy; she knew how to defend herself. She would also stick up for the girls who couldn't defend themselves. How fascinating that this led to her defending women's rights all over the world!

My mother taught me many valuable lessons, but the most important one has to do with the gravity of unconditional love. The strength of the love our family shares has carried us all through difficult and challenging periods as well as happy and joyful occasions. Whatever phase we might be in, we have all always had each other's back and always will. This is what unconditional love is all about. It is the highest aspiration that each and every one can strive for every day, expressing unconditional love for ourselves first and then for everyone and every living thing around us as a unified whole.

This brings to mind a Buddhist prayer that says, "You who love all beings without exception are the source of happiness and goodness." We can be a source of happiness and goodness every day by expressing our love of all beings without exception. Once you truly grasp the essence of this unity, you realize that however you feel towards others is just a reflection of how you feel about yourself. "Do unto others as you would have done unto yourself" has a much deeper meaning than just reciprocation. When you realize that you and "others" are one and that you and the Creator are one, you begin to see that you are all sharing the same energy field and responding to the same gravitational pull. This inspires you to think and act accordingly; this is the gravitational pull of pure love.

MY PARENTS AND I FROLLICKING IN THE DESERT

Self-Reflection
Time Period: 1996 - 2008
Topic: Harmony

Memories, Thoughts & Feelings:

The remoteness of the desert paradise gives my family the blessed opportunity to spend quality time together. The memories that we have of our extraordinary adventures and quiet times will be cherished. I realize that I have been incredibly fortunate to be blessed with such loving and caring parents. Their success as individuals, against all odds, has been truly inspiring for me. My mother's deep love and devotion represents the unifying love of the Creator that holds our whole universe together.

Suspected Causes:
Related past history

I believe my family was brought together in this special place and time for the divine purpose of sealing our family bond. This, for me, represents a divine cause in motion. The cause for the closeness that each of us has for one another is the love that filled our home growing up.

Effects:
Occurring as a result of the causes identified

I grew and flourished as a result of the love and support my family offered during this transitional period of my life. I was able to pursue my dreams and follow my heart. My sister was able to heal from her war wounds, both physically and emotionally. The quiet and undistracted environment also allowed her to study for law school, graduate and pass the bar with flying colors. My father, after working for fifty years, had the chance to spend precious time with his girls exploring the desert. He also joined the paleontology group at the state park. My mother had the opportunity to express her love of the arts and socialize with like-minded people by joining the local Art Guild and participating in the Performing Arts Center. Most importantly, we were all drawn together in this magical place to create beautiful memories as a family and flourish as individuals.

Lessons Hidden Within:

Be grateful for family each and every day. Embrace every opportunity to spend precious time together.

Never underestimate the power of love within a family unit. This strong force is the same gravitational field that unites the sun and the moon and stars.

Admiring how my parents overcame hardships and barriers, I have been inspired to keep this spirit alive and uphold the family tradition of hard work, perseverance, and success.

Lesson Plan:

I will always cherish my parents and never take them for granted.

I will let them know on a regular basis how amazing I think they are and how grateful I am for their love and inspiration.

I will cherish all the beautiful memories we have shared together and keep them alive in my writing, scrapbooks and especially, in my heart.

I will dedicate my love, time and effort to caring for my parents in their times of need in the same way they have always been there for me.

DAY FIVE
The Spiritual Essence of Harmony

A Conversation with Spiritual Counselor & Minister, Janet Myatt

SUZANNE: Good afternoon Janet and welcome back. Today we are interested in exploring the nature of harmony. There are times in our life when we seem to enter a "life-stream" that flows effortlessly, and everything just falls into place beautifully. We begin to move in perfect harmony with the world around us. But how can we help this experience occur?

JANET: This requires a subtle practice of keeping the mind, heart, and will steady in the light. This means we have to let go of attachment to outcomes and be willing to allow our experiences to unfold within and around us. We have to be willing to remember that everything that happens here in the world of forms is like a dream — or a story we're playing a part in, for the purposes of learning about our creativity and revealing our divine nature in manifest form.

SUZANNE: There is a common theme running through all of our conversations, and that is accepting this precious opportunity called life for what it is: an opportunity to learn, grow, and activate the divine potential within us. If we can step back for a moment and realize that the physical aspect of our lives is just a vehicle through which our soul can express itself, we can use this incarnation wisely and make significant progress on our evolutionary path. This life is all about the important life lessons we need to learn in order to evolve. That's why it is so important to go through this process of uncovering and applying these lessons. New and more advanced lessons will continually be revealed as we go along. When we allow our soul's life-stream to flow naturally, without the resistance of our ego, our lessons will unfold in a synchronistic and harmonious way. When we focus on the highest aspect of ourselves, we will fall into the perfect harmony of the divinely guided life-stream.

In an excerpt from a prayer in "The Seven Sacred Rays" by Aurelia Jones, a request is made: "Direct my life stream in ways that, daily and hourly, my true identity in God manifests."

JANET: As we evolve, we are coming to understand that the forms we use to express ourselves in physical reality are not absolutely real because they are not eternal. They are created and they are destroyed. And, creating and destroying is the *activity* of God both within us and all around us, but not *who* God is. God is love – that mighty pervasive all-knowing, eternal, loving Presence that underlies all of Creation and gives life to all within it. Thus, we as his children are also love. *All* forms then, whether they are objective physical bodies, or subjective emotional/ behavioral patterns, or thought-forms, are only temporary vehicles through which spirit can express and experience. When we remember this, we acquire a new level of equanimity. We come to remember that we are spirit. We are consciousness. And, these things are eternal. Life here on earth is temporary and serves as a creative playground or schoolhouse where we can learn how to reveal ourselves in objective form. With this greater perspective in mind, we are able to detach more readily from specific outcomes and instead seek the highest good. We seek the harmonious road, or the middle way between the pairs of opposites we are constantly navigating our way through in the world of duality.

When our life is in equilibrium, we know we are in harmony with ourselves, others and the world around us. When we experience disequilibrium, we know we have swung out of harmony either with ourselves, others, and/or the world around us. This is not inherently bad because it can serve as a catalyst for important and necessary change. When things get out of whack, we can stop, go within, ask for divine guidance, and open up to new possibilities. In short, we can tap into our intuition and discover more effective ways of revealing our divine nature in whatever situation we are struggling with.

SUZANNE: Harmony prevails when we are in alignment with the most divine aspect of our being, whether you call it the "Christ-mind" or "Buddha-mind" or "higher Self." That is our true nature without the illusion of our ego identity, which seems so real.

141

JANET: We can step back and realize that nothing happening here is permanently real. Everything is temporary and changing. And, we can use that changeability to alter things for the better. Our life here on earth provides us with a grand opportunity to learn how to reveal our divine nature in objective form. Because we don't fully know how to do this yet, we are learning through trial and error, cause and effect. It's valuable to develop a tolerance for this process so that we can more easily forgive ourselves and others when things go wrong. Detaching from specific outcomes and focusing instead on what is needed to create or restore a state of genuine equilibrium, or inner peace, is a powerful way of developing our ability to express our divine nature.

SUZANNE: If we can see the drama of everyday life for what it truly is — a test of our true nature, an opportunity to transmute negative emotions (or darkness) into positive energy (light) — than we can make real progress. The Bible says, "We reap what we sow" and Buddhism expresses the same idea as karma. We attract the energy into our lives that we have generated, or allowed to come in. When we make a firm decision that we will only radiate positive emotions and think and behave in ways that harmonize with our highest self, we will begin to attract a higher vibration of energy toward us and deflect the lower energies away from us. This alone will create more harmony in our lives.

We have the power to use our intention and will to create harmony and peace within our lives and the world around us. We have the power to transform chaos into order by being a powerful beacon of light. Light always overcomes the darkness and our bright light has the power to diffuse or transmute darker energy. This is the power of the Christ-mind, or Buddha-mind, that is within each and every one of us. We just have to use our lives to activate our divine potential so that we can do what we really came here for — to create and evolve!

Now it's your turn!

SELF-EXPLORATION #5 – LIVING IN HARMONY
Theme: Harmony

Close your eyes and think deeply about a period of your life when you were especially happy and everything seemed to be flowing along perfectly. This period was probably marked by a harmonious series of synchronistic events that all fell into place beautifully. Relationships with your friends and family were free of conflict, and everyone was reaching out to help one another and improve each other's lives. During this period, your professional life would have also been flourishing. Your co-workers would be supportive of one another and the working environment would be upbeat. Your career would be on an upward track and you would be successful in all your pursuits. All in all, you were feeling really good about yourself — proud of your success at work and pleased about your loving relationships at home.

Explore Your Heart and Mind

Try to identify the feelings that surfaced during this harmonious period of your life. Recall the circumstances that led into harmony, and the effects that it had on you and those around you. Start by defining what "harmony" means to you.

What are the specific things and circumstances that create harmony in your life? In other words, what makes you happy?

_____

_____

_____

_____

_____

_____

How would you prioritize these elements of harmony? What are the most important requirements for you to have inner peace and pure joy in your life? Do they include material wealth, spiritual fulfillment, or both?

_____

_____

_____

_____

_____

_____

What are the specific characteristics which define a harmonious relationship between yourself and others? Does it feel mutually beneficial, or are you happier when you are more on the giving or receiving end? Be honest with yourself as you reflect upon these various relationships:

You and your spouse/partner:

_____

_____

_____

_____

You and your siblings:

_____

_____

_____

_____

You and your parents:

_____

_____

_____

_____

You and your friends:

_____

_____

_____

_____

You and your co-workers:

_____

_____

_____

_____

Take the time to focus on the people who affect the quality of your life the most and the emotions that arise when you think of your relationship with them. Recognize those things that create harmony and dis-harmony in these relationships.

Identify Lessons and Shifts

Start by accounting for the major circumstances of your life, harmonious or not, and identify the specific role you had in creating them. You can give credit to others who helped create them as well. It is important to recall the most harmonious times and compare them to the least harmonious ones.

Harmonious Times and Extenuating Circumstances

Love, Family, Health, Wealth, Success, Growth

_____

_____

_____

_____

_____

Dis-Harmonious Times and Associated Causes

Break-Up, Financial, Distress, Failure, Regression

_____

_____

_____

_____

_____

Time for your Reflection

Now that you have a clearer picture of what harmony looks like to you, single out a specific period in your life when you were particularly happy and at peace with yourself and the world around you. Identify the causes and recognize the effects. Hidden within this reflection is a special appreciation for those people, places and things that make you happy. Understanding the circumstances that produce a harmonious flow of positive energy in your life will help you to re-create them. You can create an environment rich in those things which bring you peace and joy by knowing what truly makes you happy.

You can make a promise to yourself that you will do everything you can to embrace the highest quality of life for yourself and others. Upon awakening every day, you can make a commitment to be the best person you can be in every way, expressing only the highest thoughts, words and actions. This is the key to creating harmony in your life.

It's time to allow your harmonious experience to unfold. Since you are reflecting upon harmonious times, this practice will give you the perfect opportunity to rejoice. You can express the joy and gratitude that makes you want to celebrate life. It is a blessing to have the chance to recognize and celebrate the beauty and grace in our lives. You can clearly see the divine nature of yourself and others revealed during times of peace and harmony. You can feel the spirit of life embracing joy in all its glory!

SELF-REALIZATION #5
Meditation on Harmony

It's time to progress on your path of self-realization.

Before journaling your experience, please engage in Dynamic Movement Therapy to open and expand your body. We will start with the dynamic movement therapy to increase blood flow and then move into the breathing practices to oxygenate your brain. We will incorporate the practice of breathing in white light and exhaling dark smoke as a way to trigger the release of leftover psychic debris from the past. You can engage in the movement and breathing practices by referring back to the written guidelines in the introduction, or or you can access the audio download for free at *www.suzannerosstranscendence. com/Up!Trilogy/WakeUp!Meditations.*

Now you are ready to go within by doing your visualization/meditation. It's not always easy to surrender to our divine nature as spiritual beings inhabiting physical bodies. It's much easier to become attached to our ego identity, and to be very identified with our physical body. We have been programmed to believe that these are the true representations of ourselves. Beneath our roles and within our physical being lies the essence of our authentic self. Our spirit struggles to shine through the shadows of our ego identity. We must make an effort to liberate our spirit and allow our true nature to blend harmoniously with our ego identity. We must learn how to become the spiritual representation of our true selves.

By setting aside the temptations of our ego, we can connect with the spiritual apect of our being. We can overcome the sense-attractions and self-centeredness of the ego and open our hearts to all that which ignites our spirit. Instead of being drawn toward material delights, we can focus on spiritual truths. We can avoid being drawn into self-centered thoughts that breed resentment, blame, anger and hatred and instead, redirect our thoughts toward compassion, understanding, patience and love. We can reveal our true nature as divine beings connected to the spiritual realm and allow it to merge with our ego identity in the physical realm.

Merging our divinity with our humanity is life's biggest challenge, and our highest purpose. When we create meaningful experiences by expressing our highest self, we are serving our divine purpose and progressing on our evolutionary path. When we create with meaning and evolve with purpose, harmony prevails and we naturally come into alignment with our spiritual nature.

This VIS-MED on Harmony will help you remove the debris of your ego mind so that the light of your spirit can illuminate your energy centers. Once these blockages have been removed, your spirit will shine through your ego identity. You will radiate love, light, compassion and kindness toward others and you will attract sweet harmony and pure joy into your life. Once your ego becomes synchronized with your highest self, you will resonate with the most powerful source of energy in the entire universe — pure unconditional love.

You can download an audio version of this guided meditation by going to my website at *www.suzannerosstranscendence.com.* On the Up!Trilogy menu, select **Wake Up! Meditations** and go to the **VIS-MED for Harmony.**

DAY FIVE
Self-Reflection

Name of the Experience: _____

Time Period: _____

Topic: Harmony

Memories, Thoughts & Feelings:

_____

_____

_____

_____

_____

_____

Suspected Causes:
Related past history

_____

_____

_____

_____

_____

_____

_____

Effects:
Occurring as a result of the causes identified

_____

_____

_____

_____

_____

_____

Lessons Hidden Within:

_____

_____

_____

_____

_____

Lesson Plan:

_____

_____

_____

_____

_____

_____

DAY FIVE
PRACTICAL SPIRITUALITY
Harmony & Equilibrium

"The immutable cosmic forces are ever seeking a balance. The operation of this law of nature is absolute and totally impersonal in its striving for harmony and balance."

— Edward Lee

I believe we all have the potential to do, be, and have anything we desire. All we have to do is focus on what we truly want in our lives and then make a clear plan of how to get there. It's really that simple and it's all about creating balance and harmony in your life.

I want you to ask yourself: What more could I do daily to be the best employee and coworker, the best husband or wife, father or mother, and the best friend? Most importantly, I want you to ask yourself: How can I truly be my own best friend? Do I value myself enough to make the effort it takes to be healthier and more successful? Not just for my own benefit, but for the benefit of those around me — those who I care about and who depend on me to bring my best self forth every day.

Ask yourself if you are making the most out of your life every day by bringing your best self forth both at work and at home. If not, ask yourself why. What is standing in your way? What barriers have you put up? What is preventing you from getting everything that you want out of your life? We all have to ask ourselves this question: "What is it that we truly want and why don't we already have it?"

We will be exploring these questions over the course of this workshop and finding the real answers to them. What you will come to realize is that you have the power within you to unleash your highest potential, and there is nothing standing in your way except for the limiting beliefs you may have created in your own mind. You can, however, take comfort in knowing this: There are no obstacles that you cannot overcome. There are no barriers that you cannot break down. No matter what it is you wish to achieve, I firmly believe you can make it happen and by the end of this workshop, you will too.

You might be thinking, "That's all easy for you to say. You don't know my life and all of the obstacles and constraints that I have. You don't know the stress and pressure I am under, or all of the demands of my personal and professional life." That may be true, but I have empathy for those of you who are trying to balance the demands of your professional life with the obligations of your personal life, because I have been there. I have been stressed out, sleep deprived, undernourished, and anxiety-ridden from living an unbalanced life. I know what it's like trying to please everyone by being the perfect employee, perfect wife, and perfect image of success. Even though I seemed successful on the outside, I was not so much on the inside and I knew if I didn't start focusing on my own health and wellness, I would burn out.

One day near the end of my rope, I seriously asked myself, "Are you happy with the way everything is going in your life?" And the answer was a resounding "NO!" I knew I needed to start making some major changes. Realizing I was at a crossroads, I chose to make the positive changes that would improve the quality of my life. I realized that I had the power to make these changes and I knew it would be worth the effort, and so I did! And believe me, if I can do it, you can too. I am no different than anyone else.

Now for me, these changes included pursuing a career in health and wellness, but I started by focusing on my own. That's what changed my life. It wasn't that I made a new career choice, it's that I made a new personal choice to value myself enough to make positive changes. I convinced myself that I was worth it and the people whom I loved and cared about were worth it too. I knew that if I didn't take care of myself, it wasn't only I who would suffer. Everyone around me would be affected, those who depended on me and believed in me. So that became my motivation: to be the best person I could be for not only myself, but for others too. I wanted to live my best life. I needed to find balance and equilibrium. I also needed to follow my heart and pursue my true calling. I knew I wasn't reaching my highest potential at work or at home — not even close — and as a result, I wasn't experiencing harmony in my life. So it started with saying "I am worth it!"

Real change often has to start with health and wellness, because if you don't have that, you cannot reach your highest potential in any aspect of your life. With optimal health, you have unlimited potential. Without it, you are limiting yourself unnecessarily. You have the capacity to improve your health and wellness.

Let's start by identifying and breaking down any barriers that appear to be limiting you from reaching your highest potential. We are in this together and by the end of the workshop, each and every one of you will be saying:

- I am an amazing human being with unlimited potential.
- I can do anything I desire and be anything I wish.
- I will reach my highest potential.
- I am, I can, I will.

Now, close your eyes. We are going to revisit the "Golden Dream" concept. Remember, this is the fantasy version of you and your life. In this fantasy, you have everything you ever wanted and have achieved everything you ever dreamed of. What do you see? Do you picture wealth and riches? Perhaps you're thinking: "If I had lots of money, I could have everything, be anything and go anywhere. Then I'd really be happy!"

Just like before, I am going to challenge you to go a little deeper once again. What does the "fantasy you" look and feel like? Do you picture yourself taller, thinner, more attractive, more successful, more popular, admired and respected by everyone? Now stop and consider for a moment: Why aren't you all of these things and more? Why don't you have everything you ever wanted? In a world where anything is possible, why aren't you living your fantasy reality? Ask yourself: Why am I limiting myself and believing that I am only capable of achieving a certain level of success, having a certain level of abundance and looking and feeling only moderately well?

It's time to shatter these limited beliefs about yourself. First, you need to make a plan by identifying where you are at now – your CURRENT SELF — and then visualize where you want to be as your IDEAL SELF. Then, draw a bridge between the two. One step at a time, you'll cross that bridge by making small, incremental changes every day.

You can start by recognizing what you already have: a good job or an unfulfilling career, a stable income or an unpredictable one, a loving family or a dysfunctional one, a decent car and decent house (or not) and good or poor health. Now look ahead into the future and see what that looks like. Visualize getting the promotion that you deserve, or pursuing a fulfilling career more aligned with your true calling. Envision yourself with abundant health and wealth. Imagine having more balance and harmony in your life — more quality time with your family, more time for yourself.

The intention of this practice is to identify the aspects of yourself that you would like to improve upon. This workshop can be a major turning point in your life. I believe that you will make the most of it because I believe in you and I know that in your heart, you believe in yourself. Together we will make the most out of this ten days. Today, you will start making the most out of every day.

Awakening through Reflection

DAY SIX

HEALING

WORKSHOP MODULES:

1. Life Experience & Analysis: "My Wake-Up Call"

2. The Spiritual Essence of Healing

3. Self-Exploration #6: A Time of Healing

4. Self-Realization #6: Meditation on Healing

5. Self-Reflection #6: Uncovering Life Lessons

6. Practical Spirituality: Healing with an Open Heart and Mind

LIFE EXPERIENCE

DAY SIX

My Wake-up Call

"All good things must come to an end," goes the old saying, but I thought I'd get an exception to the rule. I was special, after all, and I had angels and guides looking out for me. But I didn't realize I had to take more responsibility for myself — and there were a few cracks in my armor that had never been mended, and would soon break wide open.

Everything began to change when my husband's family decided to sell the business they owned in the desert for over 25 years. His parents were ready to retire and Scott wasn't interested in taking over. His brother had moved to central California and was doing well in the cell communications industry; he had started his own business and offered Scott a job. After exploring other options closer to home, Scott decided the opportunity up north with his brother was the best choice. It wasn't long before he was running his own crew and excelling in the industry. Meanwhile I wasn't doing so well back in the desert.

The region had been hit hard by two events that had occurred back to back at the turn of the millennium. First, there was the SDG&E crisis in 2000, causing electric bills to go through the roof. If you failed to pay your utility bill, SDG&E marched in and closed you down until or unless you could pay up. It was frightening. Some businesses shut down and most of us never fully recovered. Then in 2001, the horrifying events of 911 happened. This also had a devastating effect on our town because the snowbirds were mostly wealthy retired golfers who were heavily invested in the stock market. When it crashed, they pulled way back on their spending. Since their desert residences were usually second and third homes, many of them sold or just walked away. Being at a point in their lives where they would have no chance to recover their losses, many just moved back to their permanent homes up north.

Soon our desert town was dying. By 2008, the main golf course community keeping local businesses alive was at 30% residency. The other major golf course community actually let their course dry up after a failed attempt at upgrading the property. Eventually, even the beautiful four-star resort, where I got my new lease on life twelve years earlier, shut down. The luscious landscape dried up and the colorful tarps that once adorned the patios were flapping in the wind, torn and disintegrating. This was all highly symbolic for me, as I was slowly dying inside and headed for a classic "dark night of the soul."

Some of us have to go through such a transition in order to rebound to a much higher place than we've ever been before. My dark night was painful and traumatic, but I can honestly say I am grateful for the experience. During my recovery from this worst year of my life, I was introduced to spirituality. I also received counseling and group therapy to heal some earlier wounds. I also became hooked on inspirational books and CDs, many of them authored by Wayne Dyer and his friends at Hay House Publishing.

Every dark night involves some deeply humbling experiences. After my husband left to work up north, I was lonely and felt abandoned. I knew in my heart, however, that Scott hadn't abandoned me. In fact, he was determined our marriage could survive the separation, but I still felt resentful and alone. As a result of being on my own and my business slowing down, I had way too much free time on my hands. This is never a good thing if you're lonely and depressed; it didn't help that I knew other people who also had a lot of free time and mostly liked to hang out and party. I discovered that partying always made me feel better. Laughing, playing pool, and dancing took my mind off everything!

In fact, I had always enjoyed getting together with my family and friends to party but now it was getting out of hand. I became a regular at the local bar, and the partying that had begun on weekends began extending to weeknights... and ultimately, week*days*. Bad behavior and poor choices were devastating my life. Fortunately, the love of my family and the unconditional love of my husband saved me from myself. After seven years, I have forgiven myself and am able to be compassionate toward the unbalanced "me" of that time period.

My experience in recovery, which I badly needed, turned my life around completely. Giving up partying was the easy part; learning to love myself again was the biggest challenge. Seeing how much my husband truly loves and cares about me was the greatest gift to come out of the experience. My newfound search for a deeper and more meaningful spiritual life was the next greatest blessing.

The classic song that clearly symbolizes this transformational period is "Amazing Grace" and that is why I am compelled to insert a short version of it here. During periods of profound gratitude and joy, I still walk around belting it out! You are welcome to sing it aloud with me now:

Amazing grace how sweet the sound,
That saved a wretch like me
I once was lost but now am found,
Was blind, but now, I see.

157

T'was grace that taught my heart to fear
And grace, my fears relieved.
How precious is that grace appeared
The hour I first believed.
Through many dangerous toils and snares
I have already come.
T'was grace that brought me safe thus far
and grace will lead me home.

Self-Reflection
Time Period: 2007 - 2008
Topic: Healing

Memories, Thoughts & Feelings:

After Scott and his family left the desert, I was left feeling abandoned and alone. My parents had built a home in Canada and were spending more time there as well. The SDG&E crisis of 2000 and the tragedy of 9/11 had devastating impacts. As a result, the town went into a decline that contributed to my own personal decline. Thanks to the unconditional love of my husband and family, I recovered.

Suspected Causes:
Related past history

Primary cause: abandonment.

This deeply rooted fear haunts all of us to some extent as it can be traced all the way back to the metaphoric Garden of Eden. We believe that we were left on our own, "separate" from the Creator, and have been struggling ever since to find our way back home. I felt abandoned by Scott taking a job far from home, and my parents moving to Canada. Finally, my dream of a fitness center was dying.

Effects:
Occurring as a result of the causes identified

My heart was broken.
My dreams were shattered.
I felt empty and alone.
I felt like a failure in both my livelihood and my marriage.

I felt abandoned by everyone who supposedly loved and cared about me.

I blamed myself and felt I had done something wrong to drive everyone away, including my beloved clients.

I sought out others who also had unresolved issues. Sometimes those who were much worse off than me made me feel better about myself.

I became dependent on alcohol to treat my open wounds.

Lessons Hidden Within:

There is no point to blaming myself for things that are beyond my control.

I must never take on the role of victim. I can prevail over the challenges that come my way and learn from them without feeling defeated.

I must overcome my fear of abandonment and never blame myself or others if the time comes when we must be separated.

Alcohol never solves any problems.

Lesson Plan:

I will never again adopt a defeatist attitude.

I will never again allow external circumstances to destroy my inner being. I will take full responsibility for mending my own fences.

I will be forever grateful to my courageous husband, who never lost faith in my enduring spirit.

I will never disappoint him or my family again.

I will never again use any type of toxic substance to alleviate my suffering.

I will dedicate my life to reducing my suffering and the suffering of others through the enlightenment of the soul.

DAY SIX
The Spiritual Essence of Healing

A Conversation with Spiritual Counselor & Minister, Janet Myatt

SUZANNE: Good afternoon, Janet. I am so pleased to have you back. Yesterday, we were talking about harmonious states of being and why we have to move through stages of harmony and dis-harmony in order to progress on our paths. When my life fell apart around me, I felt like I hit the ground hard. In retrospect, I realized that it was necessary in order for me to wake up. But I was wounded at first and needed to heal before my awakening could unfold.

JANET: Healing is all about becoming clear, aligning with our greater purpose and transforming energy from one state to another. Healing is not always about "cures" or prolonging life (even though that can happen). In very broad terms, healing means moving from chaos and disorder into harmony and order. This holds true for healing illness in the dense physical body as well as healing the psyche.

Everything contains energy and energy follows thought. Therefore, what we think is what we create. *A Course in Miracles* explains that *all* healing is simply a matter of changing our minds; whatever we do externally is called "magic." That is, we believe that symbols, like medicines, have the power to create change. For instance, a pill represents our decision to get better, to change the energy in our body from a malefic pattern to a beneficent pattern. Because we *believe* the pill has the power to heal us, we *allow* the necessary energetic changes to take place and we heal. This gives us insight into why medicine works quite well for some people but not for others.   If there is a stronger counter-belief in play, or a deeper lesson to be learned by the individual, the effectiveness of the medicine is compromised. Or if the soul has decided to withdrawal from the body, then the "power" of the medicine will be negated.

SUZANNE: That is so fascinating. It helps to explain why, when people engage in a clinical study, they experience the healing effect of the drugs even when they are given placebos.

JANET: Well, *A Course in Miracles* also suggests that until we fully realize our true power to change energy, we should take the pill. It's like a ritual in which we have invested a degree of power. Rituals and ceremonies can invoke change by helping us consciously direct our thoughts and feelings toward desired results.

However we go about it, what underlies all healing is the alchemical process of changing energetic patterns from one form to another. We have not yet mastered this process because we do not have total awareness and self-control over all the emotional and mental patterns we've set in motion in our lives. On a deeper level, we have not yet fully learned how to transform all the chaotic energy patterns inherited by us in the matter we clothe ourselves in. Mastery of matter happens quite slowly over the course of our evolution as a species.

Matter aside, our focus needs to be on mastering our thoughts and emotions because they account for most of what ails us. When we learn how to live in a balanced, harmonious, inspired and intuitive way, we thrive. Our bodies respond to this ordered, loving inflow of energy and reflect it back to us. Our lives begin to work synchronistically and we learn how to be emotionally and mentally present in the moment, unburdened by past hurts and misconceptions. Additionally, others around us have more room to thrive and a greater opportunity to find their own way of being balanced, loving, and well.

In a nutshell, then, healing ourselves is vitally important not only personally, but globally and universally. We must actively seek out what is in disarray within us and extend to it our divine, unconditional love. We must embrace ourselves and restore that which sits in pain, ignorance, and fear, to love and harmony. Deep within us there exists everything we need to do this. When we ask this part of ourselves for help, for guidance, and for forgiveness — and we listen and act upon what we learn — then we heal.

Suzanne: If we focus on healing dysfunctional energy created in the past, we will experience some degree of energetic healing in the present. As we continue to heal the past over the course of this workshop, we are creating more harmonious states at all levels of our being – mental, spiritual and physical. We are empowered to reach our highest potential when our mind, body and spirit are aligned in perfect harmony. I'd say it's well worth the effort! Thank you for your fascinating insight on energetic healing, Janet.

Now it's your turn!

SELF-EXPLORATION #6 – A TIME OF HEALING
Theme: Healing

Close your eyes and think deeply about a time when you were especially challenged and nothing seemed to go your way. Recall the events that led to this difficult time in your life. Think about the way that you handled yourself during this time. What things did you do to help you deal with the challenges? Did you choose positive or negative strategies for dealing with your problems? What did you or others do to pull out of these difficulties? Focus on the healing that was required once things began to turn around.

Explore your Heart and Mind

It's important to understand how and why the circumstances came about and what your role was in creating it. Think about the roles others played in creating them as well.

Explore how you feel about the way you handled this critical time in your life. Did it lead you to do or say things that you later regretted? What stands out in your mind that you wished you hadn't said or done? Explain what you would do differently, given what you know now.

_____

_____

_____

What steps did you take to remedy the situation so that you could move forward in a more positive direction? Did others step in to help you?

_____

_____

_____

Did you find it necessary to seek professional help to heal your wounds? Which therapeutic or healing modalities were the most helpful?

_____

_____

_____

_____

Were you able to fully recover from this difficult time, or do you still struggle with related issues? If so, what are you doing to address these?

_____

_____

_____

_____

Identify Lessons and Shifts

Taking full accountability for your role in events that negatively impacted your life is difficult. It's much easier to blame others. Are you able to recognize your role in creating challenges for yourself? If so, describe your role and explain how you are taking accountability for the circumstances, good or bad, in your life now.

_____

_____

_____

_____

Are you willing to make an effort to apply compassion, patience and love to the things you think, say and do? If so, give specific examples of how you might have applied these qualities to past circumstances, then how you can apply these virtues to your life today. Be specific.

_____

_____

_____

_____

Have you forgiven yourself and others for the issues that led to past challenges? If not, are you prepared to make a sincere effort toward healing those wounds once and for all? If so, how?

_____

_____

_____

_____

Sometimes, simply confessing those deeds you are ashamed of works wonders for the soul. Asking forgiveness from a higher power can be very purifying. Are you willing to sit quietly and call on spirit guides to listen and forgive? Are you willing to confess and ask forgiveness? If so, just start by writing your confession and then read it out loud:

_____

_____

_____

_____

_____

Now just ask forgiveness from a higher source. It may be a spirit guide, a higher power or even your higher self.

You may want to consider reaching out to those who may have been hurt by your thoughts, words, and actions in the past. Do you still harbor resentment, so that you are not willing to mend fences? Sometimes it is better to let bygones be bygones; however, it is never healthy to let still-open wounds fester. You will always benefit from making an effort to be compassionate toward yourself and forgive your own past mistakes. As long as you learn from them, they won't have been in vain, and can actually be viewed as necessary and beneficial for your soul's evolution.

Time for your Reflection

Healing from a traumatic experience, regardless of how big or small, can be very challenging. At the same time, it can also be very rewarding and lead to a transformational shift in your perception. Having survived the crisis, you may have felt a new surge of growth and a stronger determination to embrace your life more fully. Engaging in the "VIS-MED for Healing" will help you heal from within.

SELF-REALIZATION #6
Meditation on Healing

It's time to progress on your path of self-realization.

Before journaling your experience, please engage in Dynamic Movement Therapy to open and expand your body. Then be seated comfortably and perform the Inspirational Breathing Practices to oxygenate your body and clear your mind of distractions. Please refer to the written instructions given in the introduction or you can access the audio download for free at ***www. suzannerosstranscendence.com/Up!Trilogy/WakeUp!Meditations.***

Now you are ready to go within by doing the visualization/meditation. We all go through difficult times in our lives that require healing. Whether we've experienced a breakup, a job loss, or some kind of failure that you blame yourself for, it will take some time to mend the wounds. Based on the extent of the failure, some wounds may be deeper than others and some may leave psychic scar tissue that will never fully heal without a conscious effort.

In times when we feel that we have failed ourselves and others, forgiveness is the only way we can ever truly love ourselves again. And it's only when we love ourselves that we can fully express love toward another person. Whether we realize it or not, every person in our life is, in some way, a reflection of ourselves. Until we forgive ourselves, we will find ourselves blaming others. If we really have failed others, we may need to reach out and ask for their forgiveness before we can completely forgive ourselves. Forgiveness is the most challenging and yet the most rewarding thing that we can ever do for ourselves and others. To love is to forgive, and to forgive is to love. Nobody is perfect and it's our imperfections that make us human. All we can do is try to recognize our faults, then make a sincere effort to improve upon them. Learning to say "I'm sorry" and learning to accept an apology are two of the most important things you can do to make forgiveness an important part of your recovery. In forgiving, there will be healing.

Close your eyes and ask yourself if there is anything you are blaming yourself for right now. What haven't you forgiven yourself for? If something comes to mind, examine it. Don't justify your words or actions, and don't beat yourself up for them either. Simply be accountable. Admit you made a mistake, release yourself from blame, and commit to handling similar challenges or situations better the next time around. Focus on ways in which you can improve your behavior toward others. Think about how you can align your thoughts, words, and actions with your highest self. Make a commitment to take the higher road when confronted with a difficult person or challenging situation.

Now think about anyone you might be blaming for something you haven't let go of. Take a deep breath and do your best to apply compassion and understanding. Try to put yourself in their shoes. Think about the reasons why they may be saying or doing things that upset you. Think about their life and what struggles they may be having. Try to empathize with them. Remember that, like you, they are only human and are doing the best they can, according to their experience and beliefs. Consider reaching out to them and mending fences. This is the first step toward taking the higher road. Always try to align with the virtues of your highest self. You are now ready to connect with your higher self and your spiritual guides by engaging in the following meditation on healing.

You can download an audio version of this guided meditation by going to my website at *www.suzannerosstranscendence.com.* On the Up!Trilogy menu, select **Wake Up! Meditations** and go to the **VIS-MED for Healing.**

DAY SIX
Self-Reflection

Name of the Experience: _____

Time Period: _____

Topic: Healing

Memories, Thoughts & Feelings:

_____

_____

_____

_____

_____

_____

Suspected Causes:
Related past history

_____

_____

_____

_____

_____

_____

_____

Effects:
Occurring as a result of the causes identified

_____

_____

_____

_____

_____

_____

Lessons Hidden Within:

_____

_____

_____

_____

_____

_____

Lesson Plan:

_____

_____

_____

_____

_____

_____

DAY SIX
PRACTICAL SPIRITUALITY
Healing with an Open Heart and Mind

"A mind is like a parachute. It doesn't work if it is not open."

—Frank Zappa

The more that I learn about science, religion, and spirituality, the more I realize that every discipline, system, and philosophy holds some semblance of truth within it. Nothing should be discarded and everything should be considered with an open yet discriminating mind. Human beings have always been trying to figure out who we are, where we came from, and why we are here.

I believe that, through a combined process of Darwinian evolution and divine intervention, we have evolved and devolved, advanced and degenerated. The highest truth of our existence is that we are spiritual beings having a physical experience. We are entangled in the web of consciousness that defines the pattern of the universe as well as well as the patterns of our individual being. Our spirits inhabit physical bodies in order to gather experience on material worlds. Between physical incarnations, our souls ascend into spiritual worlds where they continue their evolutionary path. In higher schools of learning, they have the opportunity to review their life experiences and reconfigure their consciousness before descending to continue on their journey of self-realization in the material world of time and space.

Sometimes we have to stop and ask ourselves, "Whose journey are we on?" We have an innate desire to know ourselves on a deeper and more meaningful level. We want to know what is the true nature of our being and the purpose of our existence. We want to know who or what is the source of life in the universe. When we get to the point in our lives when we know there just has to be more to our existence than the endless details of our daily life, we begin to explore what lies beyond. Our journey of self-realization truly begins when we first look up and start to wonder about the magic and mystery of it all. Fortunately we have endless resources at our fingertips to enlighten us on our journey. Since we are unique individuals, each on our own path, we will pulled in different directions. We will be drawn toward the same light by different routes.

No matter what path you have chosen, you must be sure you are following your heart and keeping your mind wide open. You must also set some precious time aside if you are to make this journey into the light. Every moment will be worth its weight in gold if you embrace it wholeheartedly. I am fortunate to have more time than most and as such, I have dedicated much of it to exploring deeper truths. I am fascinated by every aspect of this exploration and have plunged headfirst into it. I am surrounded most days by stacks of books on everything from science and religion to meditation and prayer. I have copious amounts of notes and drawings, as I am constantly scribbling my thoughts down on paper.

After five years of searching, I have arrived at a place where answers are unfolding in miraculous ways every day and all around me. I see the true nature of reality in a way I never thought possible before. I attribute this awakening to the fact that I have kept my heart and mind wide open throughout the entire process. I have let everything in and then decided what to keep, based on how it fits within the puzzle. I also spend time just going within to listen to my own heart and explore my own mind to discern what resonates for me..

As a result of this intensive inner and outer exploration, I have formulated my own belief system, called "Eternalism," based upon a wide range of scientific, religious and spiritual truths that all come together as one. Upon accumulating a vast amount of research and looking in many different directions, I asked myself one day what it is that I truly am. Am I a string theorist or a Buddhist? Am I a philosopher or a devotee? Do I believe in Catholicism or Hinduism? Finally I decided that what I really believed in was eternity. I felt very pleased with this new revelation and was satisfied by the fact that it embraced an infinite array of possibilities.

For today's practice, I want you to write down the spiritual and/or religious beliefs that resonate within you as fundamental truths. Just write down the first five beliefs that come to mind without thinking too much. The ones you truly believe will flow right onto the page effortlessly, ie. : "God is love" or "The universal source is infinite — without beginning or end."

1._____

_____

2._____

_____

3._____

_____

4._____

_____

5._____

_____

Hold these beliefs close to your heart while keeping your mind open to new possibilities that may align with these fundamental truths. The world's religions and belief systems have many parallels. When we learn to recognize the beliefs we have in common rather than focusing on those that differ, we will begin to develop a stronger sense of unity. We will create a more synchronized universe – one verse, one song, one symphony — that we can all harmonize with. That's how we can truly heal ourselves and our planet.

Awakening through Reflection

DAY SEVEN

REAWAKENING

WORKSHOP MODULES:

1. Life Experience & Analysis: "Discovering Dharma"

2. The Spiritual Essence of Reawakening

3. Self-Exploration #7: Reawakening the Spirit

4. Self-Realization #7: Meditation on Reawakening

5. Self-Reflection #7: Uncovering Life Lessons

6. Practical Spirituality: Beyond the Chaos

LIFE EXPERIENCE

DAY SEVEN

Discovering Dharma

After surviving my fall from grace, I decided to visit my parents in their summer home up north. As "snowbirds" they chose to return to their roots in Canada for six months out of the year. My mother was born near Calgary, Alberta in a small Mennonite community. The landscape is dominated by grain agriculture and spotted with rustic red barns and monstrous tractors. Fields of hay, wheat, and flax surround the tiny farming villages which typically have little more than one general store, a coffee shop, and post office.

This sparsely inhabited countryside fills me with a deep inner peace, and the big open sky always makes my mind feel expansive. My parents had both been very supportive during my recent trials and tribulations, and I knew it would be good for us to spend time together following my recovery. During my visit, I noticed a book entitled *The Jewel Tree of Tibet* by Robert Thurman. This was the book that had inspired my sister to join a Buddhist center near her home in San Diego. As I read, I was becoming intrigued myself.

I have often heard the phrase, "When the student is ready, the teachings will appear." And so they did. After studying the teachings of compassion and forgiveness in Thurman's book, I made a commitment to pursue the study and practice of Buddhism as soon as I got back home. I would start by asking my sister how the practices had transformed her life, and what she felt was the best way to begin. It turned out that she was planning to go to a retreat in a few weeks and gladly invited me to join her. In the meantime, she suggested some reading material. Little did I know this was the beginning of a spiritual quest that would drastically change my entire perception of reality.

The possibility of developing a blissful state of mind gave me the hope I needed to emerge from the darkness and step into the light. I was definitely ready to embark upon a new and more enlightened approach to my life. My first experience with attempting a meditative state began with an imagery of light and perfection inspired by the following verse:

Through the great bliss state,
I myself become the mentor deity.
From my luminous body,

Light rays shine all around,
Massively blessing beings and things,
Making the universe pure and fabulous,
Perfection in its every quality. [1]

Robert Thurman suggests that one should first approach meditation as a contemplative visualization. This wise approach has become the cornerstone of my spiritual practice. Meditation focused on light-ray visualization and conceptual contemplation has been extremely valuable to me, and I have taught this form of meditation to many of my students. Beginning a meditation session by focusing on the image of light rays emanating from the very core of your being, and then expanding outward to bless all living things, has the effect of opening a gateway into the higher realms of perfection and bliss.

I am firmly convinced that there is a higher 'omnipresent' power just waiting for us to open and surrender to it. I have learned that all we have to do is remove ourselves from the distractions of daily life, and still our mind by focusing on our breathing and engaging in meditation or visualization. This technique magically opens the door to the omnipotent light of love that immediately engulfs you in its embrace. Once you have entered the light and are able to stay focused on its brilliance, images and thought patterns begin to form as you are lovingly guided along a path toward enlightenment. As long as you allow your mind to remain open to the experience as it unfolds, you will benefit greatly from these divine adventures. Over time and with consistent practice, the meditations become more and more enlightening as the teachings are absorbed. This greatly enhances your spiritual understanding and development.

The momentary stilling of chatter and focusing of the mind produces a balanced state that precedes the unfolding of a harmonious sequence of events throughout the rest of the day. This is because your whole perception and approach to daily life is more calm and confident. Fortunately, with patience, persistence and gentle nudging, I am able to persuade those who are interested in enhancing their lives to attempt just a few moments of contemplative visualization each day. I encourage them to briefly step aside from the demands of their day, close their eyes for a few moments and just repeat the lines from that very first verse that changed my life forever.

Radical change is always intimidating. Even if you are not happy with the way that your life is going and you know there must be a better way, you may still feel insecure about changing a very familiar way of doing things. Sometimes I see this with clients who are in a chronic state of pain but make no real attempt to alleviate it; taking away their pain would be like stripping away a part of their identity. It is the fear of the unknown that intimidates us from embarking upon new and transformative ways of being or alternative ways of living.

The Buddhist center near my sister's house in San Diego practices "The New Kadampa Tradition" or simply, NKT. The practices embraced by this tradition are inspired by the master "Atisha" who translated the 84,000 original Buddhist teachings into "Lamrin," or stages of the path. Currently, Geshe Kelsang Gyatso, who became an ordained Buddhist monk in Tibet at the age of eight, is recognized as the leader of the tradition.

My understanding is that he has very artfully and effectively translated the Tibetan Buddhist teachings, with the guidance of Atisha's Lamrin, into a format that Westerners can fully appreciate. My sister suggested that I immerse myself in these teachings by reading and interactively engaging in his book, *The New Meditation Handbook*. This book became my new best friend. I took it with me everywhere I went and read and practiced the teachings in every free moment I had.

My sister was impressed when I saw her two weeks later, and I told her I had memorized "The Liberation Prayer." In this moment I felt a deeper connection and more powerful love toward my sister than I had before. I always adored her but this was a special moment that transformed our relationship, and we decided to call each other 'Buddha buddies.' In the past, we probably would've engaged in activities that were fun but always included partying. Now that I had changed my ways, she decided that she would support me by also giving up alcohol altogether. Her commitment to make this lifestyle change touched me deeply.

We decided to attend a retreat together in Petaluma, not too far from my new home in Northern California. My sister and I booked a room at a local hotel which gave us a chance to spend quality time in an intimate environment conducive to openly sharing our thoughts and feelings. Neither of our significant others were interested in Buddhism, or spirituality for that matter, so that's why it was important for us to have this opportunity to get away.

At first, joining a large group of people all singing and chanting while seated in front of an ordained monk, was rather intimidating. I felt somewhat uncomfortable and out of place; however, I was intrigued by the practice and found the teachings inspirational, so I persevered. My sister introduced me to the ordained monk associated with her Buddhist center in San Diego. Meeting him felt like an honor. I felt as if he was a sacred being and I was privileged just to be in his presence.

Due to a car accident that I had in my youth, I have chronic back pain and the fold-out chairs we had to sit in for hours during meditation were causing me to have painful back spasms. Toward the end of the second day, these spasms became so debilitating that we had to leave early. We approached the monk who was hosting the retreat to apologize for our early departure. My sister explained that it was due to my intense back pain. I'll never forget his response. He said, "You know it doesn't have to be that way. The pain of suffering in your mind is manifesting as physical pain in your body." I said, "Well, I certainly look forward to the time when my mental capacity is such that I am able to overcome my physical pain. I promise to work toward this goal." And I meant it.

After the inspirational experience of attending a formal retreat, along with the promise of greater things to come, I was more motivated than ever to make a strong commitment to my Buddhist practice. Every day, I would either sit in meditation or do what I call a 'walking meditation' out in nature. During the sitting meditations, I would engage in all of the preparatory practices recommended in *The New Meditation Handbook*. These preparations include cleaning the room you intend to use for meditation, as if you are expecting honorary guests. It is also recommended that you wash your hands and face as a symbol of purification.

Then you set up your shrine. My sister had helped me choose items for my own unique shrine. They included a small gold statue of the compassion Buddha, Avolakiteshvara, a stupa, Buddhist texts and an offering of tea leaves in a small teacup. These are placed on a satin matte. Once seated in front of the shrine, preparatory prayers are done in a particular sequence intended to progressively deepen your focus and increase your awareness. They emphasize the Buddhist principles of inner peace, compassion, wisdom and joy. The first time I engaged in this process with an intense focus and open mind, I had the most profound experience. While vividly imagining being surrounded by Buddha and the bodhisattvas, I suddenly felt a cold breeze pass right through me and then I became aware of a very loving and comforting presence. It felt reassuring, as if the presence of the spirits was a sign of approval — their way of showing me that they were supportive of my practice and would always be there for me.

As I said in the introduction, the powerful message I often receive when I go within is to share my journey and illuminate the path that I have taken. I have also heard from others, "Write what you know" and "what I know for sure is"...that the path I have taken, starting with Buddhism and expanding into a broad perspective embracing many disciplines, has worked wonders in my life. I share what I know, and invite you to design your own path based upon your experiences. This way, you can discover what path provides illumination for you.

WAKE UP!

I offer this beautiful Kadampa prayer to enlighten you on your journey:

The Liberation Prayer

Borrowed from Geshe Kelsang Gyatso's *The New Meditation Handbook*

O Blessed One Shakyamuni Buddha,
Precious treasury of compassion,
Bestower of supreme inner peace,

You who love all beings without exception,
Are the source of happiness and goodness;
And you guide us to the liberating path.

Your body is a wish-fulfilling jewel,
Your speech is supreme, purifying nectar,
And your mind is refuge for all living beings.

With folded hands, I turn to you,
Supreme unchanging friend,
I request from the depths of my heart:

Please give me the light of your wisdom
To dispel the darkness of my mind
And to heal my mental continuum.

Please nourish me with your goodness,
That I in turn may nourish all beings
With an unceasing banquet of delight.

Through your compassionate intention,
Your blessings and virtuous deeds,
And my strong wish to rely upon you,

May all suffering quickly cease
And all happiness and joy be fulfilled;
And may holy Dharma flourish forevermore.[2]

References

1. Robert Thurman, *The Jewel Tree of Tibet,* Free Press, New York, NY 2005, page 10.

2. Geshe Kelsang Gyatso, *The New Meditation Handbook,* Tharpa Publications, Glen Spey, NY 2009, page 28.

REAWAKENING MY SPIRIT

Self-Reflection
Time Period: Fall 2008
Topic: Reawakening

Memories, Thoughts & Feelings:

After spending the summer trying to work through some of the issues that led to my downfall, I decided what I really needed was a big hug from my mom and dad. While spending time with them in Canada, I found a book on Buddhism and the messages within were exactly what I needed to hear at this turning point in my life. This inspired me to make a commitment to the study and practice of this ancient belief system. With my sister's guidance, I was able to find the perfect path. The "New Kadampa Tradition" became a powerful source of inspiration just when I needed it most.

Suspected Causes:
Related past history

It's no coincidence that I found this book on my nightstand. My sister had just been there and knew I was coming. Maybe she left it, intentionally or not. Or perhaps my mom put it there. Either way, there was a higher consciousness involved who lovingly extended a gift — one that would inspire me and reignite my spirit since its flame had been nearly extinguished.

Effects:
Occurring as a result of the causes identified

An awakening began to restore my faith in the beauty of the world. I had glimpsed the uglier side, and desperately needed reassurance that love, compassion, forgiveness, and joy were all out there just waiting to be rediscovered.

I was given another chance to emerge from victim-mode and become a victor once again. I had been given a fresh start and I knew that the choices I would make going forward were totally up to me. I could squander it and immerse myself in self-pity, or I could express my deepest gratitude by living my life on purpose. I chose the latter. I wanted to repay the gift by dedicating the rest of my life to the renewal of spirit in the world.

Lessons Hidden Within:

Choose to embrace second chances.

The brilliant sun is always shining behind even the darkest clouds.

Upon asking for forgiveness, I will make a strong commitment to forgive myself and extend forgiveness to everyone from that point forward.

I will always express compassion and empathy toward myself and others. Having experienced and heard painful hard-luck stories, I have developed a strong empathy for everyone who struggles. I promise to reach out, lift up, and do whatever I can to rescue those in need.

Lesson Plan:

I will make the most of every day and not waste my time engaged in meaningless activities.

I will be forgiving, understanding and compassionate to everyone, and if I can provide any type of support or encouragement, I will.

I will seek the truth about our existence and uncover the true meaning and purpose of our lives.

I will discover the path to a higher consciousness and make every effort to connect with it. Once I do, I will live in that awareness and hopefully inspire others to see the light of truth as well.

I will seek to raise the individual and collective consciousness of the human spirit.

DAY SEVEN
The Spiritual Essence of Reawakening
With Spiritual Counselor & Minister, Janet Myatt

SUZANNE: Good afternoon, Janet, and welcome back. I am really looking forward to exploring our topic "reawakening" today. Especially since my own personal experience of reawakening was so remarkable. It dramatically altered my perception of life and enhanced the way I experience it.

JANET: Not everyone gets a second chance. You are fortunate for having the personal courage to try again, and also for the unconditional love and support from your husband and family.

SUZANNE: Indeed I am. After being reawakened, I experienced a divine miracle that rocked the very core of my being, so I felt like I had angels looking out for me as well! Since then, I have dedicated every day of my life to my spiritual growth. Everything I think, say, and do has been affected by my revelations, and every aspect of my personal and professional life has been joined to my spiritual path. I see them as all being connected in my holistic view of life and I am always searching for the ways in which each and every interaction and experience contributes to the greater fulfillment of my divine purpose.

My first awakening 20 years ago, was incredible, but because life is dynamic and we are always creating and destroying, I fell asleep again. When I was reawakened, I took a greater leap. This time, I realized that if I didn't fill the spiritual void in my life, I would continue to fall asleep and wake up, fall asleep and wake up, yet not make much progress on my path. So when I recognized that I needed to fill the spiritual void once and for all, things really started to expand in every direction.

JANET: This is how the law of inertia works. When we first begin on our path, it often feels like we're sort of stuttering - starting and then halting. We find our balance point and then lose it. But each little step that we take still has a cumulative effect, and moments of awakening begin to lengthen and cohere.

Ascension is not a linear process, but works in an upward spiral of ever-expanding cycles of growth and awareness. As our understanding of the nature of the universe and our role in it deepens, we return more and more of our energy and our consciousness into the rhythm of divine, unconditional love. We experience sudden shifts or expansions in our awareness that liberate us from ignorance. I compare it to living in a windowless basement and after careful exploration, suddenly finding a doorway. As we step through, we realize that we now have access to a much larger, more comfortable space. At first this is thrilling and there is much to explore, learn, and master in this new space. However, eventually there comes a time when this space begins to feel limiting. We find ourselves hitting the boundaries of the space, and a new dissatisfaction emerges. We long for more freedom. This dissatisfaction is a gift when we use it properly. When it motivates us to find the next doorway it serves a divine purpose. When it turns us bitter and we become depressed, hopeless, angry or lethargic, we miss our opportunity to evolve — to turn chaos into order, fear into love.

When we begin to feel limited, we must look at what needs to die so that we may be reborn into a higher version of ourselves. We need to find the next level in our ever-expanding consciousness. It is our task to move from one level of awareness to the next, learning, growing and evolving as we do. As we do this, we take with us what is eternal and true and begin to seek new levels of awareness and mastery. We must ask ourselves, "What needs to be completed? What needs to be released or let go of? What needs to change?" And, "What needs to come in? What needs to arise?"

Life in the physical world is the gift we give ourselves to learn and master the forces of creativity within us. It is cyclical, expansive, and progressive. With each new awakening there will be a cycle of birth, discovery, exploration, learning, mastery, detachment, death and then rebirth. The death process is as important as all of the others, for it allows us to cast off that which no longer serves the highest good, and carry forward only that which does. It is important for us to realize and remember that Life is eternal. Only the forms of existence are temporary.

SUZANNE: It's reassuring to know that death can be an opportunity to shed our skin and start anew with that which serves the highest good. If we spend this lifetime wisely, consciously mastering our lessons and actively balancing our karma, we can rest assured that our experiences in both the here and hereafter will be greatly enhanced! Thank you for your inspiring message, Janet.

Now it's your turn!

SELF-EXPLORATION #7 – REAWAKENING THE SPIRIT
Theme: Reawakening

At times you may fall asleep and lose touch with your own true nature, requiring drastic measures to wake you up. This may come in the form of a dramatic event, health scare, or downward spiral in your well-being or relationships. Think deeply about a difficult time or traumatic episode that awakened you to a new perspective. Reflect on how this reawakening changed the way you perceived your life and those around you. Think about the changes you made as a result of this shift.

Explore your Heart and Mind

Focus on an event or sudden change in life circumstances that rocked your world. Reflect upon the way you perceived yourself and the world around you before and after. Did the episode cause a transformational shift in your consciousness? If so, try and recall the specific changes in your perspective.

_____

_____

_____

_____

Challenging times often bring people together; they can also tear people apart. Either way, significant aspects of your relationships are revealed. Examine the nature of your relationships before and after a major change.

_____

_____

_____

_____

Do you feel this experience allowed you to identify the people who have the most positive influence on your life, as well as those who have a negative one?

_____

_____

_____

_____

What were the most important changes you made in your life upon reawakening? Consider the things you changed about yourself — attitude, plans, hobbies, career, or other interests. Now consider how these changes have impacted your life since that time.

_____

_____

_____

_____

Identify Lessons and Shifts

Significant shifts often help you to see the bigger picture of your life more clearly. The more meaningful aspects of your life may be illuminated while the trivial ones fade away. This is the first sign of your higher Self awakening and your ego-self diminishing. Think back on the things that were important to you prior to your shift, and compare them with whatever became a priority afterward.

_____

_____

_____

_____

In retrospect, are you able to see how this shift allowed you to progress on your path toward a higher consciousness? In what ways do you believe your mindset evolved?

_____

_____

_____

_____

Have you noticed a higher level of awareness with respect to the world around you? Are you more aware of the way you interact with others? Are you less consumed with yourself and more connected with others? If so, in what ways?

_____

_____

_____

_____

_____

If not, think about ways you can raise your awareness of the people, places and things around you.

_____

_____

_____

_____

Do you feel a greater connection to the natural world around you? Do you feel drawn to be out in nature amongst the trees, plants, and animals? If so, how does this make you feel?

_____

_____

_____

_____

If not, make a commitment to spend more time in nature and then focus on being present with the plants and animals you pass along the way.

Time for your Reflection

After experiencing a shift in consciousness, it is common to feel as if you have awakened from slumber. We tend to drift into a narrow focus when our lives become overwhelming. Upon reawakening, the world seems bigger, brighter and more abundant. We may find ourselves drawn to those who are more enlightened, and drift away from those who are less so. At the same time, we may feel compelled to lift the hearts and minds of those who are still sleeping. The greatest benefit is the feeling of unity that connects us to the beauty within all living things and beings. A positive shift allows us to embrace our lives more fully every moment of every day.

SELF-REALIZATION #7
Meditation on Reawakening

It's time to progress on your path of self-realization

Before journaling your experience, please engage in Dynamic Movement Therapy to open and expand your body. We will start with the dynamic movement therapy to increase the blood flow and then move into the breathing practices to oxygenate your brain. You can engage in the movement and breathing practices by referring back to the written guidelines in the introduction or by going to my website for an audio download that will guide you through the practices. Access the audio download for free at *www. suzannerosstransendence.com/Up!Trilogy/WakeUp!Meditations*.

We all have a tendency to fall asleep amidst the chaos of our busy lives, especially when confronted with difficult circumstances. When the distorted thoughts of our ego override our spirit, it may be eclipsed. We may find that our ego pushes us into a corner from which there is no escape without the guidance of our higher self. At that point, we surrender to spirit and open to the guidance it has to offer. We are reawakened to the power our spirit has to lift us up, lead us out of the darkness and turn us back toward the light.

In an effort to reawaken, spirit may attract a special person into your life or drop a powerful book into your lap. If you try to remain in a higher state of awareness and observe all that is unfolding all around you, you will be more likely to recognize these signs from spirit. Making an effort to remain present by ignoring the chatter in your mind about past and future will help you connect with spirit. Taking long walks alone out in nature and appreciating the beauty all around you will help as well. Going within during guided meditation will ignite the spirit within you and open your heart to the spirit all around you.

Now retreat into your sacred space and perform the "**VIS-MED for Reawakening.**" You can download an audio version of this guided meditation by going to my website at *www.suzannerosstranscendence.com*. On the Up!Trilogy menu, select **Wake Up! Meditations** and go to the **VIS-MED for Reawakening.**

DAY SEVEN
Self-Reflection

Name of the Experience: _____

Time Period: _____

Topic: Reawakening

Memories, Thoughts & Feelings:

_____

_____

_____

_____

_____

Suspected Causes:
Related past history

_____

_____

_____

_____

_____

_____

Effects:

Occurring as a result of the causes identified

_____

_____

_____

_____

_____

Lessons Hidden Within:

_____

_____

_____

_____

_____

Lesson Plan:

_____

_____

_____

_____

_____

DAY SEVEN
PRACTICAL SPIRITUALITY

Reawakening: An Expansion of Consciousness

"Eventually we may arrive at the insight that all our thoughts are merely borrowed from the great database of consciousness and were never really our own."

— David R Hawkins

It is my firm belief that in order to understand the reality of one's self, or "self-realize," it is necessary to grasp the true essence of the reality within which one exists. The reality that we perceive depends on our choices and expectations; in other words, consciously or subconsciously, we choose our perception of reality. We also have access to the universal mind. The source of this creative intelligence is always working through us individually as our "higher Self" and collectively as the "Great Self."

We are in constant communication with both the immediate and greater fields of consciousness. Our brains are simply transmitters and receivers. At this point on our evolutionary path, we are able to access only a limited bandwidth of knowledge. As we become more advanced beings, we may be able to access it telepathically. For now, however, we can work on increasing our bandwidth in three important ways.

First, we can access the endless stream of information available to us in books and online. Second, we can expand our consciousness during meditation and contemplation. The third way is to heighten our sense awareness by increasing our sensitivity to the world around us. This practice brings us into the present moment where the real power lies.

We tend to live in a narrow field of awareness that seems like "our own little world." But we can choose to step out of that world and look beyond it. All we have to do is put away our electronic devices, shake off all the whirling thoughts related to our private world, and look beyond it into the breadth and depth of the greater world around us. When we do this, we will notice how far we can actually see. The farther we look out into the horizon, especially when we look at celestial bodies, the farther we are looking into the past. We can also see things close-up and appreciate their most intricate details. We can actually see things that are both far away and in the past, or up close and in the present, simultaneously. We can also hear sounds occurring right next to us and sounds emanating from far away at the same time.

We have much greater access to the field of consciousness around us than we typically recognize or use to our advantage.

An enhanced awareness increases your ability to consciously direct reality. Unless you are consciously aware of the thoughts and feelings you are allowing, they will permeate your mind and distort your perception. You have the power to become the master of your mind, however, and to consciously redirect your thoughts and feelings according to the guidance of your higher self. There is only one key that will unlock this potential within you and that is a strong belief in your own divine nature.

Our thoughts and our feelings are very powerful. If they reflect the divine attributes of love, compassion and unity, they can create a harmonious perception of reality. If these thoughts and feelings reflect ego-driven fear and anger, they will create a chaotic and distorted perception. We must make an effort to tame our minds by controlling our thoughts and aligning them with the highest attributes of love, gratitude, compassion and kindness. In this higher consciousness, a harmonious reality will unfold right before our eyes.

Awakening through Reflection

DAY EIGHT

SYNCHRONICITY

WORKSHOP MODULES:

1. Life Experience & Analysis: "Hospice in my Home"

2. The Spiritual Essence of Synchronicity

3. Self-Exploration #8: Going with the Flow

4. Self-Realization #8: Meditation on Synchronicity

5. Self-Reflection #8: Uncovering Life Lessons

6. Practical Spirituality: Synchronicity & Awareness

LIFE EXPERIENCE

DAY EIGHT

Hospice in my Home

As I write this, I am sitting in the bedroom where my mother-in-law passed away one year ago. I'm not sure of how to begin this story; in the end, she was the one who got us through her struggle of transition, not the other way around. Her fighting spirit was a true inspiration to everyone and she never ever gave up, even when her body ultimately failed her. Throughout the ordeal, her spirit was alive and well and we were all quite aware of it.

It was the summer of 2012 when my husband asked me how I felt about his parents coming to live with us during his mother's final battle with cancer. I supported the idea and assured him that I would do whatever I could to provide the love and care they all needed. Strangely enough, I was then enrolled in a hospice volunteer training program at Kaiser, which proved to be very helpful over the next ten months. I started out by volunteering as a "Friendly Visitor" with the County Outreach Services, where I met Charlotte, a lovely woman in her late 80's who was living in a nearby board and care facility. Her husband had passed several years earlier and her children were busy working and traveling. They felt she couldn't be left to live on her own because she had taken a few falls and left the stove on one too many times. She suffered from dementia and every time I visited, I would have to reintroduce myself as "the lady who walked her."

The caregivers in the home seldom had the chance to take her for a walk around the neighborhood so I decided this was my main purpose for visiting: let her feel the warm sun and fresh air, work her leg muscles and promote oxygen flow through her body. What became more important to her were the flowers she would see along the way, and the conversations we would share. One of the sadder things was that she kept telling everyone she was going home any day now, when the truth was that she would never go home again. She never watched T.V. with the other residents and preferred to put puzzles together or play Scrabble. I used to bring her puzzles and she would share with me the best strategic approaches to putting them together. When each one was complete, we'd sit back and admire our achievement. One of the caregivers would glue it all together, mount it on poster board and hang it in her room.

One time when we were sitting in the quiet of her room admiring her puzzle-posters, she said how much she missed listening to church music. On my next visit, I presented her with a brand new radio. It was simple with big numbers so she could easily use it. Once I got it set up and helped her find a church music station, we sat there on the edge of her bed and listened. She was delighted when a livelier song came on and said, "Turn it up!" So I did and we tried to sing along. We laughed at each other's feeble attempt to get the words right. It was a truly precious moment and I'll never forget it. I knew I had brightened up her life a little with a simple gift from my heart.

After Charlotte passed, I decided to move onto something even more challenging. During hospice training, the instructor would look at us all and say, "You do realize what you're signing up for here, don't you?" Impressively, out of eight volunteers, only one bowed out during the process. I was inspired to do this work by one of my favorite spiritual guides, Ram Dass, while listening to one of his audiobooks, "Path to Service," where he talks in depth about the spiritual value of working with the dying. I also became involved with a local inspirational center connected with the Himalayan Institute, focusing on the traditional Vedantic teachings.

These developments came along at the perfect time to prepare me for what was coming. My experience with Charlotte gave me greater empathy for what it must be like to be taken out of your home and placed in the care of others uncertain about your fate on a daily basis. The hospice training prepared me for the harsher realities of facing one's mortality. I became more familiar with the absoluteness of death and the process of dying as I progressed through the course and read books on the subject. Finding a spiritual community that I could turn to for support and encouragement was probably the most valuable outcome. The fact that they specialized in working with the dying was harmoniously aligned with my path.

In August of 2012, my mother and father-in-law moved in with us. When we were buying the house a few years earlier, I had been adamant that we needed extra bedrooms for our parents. We knew it would cost more to buy a bigger home but we both agreed it was important. A huge master suite turned out to be a blessing for my in-laws and they used every inch of it. They transformed the room into comfortable new living quarters that included a fridge and microwave as well as a dining room table and reclining love seat. They set up an office for all of their administrative needs, as they were still in charge of the operations at their horse ranch in San Diego. They bought a big screen T.V., purchased new blinds, hung family photos and made it as homey as possible.

My mother-in-law was being a real trooper. She faced a long, hard battle with cancer, and all of us wondered if the suffering from both the illness and the treatments was worth it. As she got thinner and weaker, we all felt deep sympathy for her. Toward the end, she would come downstairs (with help) and try to sit with us but she spent much of the time just moaning in pure agony. She had trouble breathing because she had asthma and also had to have a colostomy bag. She was miserable and one day, as I sat on the bed next to her while she was vomiting, she just looked at me and said, "I can't live like this anymore." Tears ran down both of our faces as we sat there wondering why it had to be this way.

At times, the tension in the house was palpable as we all waited for the next crisis to arise. There was little joy left in the house and I sometimes wanted to escape, but I knew that we all needed to be there for Jenny and each other. I would take deep breaths, swallow my feelings and say over and over in my head, "Let it go, let it go." This is when I decided that I had a lot more work to do on myself, and so I made a strong commitment to go even deeper into my spiritual practice. I knew in my heart the whole experience had a greater purpose for all of us.

One morning, my father-in-law came downstairs looking ragged. "I don't think Jenny is going to make it through the day," he said quietly. My heart sank; I went over to console him and asked what I could do. He said he would really appreciate it if I could go upstairs and be with her while he stepped outside and made a few phone calls. I said, "Sure, of course." My husband had already left for work so after he stepped outside, it was just her and myself in the house. As I walked up the stairs, I had to stop and catch my breath, feeling the momentary urge to flee. I stepped into my bathroom, and looked in the mirror and said, "You have to do this. Be strong. Gather your courage, girl."

When I entered the bedroom, my mother-in-law was lying face up with both her eyes and mouth wide open, yet totally non-responsive. She was gurgling fluid in the back of her throat, and was clearly in the process of dying. Suddenly my fear subsided and a sense of peace washed over me. It was like a "spirit-to-spirit" bond as mine reached out to hers and she responded. I sat down on a chair next to the bedside and held her hand. The song, "Amazing Grace" came to mind and as I sang it, she squeezed my hand. I explained to her softly that she would soon be with her beloved parents and they would be so happy to see her. They would welcome her with open arms. She had lost a baby when he was just an infant and I told her she would see him too. She wasn't open to this before, but it just felt right to comfort her with these thoughts now. It was a beautiful moment for both of us and I'll never forget it.

It was such a blessing that we were able to gather more family members together before she drew her last breath. In fact, she sustained for another eight hours, which surprised us all, even the hospice workers. A minister arrived, sang a song for her, then closed his eyes, held one of her hands and said: "Yea, though I walk through the valley of the shadow of death, I will fear no evil: for thou art with me; thy rod and thy staff will comfort me." This brought tears to everyone's eyes as the reality of her death began to sink in even more.

I've read that as Steve Jobs passed over, he kept saying, "Wow" over and over. We experienced something similar with Jenny. Her eyes were peeled wide open the whole time, which seemed odd since she didn't appear to be conscious. You could hear her labored breathing and sometimes she would gasp for air. The most fascinating part was that she kept saying, "Yaaa..." over and over. It was haunting at first but then we all got used to it and would sometimes reply with comforting words. Her sons took turns sitting with her and Dick would rub her head and caress her hair. It was very sweet and touching to observe them expressing their deep affection for their beloved mother and wife.

Finally, she drew one last deep inhalation and then became completely still. Her spirit had left her body. Suddenly it seemed so obvious to me that we are all just skin and bones without the spiritual breath of life and spark of personality to illuminate our being. Each of us approached her and said our final goodbye. I kissed her on the forehead and told her I loved her and would see her soon. I knew her spirit was still present to hear every word and witness every gesture. In fact, you could still feel her presence even as we moved into the downstairs rooms. Her husband kept going back upstairs to check on her while we waited for the medical examiner and hearse to arrive. You could almost see her spirit follow him as he paced and went up and down the stairs. After several trips, my husband stopped him and in a loving way said, "Dad, maybe you shouldn't keep going up there."

As we waited two hours for the medical examiner, we were all pretty solemn and even a little awkward knowing that her lifeless body was lying upstairs. We had all been caring for her for so long that there was a sense that someone should be up there tending to her needs. We were all a little on edge until my sister-in-law broke the ice, finally saying "Sheesh! By the time they get here, she'll already be reincarnated!" There was a brief pause before we all broke into laughter; that was just what we needed.

After that, things seemed much less intense and we started to chat more comfortably. Everyone felt much more at ease until the hearse arrived. Unfortunately they left the stretcher with her body on it sitting in the downstairs hall until the medical examiner arrived, and that was especially stressful for Dick. He wouldn't leave her side and began to sob. We all shed tears and our hearts felt heavy with sadness. After the hearse finally drove away, we all just sat there stunned. Suddenly my father-in-law admitted, "I need a drink." My husband drove to the liquor store to get his dad the 'liquid courage' he needed, and in fact the alcohol helped him relax and share his feelings. He expressed his deep gratitude to all of us for giving them both so much love and support for the past ten months, and said he wanted us to all take a "memorial trip" together to honor her one last time.

After a few more drinks, he began to regale stories about her and the boys when they were younger. Everyone laughed and the boys joined in with their own version of events. I finally went to bed around ten to give him and the boys some precious time alone. They had just lost their mother and wife and needed time to grieve and reminisce together as a family unit.

The funeral was lovely and there were so many people there to honor and bless her. The service was held in a small church although my mother-in-law wasn't religious in the traditional sense. When she was staying at our house, she couldn't figure out what I was! She would see my Buddhist shrine, picture of Jesus, archangels and crystals along with the Bible and books on spirituality, and finally concluded, "Well I know you're not religious because you don't go to church." I replied, "I am spiritual. That's all."

She'd answered, "Well, some people need that in their life to make them feel better about themselves." I kept quiet and thought, *She's right. It does make me feel better about myself, and everything else.*" One night over dinner, someone mentioned heaven and I said to her, "Jenny, you have been such a good person your whole life, so honest and kind. Your main concern has always been taking care of your family. If there is a heaven, you are definitely going there." She smiled and thanked me. I knew I had lifted her spirits and given her something pleasurable to think about amidst all her agony. Hopefully she had glimpsed a little light at the end of the tunnel.

In Honor of

VIRGINIA DIANE TYNAN

April 3, 1943 - May 4, 2012

Self-Reflection
Time Period: May 2012
Topic: Synchronicity

Memories, Thoughts & Feelings:

There is no doubt in my mind that I had become aware of a higher source and was intuitively following its guidance. I was led to Ram Dass and his book *Path to Service*, which motivated me to pursue hospice volunteering. This in turn led me to "The Awakening Center," a spiritual community. Hospice training served me well during my mother-in-law's battle with cancer and the community provided much-needed support during that time. This inspired me to seek spiritual counseling and I found an 'intuitive' who has become a very important part of my journey. These synchronistic events enabled me to deepen my spirituality in many ways and as a result, I am compelled to share my experiences for the benefit of others.

Suspected Causes:

Related past history

Primary cause: heightened spiritual awareness

Following my reawakening in 2008, I made a strong determination to seek spiritual truths and integrate spiritual practices into my life. As a result, I continue to advance on my spiritual journey toward self-realization.

I became aware of a strong connection to a higher source of spiritual guidance and surrendered to its will.

I became aware that my intuition was the voice of this higher source and if I listened to it, I would be led down the right path.

I developed a strong faith in the power of this source to increase my potential and lovingly expand my consciousness.

Effects:

Occurring as a result of the causes identified

In this higher state of awareness, I am in harmony with my higher Self. Without resistance from my ego-self, events unfold harmoniously to advance my spiritual growth.

My ability to surrender to the will of a higher power benefits both myself and others as I radiate love and light to the world. I begin to emulate the qualities of this higher source, emphasizing unity, compassion, patience, and kindness. The expression of these virtuous qualities fills me with a deep inner peace and exuberant joy.

My thoughts, words and actions are motivated by unconditional love for all living beings, both in the physical and spiritual realms.

This heightened state of spiritual awareness illuminates the synchronicity of sequential events as they unfold before me.

Lessons Hidden Within:

These experiences reinforce the many benefits of the spiritual path. I learned that seeking and surrendering are the keys which unlock the door to a world where loving guidance and support are readily available.

Through meditation and visualization, I have learned how to access sacred wisdom and open my heart and mind to its teachings.

I have realized that I need to preserve my ego-self for its basic survival instincts, but have learned to distinguish and follow the loving guidance of my higher Self.

I have become aware that love and faith allow life to unfold naturally, and that fear and doubt create resistance to the harmonious flow.

Studying, practicing, and exemplifying spiritual truth elevates my experience of life. This pursuit has allowed me to attract and radiate the light that spreads love and compassion and most importantly, promotes the desire to be united as one.

Lesson Plan:

I will make time every day to meditate and go within. I will listen carefully to the guidance I receive.

I will continue to read and study the spiritual material that comes my way. I will provide insight to those who willingly request my guidance.

I will focus on increasing my awareness of the world around me. I will be in tune with the harmonious flow of energy that I transmit and receive.

I will pray and surrender to the higher powers which surround me. I will verbally pronounce my dedication to performing the will of the Creator and declare my willingness to be an instrument through which the highest thoughts, words and actions can easily flow.

I will make a sincere effort to think, say, and do that which is motivated by the purest intentions and characterized by the highest virtues. I will redirect less virtuous tendencies in my heightened state of awareness.

Every day, I will frequently express my sincere gratitude and infinite love for the Universal Father, Eternal Son and Infinite Spirit. I will bless them for breathing life into all living things and for directing all of creation with the essence of pure love.

DAY EIGHT

The Spiritual Essence of Synchronicity

With Spiritual Counselor & Minister, Janet Myatt

SUZANNE: Good morning Janet! Thanks so much for joining us today. We are engaging in the Wake Up! Workshop to uncover important life lessons from our past so that we can develop a lesson plan for our lives today. We can set an intention to learn and grow by creating meaningful experiences that incorporate these lessons. In this way, we can fulfill our true purpose which, I believe, is to progress on our evolutionary path.

JANET: It's my pleasure. I also believe that we will make more progress on our path if we learn how to intentionally create and consciously evolve.

SUZANNE: I was able to open to spirit because of Buddhist practices that involved envisioning light and nectar flowing down and filling my entire body, from the crown of my head to the soles of my feet. Then I would turn my attachments over to the higher beings so that I could be liberated from suffering. At first I didn't realize how powerful the practices were, but I did feel more radiant and joyful. I also began to develop an insatiable curiosity about all things spiritual and scientific. I was searching for a clear definition of the meaning and purpose of life. Then, one day, I headed out on a nature walk obsessed with this thought, and determined to find the definitive answer I was seeking. Suddenly I felt compelled to look up in the sky and written in puffy white lettering, it clearly said:

Meaning – To Create
Purpose – To Evolve

At first I was stunned, but then I recognized that I had been offered a divine revelation. I was relieved that I had been given this simple answer, and felt completely satisfied and very grateful. After that experience, synchronicities and amazing opportunities began unfolding all around me. Everyone around me became so helpful and wanted to participate. You are one of those people that jumped on board during this time.

JANET: The way I see it, we don't create synchronicity at the individual, incarnated level. We participate in it. For me, synchronicity is the experience of coming into alignment with the Divine Plan. Pieces come together in ways that feel surprising because we cannot see the overall pattern. It is much like playing in a symphony. Each individual contributes their part to the whole while simultaneously attending to the conductor and experiencing the whole. Each part is necessary for the expression of the whole, yet the whole is greater than the sum of the parts.

When we learn how to live in present time, taking our direction from our inner divine Director, we begin to experience synchronicity. Opportunities, ideas, resources, connections, people, and relationships all begin to come our way because we are now operating within the greater field of life rather than in resistance to it. Imagine that the world is made up of intersecting lines of creative force that look like an enormous golden web or grid. When we live in the boxes in between those intersecting lines, we experience isolation, stagnation, and stuckness. That's because we are out of alignment with the greater energetic field, so our life becomes effortful and difficult. When we bring our consciousness into alignment with this web of creativity through meditation and quiet reflection, we place ourselves on the divine super-highway. We can't help but interact with all of those creative lines.

We are automatically led in the perfect direction to meet up with the just the right people and situations at just the right time. This is living synchronistically.

Your story is such a great example of how this can work for us. You took the time to get into alignment with spirit instead of merely focusing on your day-to-day life. Like you said, the people and the conversations come to you. The insights, intuition, illumination, and inspiration come to you because you are connecting to the matrix of spirit.

SUZANNE: If we keep our eyes and ears wide open, we can see the synchronicities unfold and act upon the connections being made. If we keep an open heart and mind, we can harmonize with the people, places and opportunities that are being presented to us. We really have to stay alert and expansive. By contrast, people who are focused on their smartphones and other electronic devices are often displaced from their current reality. They are contracted, sitting in a slouched position and totally unaware of their immediate surroundings. They are projecting their consciousness into another aspect of reality through their device. It's sort of a modern phenomenon that's rather confounding to me.

JANET: Using the symphony analogy, you can imagine that if one of the violinists was sitting there with headphones on and facing the back, chances are that violin player would get out of sync with the rest of the symphony playing around him. This not only affects his ability to carry out his part, but affects the whole as well.

SUZANNE: Exactly! So, even though people using their phones might be making connections with people elsewhere, they are missing out on the symphony playing all around them. They aren't able to see or act upon the synchronicities unfolding right in front of them! What's important is making a conscious choice to live in a higher state of awareness with your eyes, heart and mind wide open. Thank you for that wonderful analogy, Janet!

Now it's your turn!

SELF-EXPLORATION #8 – GOING WITH THE FLOW
Theme: Synchronicity

Close your eyes and think about a time when the events unfolding in your life were synchronistic —a series of occurrences which seemed to fall into place perfectly, one right after another. This would have happened during a time when you were able to set aside your need to control and you allowed things to unfold naturally. Your optimism and ability to see the opportunities allowed for this continual flow of constructive events. This is in contrast to the times when barriers are thrown up by feeling pessimistic and resistant to the world around you.

Explore your Heart and Mind

Focus on harmonious times when everything was going your way and your life was headed in a positive direction. During this time, the right people, places and things appeared before you at just the right time and you were receptive to them. Can you recall a series of events which led to abundant opportunities and your health and wealth prospered as a result?

_____

_____

_____

_____

_____

As you recall a time like this, focus on the circumstances just prior to it. Can you recall something which may have triggered a heightened awareness or greater ability to open your heart and mind to new possibilities?

_____

_____

_____

_____

Close your eyes and think about your mindset during this period. How did things become aligned so perfectly? Were there positive influences in your life that helped you to open your eyes and see opportunities rather than barriers?

_____

_____

_____

_____

Try to remember who or what inspired you during this synchronistic period of your life. Sometimes a book or movie delivers an inspirational message. Recall the types of things you were involved with at the time. Think of the specific ways in which you may have been inspired.

_____

_____

_____

_____

Identify Lessons and Shifts

During this time when positive energy was flowing in your life, were you aware of the blessings being offered, or did you feel like you were finally getting what you deserved?

_____

_____

_____

The difference between the influence of your ego-self and the awareness of your higher Self can simply be the contrast of arrogance and gratitude. If you feel a sense of entitlement, your ego is probably in charge. If you have an attitude of gratitude, your higher Self is emerging. Focus on the way in which your newfound abundance affected you.

_____

_____

_____

_____

Times of prosperity boost your confidence and can increase your potential if you stay focused on applying yourself with integrity and determination. Expecting things to come your way will open the door to abundance. Without pure intentions and generosity, however, you won't be able to walk through it and stay there. Selfishness will eventually close the door. Openly sharing the wealth and spreading good fortune will keep the door open and the abundance flowing. Can you recall the approach that you took during a time of prosperity?

_____

_____

_____

_____

Time for your Reflection

Think about the actions which contributed to your ability to maintain the flow and those which seemed to obstruct it. Try to recognize the virtuous and non-virtuous nature of your actions. Performing the "VIS-MED for Synchronicity" will illuminate the thoughts, words and actions which led to the flow of synchronicity and those which stopped it. The difference between viewing things as opportunities or barriers will become apparent.

SELF-REALIZATION #8
Meditation on Synchronicity

It's time to progress on your path of self-realization

Before journaling your experience, please engage in Dynamic Movement Therapy to open and expand your body. Then be seated comfortably and perform the Inspirational Breathing Practices to oxygenate your body and clear your mind of distractions. You can engage in the movement and breathing practices by referring back to the written guidelines in the introduction or access the audio download for free at *www.suzannerosstransendence.com/ Up!Trilogy/WakeUp!Meditations*.

Now you are ready to go within by doing your visualization/meditation. At times in our lives when synchronicities are unfolding and we are attracting abundance, we know that we are on the right track. We are following the guidance of our higher Self and the power of our pure intentions is creating a harmonious flow of positive energy. That's how synchronicity and the law of attraction work together to create harmony. As long as we stay in spirit, we remain open to this flow.

We all become vulnerable when we give into the temptations of our ego or become distracted from spirit in the chaos of our busy lives. When we allow the ego to control our minds, we tend to make decisions that aren't conducive to our well-being or the welfare of others. When we become too distracted and act impulsively without thinking, we shut out spirit. This is why living in a higher state of awareness is so important. We must always make an effort to represent the highest version of ourselves. We must stay connected to our spirit and call upon the guidance of our higher Self. We must resist the temptation to act, or react, impulsively. We must take the time to stop and ask ourselves: Is this the highest thought, word or action I could be engaging in at this time? If the answer is no, redirect!

The more that you engage in these powerful VIS-MEDs, the greater your connection to spirit will become. The more that you call upon your higher self, the more you will become one with it. In this higher state of awareness, you will remain open to the synchronistic flow of positive energy. The following VIS-MED for Synchronicity will help you stay connected to the universal flow and you will become a magnet for abundant health, wealth and prosperity.

You can download an audio version of this guided meditation by going to my website at *www.suzannerosstranscendence.com.* On the Up!Trilogy menu, select **Wake Up! Meditations** and go to the **VIS-MED for Synchronicity.**

DAY EIGHT
Self-Reflection

Name of the Experience: _____

Time Period: _____

Topic: Synchronicity

Memories, Thoughts & Feelings:

_____

_____

_____

_____

_____

_____

Suspected Causes:
Related past history

_____

_____

_____

_____

_____

_____

Effects:
Occurring as a result of the causes identified

_____

_____

_____

_____

_____

_____

Lessons Hidden Within:

_____

_____

_____

_____

_____

Lesson Plan:

_____

_____

_____

_____

_____

DAY EIGHT
PRACTICAL SPIRITUALITY
Synchronicity & Awareness

Presence is the infinite space in which the unfolding sequence of life emerges. It is that universal atmosphere in which the flowering of human awareness blossoms into its full glory. Presence is the stillness inhabiting the core of our existence, giving us the light of life.

— Sean Calvin

Today's practice focuses on heightening your awareness so you can recognize and embrace the synchronistic opportunities that are always presenting themselves in the form of people, places and events. First of all, you have to be committed to engaging in the reality which surrounds you, and this includes leaving your mobile device alone for a while. You mustn't allow your devices to distract you from your present circumstances for a given period of time each day.

We must also make an effort to disengage from the flurry of thoughts swirling through our head that distract us from fully appreciating our surroundings. A powerful practice that I use is to say out loud or in my head, "MOMENT!" This immediately draws my attention back into the present and I can more effectively engage with the world around me.

A concept that reinforces the importance of engaging with others is the scientific theory of entanglement. This theory states that whenever we exchange energy with another living being, that energetic connection will remain intact for all time. Many scientific experiments have been done that prove the validity of this concept. This means that every interaction you have with another living being will remain forever imprinted on both of you. With this in mind, I want you to ask yourself: "What type of karmic imprint do I want to leave on myself and others throughout the day?" and "How can I improve the quality of the energetic connections I am making?"

Finally, consider that our paths are predestined. We have come here to learn the life lessons that will allow us to progress on our paths. As such, we will naturally create the experiences that are most likely to help us learn and grow. We will attract the people, places and things that are most conducive to our soul's evolution. Our spiritual guides may also place certain beings in our path to assist us on our journey. The key to recognizing these people and places as opportunities to learn and grow is to continually search for the deeper meaning of our interactions with them.

We have to ask ourselves questions like, "Why have I been placed in this particular location at this particular time, and how is this situation conducive to my growth" We also have to explore relationships on a deeper level by asking ourselves, "Why have I been connected with this person and how can we benefit each other?" and "What lessons can we learn from each other?" By making a sincere effort to uncover the meaning behind our everyday experiences and interactions, we can reveal their higher purpose and "go with the flow."

Here are three powerful ways to remain open to the synchronistic flow of life's stream:

1. Use the practice of saying, "MOMENT!" whenever you notice that you have become disconnected from the present moment.

2. Be aware of the karmic imprint you are leaving on yourself and others with every reaction and interaction.

3. Recognize that the people, places and things you have attracted into your life all represent opportunities to learn the lessons that are most conducive to your evolutionary path.

By opening yourself up to the world around you in this way, you are opening to spirit. Aligned with spirit, magical synchronicities will unfold as you meet opportunity at every intersection. The power is in the present moment. As the Aramaic prayer says, ""Enter deep, its breath, its light."

Awakening through Reflection

DAY NINE

SUFFERING

WORKSHOP MODULES:

1. Life Experience & Analysis: "My Father Sees the Light"

2. The Spiritual Essence of Suffering

3. Self-Exploration #9: Feeling the Pain

4. Self-Realization #9: Meditation on Suffering

5. Self-Reflection #9: Uncovering Life Lessons

6. Practical Spirituality: The Healing Power of Pure Intentions

LIFE EXPERIENCE

DAY NINE

My Father Sees the Light!

Less than a week after my mother-in-law passed, my husband and I headed down to San Diego for the funeral. About halfway there, I receive a frantic phone call from my mother, telling me that my father, who is going through chemotherapy, has had an adverse reaction to the drugs and is in ICU. He is going in and out of consciousness and she suggests I get down there as soon as possible.

Thank goodness for my spiritual training at times like these. In the past, I probably would have been a mess, but I had a calmness and faith that enabled me to deal with challenges in a much more rational and emotionally balanced way. With a heightened awareness focused on selflessness, I am able to "serve" everyone involved with support and compassion.

My husband dropped me off at my Mom's house in Carlsbad and continued on to his parents' ranch, farther south. My mother was very relieved to see me and I was grateful to be there for her. My father had been suffering from colorectal cancer since 2008, and had been forced to adapt to wearing a colostomy bag. This changed his demeanor; it was like he had been given a life sentence that could never be revoked. He never took a sick day in fifty years of working for the same company, so he just didn't know how to handle a permanent impairment.

I agree with Louise Hay that all diseases and conditions are emotions or mental afflictions reflected on the body. This doesn't mean that we are to blame ourselves; it just means that if we truly reflected upon our lives, we may recognize mental or emotional states as potential causes for the particular ailment we are suffering from. In her groundbreaking book *You Can Heal Your Life*, she suggested the following associations for ailments I've suffered:

Kidney-distress: Criticism, disappointment, failure. Shame. Reacting like a little kid.

Back Breaks/fractures: Rebelling against authority.

Cancer: Deep hurt. Longstanding resentment. Deep secret or grief eating away at the self. Carrying hatred. "What's the use?"

Looking back, I can see that my kidney-distress ailment probably began with feelings of failure, disappointment and shame related to a major track and field loss that took place the year before my problems started. My future as a track and field star was shot down by a loss at the California State finals with my father watching in the stands. I was so overwhelmed with shame and a sense of total failure that I gave the whole thing up altogether, deciding to spend the next summer just hanging out with my friends at the beach. In fact, I never stepped on the track again. I would definitely say I acted like a little kid, and not long after began to experience kidney distress. Leading to several major surgeries, infections and ultimately bladder dysfunction. I have been battling serious kidney and bladder issues ever since.

This gets even more interesting as I look at the broken-back issue of rebelling against authority. At age twenty, I was hired as a manager for the retail chain "Toys R Us". The hours were brutal and my boss was extremely demanding. Nothing was ever good enough and he always expected more than I could possibly give. I was at the end of my rope and thought about quitting. The main reason I hung in there was because my boyfriend's father was a bigwig with the company, and I didn't want to disappoint him. Soon I had a traumatic car accident and fractured three vertebrae, shattering one. I was laid up for six months, and of course that was the end of that employment.

Now for the grand finale — cancer — associated with "deep hurt and long-standing resentment." I can point to my first husband moving me far away from all of my family and friends and then abandoning me by never being home. Many scary things happened to me on the East Coast (house and cars broken into, major surgeries, sexual harassment at work) and he was never there for me. A year after I left him, I was diagnosed with cancer.

As Louise Hay suggests, we have to "heal our lives" to prevent our bodies from manifesting the dis-eases of our minds. I hope this book helps readers find greater harmony within, which will help reduce suffering, both mental and physical.

The last chemotherapy treatment my father had almost killed him. When he wasn't delirious, he would express his anger about the effects of the treatment to anyone who would listen. "No one over the age of 70 should ever be submitted to the ravages of chemotherapy!" he'd protest. "It's immoral to put an old person through this." We would have to calm him down but we all agreed. We did take the step of finding a new doctor who was more caring and sympathetic to my father's needs.

After my father was stable enough to be moved out of the hospital, he was transferred to a nursing home. It was a nice set-up and he seemed well taken care of. He was prescribed physical therapy which was exactly what he needed for his body and spirit. The therapy girls were cute and sweet and they always encouraged him by telling him how strong and handsome he was. He had a room with a view of a beautiful flower garden and in the distance you could see the ocean. I felt comfortable going back to Northern California after seeing how well he was doing at the home.

After only about three weeks, my sister called to say that he was well enough to go home. This presented a problem. We had already sent my mom up to their home in Canada because she had mild dementia and couldn't be left alone in Carlsbad with access to a car. I felt compelled to sit and ponder this dilemma in silence for a few moments, so I told my sister I'd call her back. Dropping my head into my hands and asking for advice from my highest Self, the answer was immediately clear: *You'll drive down to San Diego, pick him up and bring him back up to live with you.* I didn't have a single doubt in my mind when I called my sister back. She was elated and marveled at how I could possibly go through another caregiving situation on the heels of what I'd just been through. My father got all choked up: "You'd really do that for me? I don't know what to say." My husband said, "Of course sweetie, family is family and our home is open to anyone who needs it." And therein lies the sweetest reward of all that nothing else can ever compare to — LOVE, pure unconditional love. That's what it is all about, my friends, and nothing else.

I am prompted to share a wonderful poem by our friend, Louise Hay, to recognize her for all that she has done, and continues to do, to heal the world and everyone in it:

> *In the infinity of life where I am,*
>
> *All is perfect, whole, and complete.*
>
> *Each of us, myself included, experiences the richness*
>
> *And fullness of life in ways that are meaningful to us.*
>
> *I now look at the past with love and choose*
>
> *To learn from my old experiences.*
>
> *There is no right or wrong, nor good or bad.*
>
> *The past is over and done.*
>
> *There is only experience in the experience of the moment.*
>
> *I love myself for bringing myself*
>
> *Through this past into this present moment.*
>
> *I share what and who I am,*
>
> *For I know we are all one in Spirit.*
>
> *All is well in my world.*

Borrowed from *"You Can Heal Your Life"* by Louise Hay

The first thing I had to do was transition the master suite from Jenny's style to my father's. This was a challenging task because the room had been left just as it was when she passed. I felt anxious and intrusive as I entered the room, and started by apologizing to her. I said, "Hello, I am so sorry to have to go through all of your things and would like to ask for your permission. It is time for us to move on and I hope that you too have moved on and are in a beautiful place, happy and peaceful now." I continued to talk to her as I cleaned and this made me feel more relaxed and peaceful.

Once when I walked past the large computer monitor that had been hers, it suddenly flashed on, displaying her colorful screensaver. I just giggled at her playfulness; I knew she was acknowledging my effort to communicate with her and this was a sign of permission and acceptance. It was an emotionally draining day; by the end of it, I had six large trash bags filled as well as several boxes of clothing and personal belongings. I took them down to the garage and once again apologized for moving her out. I had the sense she understood.

Now I had to embark on the creative task of redecorating in a way that would make my dad feel welcome. He absolutely loved living in the desert and cherished all the sights and images associated with it, so I decided this would be the theme of his room. I also found family photos that I knew would be meaningful for him and placed them around the room. He had tears in his eyes when he entered the room and saw what I had done.

The month that he stayed with us provided a wonderful opportunity to bond with my father on a deeper and more spiritual level. On the second morning, after my husband left for work, my dad and I were seated at the coffee table across from one another and he said, "I am open to whatever it is you and your sister are seeking spiritually and am willing to learn more about it now. Will you share some material with me?"

I was floored. He proceeded to explain that he had just faced his mortality, and the experience had left him feeling empty. He had the strong urge to gain a more spiritual perspective before moving on into the afterlife. I took a deep breath. I had heard that if you are going to inspire others with spiritual insight, it should only be done in response to their specific inquiry, and you must start where they are currently at with their conceptual understanding of spirituality.

I knew my father was very intrigued by anything scientific and I had just listened to a very lengthy audio download of David Wilcock's book *The Source Field*. I knew Dad would be drawn into the scientific evidence that connected to mystical implications about the true nature of reality. Also, the fact that he could lay in bed, or sit in the easy chair, and just listen was a major plus! My father became so totally absorbed in David's book that he listened to it the whole day while I was at work. Then at night when I got home, we would sit at the kitchen table and discuss it in detail. We were both fascinated by the implications of the material and this made for lively and enthusiastic conversations.

My father was also interested in the Buddhist teachings that my sister and I had been studying, so I shared with him a simple little book by Thich Nhat Hanh entitled *Beyond the Self*. He really enjoyed the book, underlining key passages, so I followed up with *You Are Here* by the same author. I was so honored to be my father's guide; "When the student is ready, the teachings will appear!" I wrote in my journal: *"Thank you higher powers for so beautifully coordinating this magical synchronicity of events. Signed, your humble servant."*

My father came down one morning about two weeks into his stay and he was looking particularly glum. He looked at me with big sad eyes and said, "I miss mom and the puppy terribly." I looked at him empathetically and responded, "We just have to get you strong enough to travel, Dad, that's all. Then we'll go together. What do you think?" In response, he stood up straight, tossed his cane in the corner of the room and said, "Two more weeks. I can do that!"

I replied enthusiastically, "O.K. then, let's do it! Let's just book those tickets now. That will give you something to look forward to." He was so uplifted that he ate a big breakfast and then we went for a long walk. He was on his way and we both knew he had been blessed with a new lease on life. This time he was going to embrace his life with a new commitment to fill his inner spiritual void with enlightened teachings, both scientific and spiritual. He had crossed the bridge to a higher level of consciousness just when he needed it most.

MY FATHER'S

Through your eyes, I saw the world –
and always felt I had a special place in it.

LAST BIRTHDAY CARD

Self-Reflection
Time Period: May – July 2012
Topic: Suffering

Memories, Thoughts & Feelings:

During my mother-in-law's battle with cancer, I witnessed a great deal of suffering, prompting me to seek a greater understanding of the meaning and purpose behind such "cruel and unusual punishment." Was it literally some kind of punishment? I didn't think so but I needed to know more. I turned to the Buddhist tradition, focused on the transcendence of suffering by using it as an opportunity to purify and cleanse ourselves. From this perspective, suffering may actually be seen as a blessing.

To understand more about the meaning behind it, I turned to the teachings of Louise Hay, from whom I learned that we can seize the opportunity to purify our minds without physical suffering! If we acknowledge the areas of dis-ease in our lives, we can take steps toward healing these wounds before they start manifesting physically.

These perspectives gave me much greater insight as to the meaning and purpose of suffering and I was grateful for the teachings. I was also grateful for the opportunity to provide love, support and compassion to those in need during their purification process. I knew that this blessed opportunity had been presented to me as another step on my evolutionary path of spiritual advancement.

Suspected Causes:
Related past history

During meditation, I had specifically asked for opportunities to progress along my path. Listening to inspirational audio CDs by Wayne Dyer and Ram Dass, I was encouraged to follow a "Path of Service." I signed up to be a 'Friendly Visitor' with Senior Outreach and then a hospice volunteer with Kaiser. At the completion of my service and training, I was presented with two profound opportunities to apply what I had learned.

I also witnessed family members' involvement and was able to clearly see how they too were given an opportunity to purify as well. My father-in-law, for example, took it upon himself to care for his wife's every need on a 24/7 basis for a very long time. He had openly questioned whether he had been a good husband to her during their marriage. If he had any misgivings, the dedicated service and loving care he provided most certainly cleared any past negative karma between them.

My husband demonstrated a sweet and loving kindness toward his mother that clearly made her feel better. Even though he has a 'tough guy' image, he was particularly gentle and kind whenever caring for her. He gladly stepped in to help whenever it was needed, and encouraged his father to take a badly needed break on the weekends when he had time to take over.

Everyone involved had an opportunity to embrace their highest self. It's not easy to place someone else's needs above your own on a daily basis for months on end. However, the opportunity to demonstrate selflessness is priceless.

Effects:
Occurring as a result of the causes identified

Facing difficult challenges, I was forced to set aside my ego-based needs and focus entirely upon the needs of others. My own selfish pursuits were replaced by an immediate opportunity for selfless acts. Fortunately, due to my spiritual awareness, community service and hospice training, I was able to embrace this opportunity fully.

The situation in my home also motivated me to delve deeper into my spiritual research and practices. I sought out books on death, grieving and suffering. At The Awakening Center, I joined a weekly focus group on Dying and Grieving. I watched shows and read books on near-death experiences and past-life recall. I met with a psychic intuitive who also provided greater insight into the phenomenon of suffering and the transitional aspect of dying. I had a strong desire to deepen my experiences and to be able to offer service from the most enlightened perspective possible.

Lessons Hidden Within:

The teachings of Buddhism often focus on the "impermanence" of all things. After witnessing death firsthand, this concept became very clear to me. I did realize that this applies only to physical matter and that our spiritual beings are everlasting. This is not to say that they are unchanging. Everything in creation is in a dynamic state of evolutionary development. From that perspective, the concept of impermanence still applies to everything in varying degrees.

These profound experiences have demonstrated the temporary nature of our physical incarnations and reinforce the need to fully embrace every moment of them. Each and every opportunity should be cherished and appreciated. These incarnations must be used to consciously evolve, purify our karma, and most importantly, to leave the world in a better place than we found it.

Lesson Plan:

I will fully embrace every opportunity I am given to serve with a selfless enthusiasm.

I will make the most of this physical incarnation. I will make every effort to consciously evolve by advancing my spiritual awareness and by applying the highest virtue to every thought, word and action.

I will benefit the lives of others not just by serving but also by being the best example that I possibly can. I do not wish to infringe upon the free will of others by preaching spirituality. Instead, I will do my best to demonstrate how my spiritual practices have positively influenced my life. By doing my best to radiate love and light in even the most difficult situations, I hope to inspire those around me.

I promise to live in a heightened state of awareness and when I recognize a fault that needs repair, I will make a note of it and commit to working on that aspect of my being.

I will recognize difficult challenges as blessed opportunities. I have come to realize that when my life is going smoothly, I become soft. It is only during times of difficulty and suffering that I am forced to draw strength from the core of my being and develop my highest traits.

I will express gratitude every day for every breath I take. I know that I have been given this great gift of a physically incarnated life in order to evolve spiritually.

Knowing that God is experiencing through me, I will dedicate my life to giving him the best journey of self-realization I possibly can. I will use every moment to seek the highest level of God-consciousness that I possibly can.

DAY NINE
The Spiritual Essence of Suffering
With Spiritual Counselor & Minister, Janet Myatt

SUZANNE: Good afternoon, Janet! Thanks so much for joining us on our ninth day of the workshop where we will be focusing on the meaning and purpose of suffering. Yesterday, we talked about synchronicity, as well as the problem of being out of sync with yourself and the world around you. This causes chaos and disorder, which leads to suffering in general. But what about intense suffering that is happening in present time? Why do we feel so helpless when we are in the presence of someone suffering?

JANET: When we see the suffering of others around us, one of the first things we want to do is fix it for them. What I've learned the hard way is that it is not necessarily our task to fix it, and that we get into a bit of competition with God when we do this. We tend to interfere because of our own suffering and our intolerance for pain. It's easier for us to fixate on someone else's suffering rather than do the work of transforming our own. That's something to think about when we want to become crusaders. What pain within our own minds is yearning to be healed, echoed by this situation?

It can be quite an intense experience for us when someone we love is suffering because we hate to see them in pain or fear. And, their suffering adds to our own suffering. It's important at these times not to project our own fear and intolerance onto the other person because when we do that, we are adding to that person's burden. We are adding our own resistance, our own judgment of suffering, and our own fear onto theirs. Now that person has to manage not only their own suffering but ours too.

Earlier, we talked about the nature of sharing. When two or more people share an idea or share a vibration of love, it becomes greater. This is also true of fear, resistance, suffering, and all emotional and mental thought forms. When we share them, we grow them. But these are not the things we want to be growing. Instead, we have the opportunity to truly be of service by keeping our hearts and minds steady in the light of love. We can attend to others with compassion and kindness, but refrain from investing in the drama of how awful it all is. Instead we can hold a clear vision in our minds of that person as someone who is experiencing something, but ultimately not damaged by those experiences. We can remember that all physical experiences are temporary, and spirit cannot be harmed in any way. So we can radiate a loving presence of goodwill to the person in suffering, and witness their journey without judging it. And, we can encourage them to go within and find their own truth about what is happening to them.

SUZANNE: When a loved one is in a great deal of pain, it's very difficult to approach the situation with a calm and centered mind focused on comforting them. We automatically go into crisis mode and tend to create more drama by reacting with fear and urgency.

JANET: This is challenging for us because we do have this internal drive, this internal mandate, this destiny to transmute suffering into love. But the *way* we do it, the way we honor that divine task, is of the utmost importance. *A Course in Miracles* teaches us about the importance of learning the difference between creating and mis-creating. We are creating when we engage in thoughts, emotions and behaviors that promote love, and mis-creating when we foster or promote fear.

One of the first things we have to do, then, is to deal with our own emotions about suffering. This takes time, and requires a reorientation of the mind from ego to spirit. Suffering is one of our greatest challenges because when we're experiencing it firsthand, it feels eternal; we almost can't imagine that it will pass. Yet, when we remember that all things pass, we can focus on what's really going on. We can get out of our own way, take the time to go within and ask, "What is fundamental in this experience? Show me how to be the embodiment of love rather than fear."

SUZANNE: When I was caring for my loved ones, who were in a great deal of suffering, I found that it really helped us both if I just took a moment to get centered first. Before I entered the room, I would stop and clear my mind of all the clutter, especially with selfish thoughts that contained the words "I" and "me". It was also important to let go of the fearful "what if?" and "how awful" thoughts. It's like you said, it requires a "reorientation" from ego to spirit so we can hold our hearts and minds steady in the light of love. Thank you so much, Janet, for helping us project love rather than fear, not just during times of suffering, but at all times whenever possible.

Now it's your turn!

SELF-EXPLORATION #9 – FEELING THE PAIN
Theme: Suffering

Close your eyes and think about a time when you offered love, support and compassion to someone who was in a great deal of suffering. It's important to reflect upon how it was beneficial to both of you. Understanding that their suffering may be a way for them to purify and cleanse, you may be able to focus on the positive aspects of this experience. Looking back, try to recognize how you were given the opportunity to be selfless, and to draw out the strength and courage that helped you both through these difficult times. If you have never experienced a dramatic period of suffering, just recall simple acts of kindness — when you helped someone who was sick or feeling down, and in need of love and compassion. Remember what you did to help them get through it and feel better.

Explore your Heart and Mind

Begin by reflecting upon the relationship you had with the person suffering. Did you find that this opportunity allowed you to set aside any prior differences or selfish concerns, or did they arise as a result?

_____

_____

_____

How was the quality of your daily interaction affected by this experience? Did the relationship grow and flourish as a result, or did the suffering cause either of you to pull away?

_____

_____

_____

_____

Think about how you felt when you first became aware that the suffering of another being would have a dramatic effect on your personal life. If you have not had a profound experience of suffering, focus on a lesser experience that involved comforting someone in their time of need. In either case, self-sacrifice was involved. These opportunities force you to set aside your selfish desires and focus on someone else for a while. Did you feel that the opportunity to be selfless was beneficial for you? If so, how?

_____

_____

_____

_____

Do you feel that this experience opened you to being less selfish in other aspects of your life as well and if so, how?

_____

_____

_____

Identify Lessons and Shifts

Sometimes when people are faced with an obligation to give up their time and energy, they may develop some resentment. This is especially true if it becomes necessary to give up those things which bring you pleasure or even provide monetary support. Try to recall the feelings that emerged after your commitment to helping another in need. Did you gladly dedicate your time and energy with an open heart, or did you harbor some resentment, knowing that it was taking away from other important things in your life?

_____

_____

_____

_____

When the experience came to an end, did you feel good about the role you played in it? Looking back, are there things you would have done differently?

_____

_____

_____

_____

_____

If you feel you should have handled things differently or done some things better, what would you do to improve your ability to serve with an open heart and mind in the future?

_____

_____

_____

_____

_____

As a result of this experience, were you inspired to dig deeper into your heart and soul for inspiration? If so, what type of soul-searching did you do?

_____

_____

_____

_____

_____

Time for your Reflection

Think of how this opportunity to serve changed your life. Did the suffering change your outlook on how you were living your own life? Did it enhance your appreciation for your own health and well-being? Were you inspired to embrace your life more fully and to express more love and compassion toward yourself and others on a daily basis? Performing the VIS-MED for Suffering will help you focus on the overall impression that this experience left on you and highlight the changes that you made in your life as a result.

SELF-REALIZATION #9
Meditation on Suffering

It's time to progress on your path of self-realization

Before journaling your experience, please engage in Dynamic Movement Therapy to open and expand your body. This will increase the blood flow in your body before moving into the breathing practices to relax your mind. You can engage in the movement and breathing practices by referring back to the written guidelines in the introduction, or access the audio download for free at *www.suzannerosstransendence.com/Up!Trilogy/WakeUp!Meditations*.

Now you are ready to go within by doing your visualization/meditation. Before beginning the practice, consider this: There will always be periods of suffering in our lives. There is no way to escape it. However, the way that we deal with the suffering makes all the difference in the world. Our perception of suffering defines the nature of it, be it our own or someone else's. If we perceive the suffering as inevitable, we will not have the power to alleviate it. If we see it as a punishment, we will simply surrender to it and give our power away.

On the other hand, if we see suffering as a divine gift sent for the purposes of awakening or transitioning, we can transform and alleviate it. We simply need to change our perception of suffering so that we can use our inherent power to heal, while still allowing it to serve its divine purpose. Even though suffering is the result of a karmic imprint, we should not see it as a punishment. Rather we should try to see it as a blessing. All suffering is an opportunity to transmute negative imprints into positive outcomes, be it a cleansing, an awakening or a passing.

Sometimes suffering is simply the result of negative energy that we are holding onto. Relieving it may be as easy as recognizing and removing its source. We intuitively know in our heart and mind what shadows are still lurking in our consciousness. They gnaw at our spirit, trigger fear in our mind, and cause disease in our body. We have to be honest with ourselves about these lingering shadows and courageously confront them. We have to look deep within to uncover any past or immediate sources of frustration, shame, or resentment. Once we identify these underlying emotions, we can transmute them. With strong determination, we can transform these lower energies with the higher vibrations of patience, forgiveness, and compassion. With love, faith, and courage, we can heal our body, mind and spirit. All we have to do is listen to the guidance of our higher selves, surrendering to the love and protection of the One Great Self.

You can download an audio version of this guided meditation by going to my website at *www.suzannerosstranscendence.com.* On the Up!Trilogy menu, select **Wake Up! Meditations** and go to the **VIS-MED for Suffering.**

DAY NINE
Self-Reflection

Name of the Experience: _____

Time Period: _____

Topic: Practical Spirituality

Memories, Thoughts & Feelings:

_____

_____

_____

_____

_____

_____

Suspected Causes:
Related past history

_____

_____

_____

_____

_____

_____

_____

Effects:
Occurring as a result of the causes identified

_____

_____

_____

_____

_____

_____

Lessons Hidden Within:

_____

_____

_____

_____

_____

Lesson Plan:

_____

_____

_____

_____

_____

_____

DAY NINE
PRACTICAL SPIRITUALITY

The Healing Power of Pure Intentions

"The great law of thought is the most fundamental, for it connects with other laws and influences all human activities and experiences, as we become seriously committed to living a life that is physically, mentally, psychologically, emotionally, and spiritually harmonious."
—Lonnie C. Edwards, M.D.

As we move through the workshop, it becomes obvious that when we are giving freely with virtuous thoughts and pure intentions, synchronistic opportunities emerge. During these times, we receive abundant gifts of prosperity and good health. We are able to see the beauty within all things and beings, and appreciate the richness of our good fortune. On the other hand, when we put up resistance and feel victimized, we block the stream of positive energy, attracting undesirable people, bad experiences, accidents and illnesses. Cut off from the healing light of spirit, we find ourselves consumed by the shadows. We begin to create a great deal of suffering for both ourselves and others as we fall deeper and deeper into the abyss.

We can prevent this downward spiral by keeping an open heart and mind at all times regardless of circumstances. A few days ago we practiced saying, "Have faith. Trust spirit. Let it go." We must stay strong in our faith, especially when life presents challenging circumstances. It is so much more conducive to our well-being, and the welfare of others, to allow life to unfold with a curious mind and faith in the divine plan. When we love and trust spirit, we can contemplate the deeper meaning and greater purpose behind all events without the hindrance of our ego.

The ego tends toward blame, anger and resentment. We feel victimized and separate from others. When our thoughts and intentions are pure and we consciously radiate love and light, we can connect with the healing power of our spirit. When suffering occurs within and around us then, we can just sit quietly and intuitively search for causes, effects and helpful resolutions. We can call upon spiritual guidance to help us find ways to alleviate the suffering. We can even use the power of our pure intentions to project healing light. For our own suffering, we can examine what negative energy we are holding onto, and then confront it with love, compassion, and forgiveness. We can see ourselves radiating light and surrounding ourselves with a brilliant bubble of white light. For others who are suffering, we can intentionally project healing light from our hearts into theirs and then envision them surrounded by radiant light. We can even send healing energy to entire cities and countries. We can envision the entire planet suspended in a radiant sphere of bright light.

In our own lives, we can start by making an effort to prevent or reduce our own suffering. We are much more capable of helping and healing others when we are strong and healthy. When we open to the universal flow and allow divine energy to swirl in and around us, harmony prevails and healing takes place. We attract this divine energy by the magnetic power of our positive thoughts and intentions. When we intentionally radiate light and love, we can deflect harmful, negative energy. Instead of feeling separate in our ego mind, we feel connected to the spirit of all beings. Our life becomes a harmonious symphony when we become love in action. The key to this harmonious unfoldment is the purity and power of our intentions. When we are aligned with pure intentions that benefit ourselves and others, magical synchronicities unfold. Flowing with spirit in this way, we can align with our true calling and fulfill our highest purpose. On the other hand, when we resist the guidance of our higher self, we stop the universal flow and the power of our intention diminishes. We become less creative and expansive. Our evolutionary path is blocked and we begin descending into darkness. The spiritual attributes of unconditional love, generosity, and selflessness transform into ego-driven patterns of power, greed, and separateness. At this point, we usually "fall from grace".

If we are wise, we will recognize the human tendency toward ego-based intentions before they dim our light and stop the flow of spirit. We can always redirect our thoughts before they manifest as negative words and actions. We have to remember that our subconscious mind is always listening to the thoughts of our conscious mind. It is subject to these thoughts and it begins to manifest them into the forms that define our experience. Our emotions are the driving force that propels these forms into action, and they become the reality we experience.

This is how the power of thought creates the reality we experience. We have the ability to create and destroy every aspect of our experience with the power of intention. We just haven't realized how to use this power to its fullest extent because we aren't evolved enough yet to use it properly. As we progress on our evolutionary path, the awesome strength of our innate power will be revealed. Until we are endowed with divine wisdom, however, we have to rely on our higher self to help us create responsibly. The power of pure intention is always the strongest when our creative thoughts are focused on benefiting both ourselves and others.

Today's practice is focused on controlling the emotions that cause energetic thought waves to create and expand. The two most powerful emotions are love and fear, and they are at opposite ends of the emotional spectrum. As a magnetic force, these emotions attract like energy. Loving thoughts attract loving forms into your experience, and fearful energy attracts frightening forms. Love is creative and fear is destructive. Love is light and fear is darkness. Love expands and fear contracts. If you wish to attract love and light into your life, you must think loving thoughts that are inclusive and expansive. If fear creeps into your mind, you must redirect it with faith in a higher source. Otherwise, you will contract in fear and whatever you are afraid of will magically appear.

Synchronicity and intention work hand in hand with cause and effect. You can open to the light of spirit with loving thoughts that expand in creative ways. Or you can let in the darkness with fearful thoughts that contract in destructive ways. Love drives all your positive emotions and fear drives all your negative ones; it's that simple. Knowing that you create and evolve with love, and destroy and regress with fear, which do you choose?

Awakening through Reflection

DAY TEN

DEATH & DYING

WORKSHOP MODULES:

1. Life Experience & Analysis: "Sharing the Wisdom"

2. The Spiritual Essence of Death & Dying

3. Self-Exploration #10: In Remembrance

4. Self-Realization #10: Meditation on Death & Dying

5. Self-Reflection #10: Uncovering Life Lessons

6. Practical Spirituality: Afterlife: Beyond this Realm

LIFE EXPERIENCE

DAY TEN

Sharing the Wisdom

In the year following my father's visit, he read several more spiritual texts, and even undertook *The Urantia Book,* a 2000+ page volume that may be the most revelatory and detailed account of creation and evolution ever written. I shared other books I was reading at that time as well, including a series written by Zecharia Sitchins based on the ancient Sumerian Clay Tablets. We had both been long intrigued by the ancient cultures of the Egyptians and Mayans, and came to believe that advanced beings from other dimensions had a major influence on the beliefs and traditions of these ancient cultures. My father and I both firmly agree that the advanced knowledge shared by "higher" beings throughout the ages, both ancient and contemporary, has been very influential in the evolutionary progress of the human race.

Believing in the presence and influence of otherworldly beings was not a huge stretch for either my father or myself. As a young man, my father had an extraordinary experience that took place in the Canadian prairie where he was born. It was around 1950 when he had a "close encounter" with a UFO. Driving through the prairies of Saskatchewan on a remote dirt and gravel road one night, my dad and three of his buddies realized they were being followed by a bright white light that would speed up and slow down as they did. The light would also disappear and then suddenly reappear way out in front of them. Whatever vehicle was shining the light, it didn't kick up any dust as it traveled along the dirt road. Intrigued, they decided to pull over and see if the light would pass them so they could get a better look. My father says he remembers the three of them leaning against the driver's side of the car waiting for the light to reappear. Eventually they spotted a much larger, bright orange light in the distance; then the smaller white light reappeared, streaked across the horizon and merged with the orange light. The orange light hovered for a few moments and then darted across the sky, getting smaller and smaller until it finally disappeared. Ever since that extraordinary experience, my father has been fascinated with stories of mysterious lights and sightings of unknown crafts. And ever since that night, my father has had a raised triangular marking on the inside of his wrist. He calls it his "alien chip."

I am delighted that my father has kept an open mind all these years to the possibilities that lie beyond the horizon. He has always inspired me to look up in the sky with a sense of awe and wonder, and imagine what secrets were hidden among the stars. I am also thrilled that, now in his elderly years, my father is looking to me for inspiration! I've witnessed a light begin to shine behind his weary eyes that's made him look more youthful and exuberant. There is no doubt in my mind that seeing the light in his eyes sparked a strong desire within me to provide illumination for others.

Just as I had hoped, the day my father decided to glimpse the light, his life took on a more spiritual essence. Life after death became an interesting prospect as he considered the eternity of the soul and spiritual evolution throughout multiple dimensions. A few months ago, we almost lost him again when a bladder infection got out of control. By the time my sister got there, he was delirious. From our phone conversations, it sounded like we might be losing him so I jumped on a plane and flew to Canada.

One day as I stood by his bedside holding his hand, he opened his eyes and whispered, "Can't you hear them?" I said, "Who, Dad?" He replied, "The angels, they're singing a mantra." A lump formed in my throat as I replied, "A mantra?" He responded softly, "Well that's what I would call it" and then he tried to sing a phrase in the meekest little voice. I leaned in close to hear the words, which sounded foreign. I said, "Is it in English, Dad?" All he said then was, "Well, I can understand it" and then nodded off. I was astounded. I was briefly concerned that the angels had come to take him, so I kept a close eye on his breathing. He looked incredibly peaceful, with a little grin on his face.

Once he became more lucid, he made it clear to my sister and I that he wasn't ready to leave this world just yet. He needed to go home and take care of my mom and the puppy, he told us. Upon hearing this, my sister and I went into high gear to do everything we could to make that happen. We communicated to the doctors that we needed to stay on top of his antibiotics and reduce the pain medications; they were making him too drowsy and then he wouldn't eat. We got him up out of bed, even if he just sat on the edge. In a few days, we had him taking short walks with a physical therapist. My sister was making arrangements for home care while I made a commitment to keep his spirits up.

Since he had been so receptive to the teachings about the 'light', I decided to read him passages from Godfre Ray King's book *Unveiled Mysteries.* He loved the stories about Mount Shasta where the author had his experiences with the Ascended Master, Saint Germain. I was born in Shasta County and that's where my mother and father bought their first house after moving to the U.S. He remembers that time as being very special and close to his heart. This gave the story an added dimension of meaning for him. I read lovely prayers with verses like, "I am a child of the light, I am illumined by the light, I am sustained by the light," and he loved it! Every time I would stop because I thought he was sleeping, he would mumble, "Don't stop. Keep reading." A few days later, he woke up one morning and looked significantly brighter. He was more inspired than ever to get better and go home to his beautiful wife and sweet little puppy.

Update, autumn 2013: I had a sense that this chapter was left unfinished when I wrote it during the spring. I knew there was more to my father's story and that it would unfold over time. In early August, I received a phone call that my father was back in the hospital, this time with a blood clot in his leg. His doctor was very concerned about his diminishing health and frailty, so I flew again to Calgary. Upon arriving, I was taken aback by his appearance. He was so thin, and lapsing in and out of consciousness. He expressed feelings of anger and paranoia that would give way to sentiments of peace and serenity. Finally, his consciousness just faded away and he became totally non-responsive. He spent several days just lying there taking deep rhythmic breaths. We knew in our hearts that it wouldn't be long until he took one final breath.

On the afternoon before his passing, I felt compelled to gather my sister and mother so that the three of us could hold each other's hands in his and express our deepest sentiments. I felt that we needed to reassure him that it was alright to look toward the light and begin his journey into the spiritual realm. I wanted him to know that, over here in physical reality, we would be just fine. We would miss him terribly, of course, but he would always remain deep within our hearts and souls. Our bedside memorial was profoundly meaningful for all of us. My sister performed a beautiful Buddhist ritual to purify and transcend his soul. I said a little prayer from St. Germain that included verses about the light. My mother reassured him that she and the puppy he adored would be well taken care of, and that her final wish was for him to be liberated from suffering. We all wept softly and found comfort in each other's faith that he would ascend to a higher realm where love, peace, and divine joy were omnipresent.

On the night of Wednesday, August 28th, my father's soul ascended. My sister and I had decided that, if he passed overnight, she would slip out and drive to the hospital while I stayed home with my mother. We felt no need for her to be awakened in a state of alarm and experience any further mental distress. It was an enlightened decision because, as opposed to a grim phone call in the night, my sister awakened us to the most beautiful message of peace, light, and surrender. She was glowing and shared with us that she had been blessed with a divine experience. She explained how she felt calm and peaceful after she received the hospital call and that, as she drove through the stillness of the night, she felt accompanied by a comforting presence. She didn't know quite what to expect upon her arrival, but wasn't fearful or anxious. She was greeted by the night nurses for whom we'd developed a great appreciation and fondness. They were kind, patient, and sincere at a time when we were faced with very difficult and challenging circumstances.

As my sister approached my dad's private room, she was struck by a vision of light radiating from the doorway, illuminating the dim corridor. As she cautiously entered the room, she became aware that the light was radiating from my father's body. She was overwhelmed by a deep inner peace at the sight of his radiant being, bathed in complete serenity. She wept tears of joy and knew that he was finally at peace. The angels had come to embrace his soul and deliver it from the suffering of the physical realm.

My mother and I were blessed to have been presented with this heartwarming story and, instead of overwhelming grief and sadness, we were filled with relief and gratitude. We all knew he was in a better place and, at the same time, we felt the comfort of his loving presence in and around us. We would always be together as one within the light of pure love.

As a tribute to my father, I would like to share the message that I offered at his funeral.

Ode to My Father
The Eulogy

In the latter years of my father's life, he would often reflect. After some contemplation, he would say one of two things: "No regrets" and "Right place, right time." He truly felt as if he had been born at the perfect time — between wars and after the Depression. He also felt like he and my mother had always lived in the right places at a time when the area was flourishing and prosperous. After he became sick and began looking back on his life, he would share with us that he had accomplished everything he set out to do in his life — beautiful family that he loved and a wonderful career that he enjoyed. He said that he had traveled everywhere he wanted to go and seen everything he wished to experience. I would listen and think, "How wonderful to feel like you had fulfilled all of your dreams and had no regrets!" You can't ask for much more than that in one lifetime.

As a dad, he wanted to make sure to teach us valuable life lessons. My father always used to say, "Everything in moderation." It's such a simple phrase but it contains the greatest wisdom.

What it really means is "balance" and as I gain more life experience, (and hopefully a little knowledge), I am able to truly grasp the importance of this message.

As a kid, I thought it simply meant, "Don't eat too much ice cream," "Don't stay up too late." In other words, "Don't have too much fun!" As a young adult, I thought, "Boring. I want to do too much of everything!" So I replaced my Dad's philosophy with my own new motto: "Work hard, play hard!" By the age of 30, I was exhausted and thought, O.K., maybe it's time to let go of the "Play hard" now I'll just "Work hard!

I'll be so successful and keep my nose to the grindstone!" Ten years later, I ditched that idea and tried "Play hard" again for a bit until finally I had to just give in and admit to myself that my dad was right:

"Everything in moderation." Balance = Harmony and you can't have one without the other.

Thank you, Dad, for that simple, yet profound truth.

Because of this philosophy, my dad was always "the rock" in our family. He was the quiet, dependable guy that you could always count on. We always had a nice home and never wanted for anything.

Once my dad retired, he moved out to the desert where I had started a fitness business. He helped me computerize all my records and organize my bookkeeping which was tremendously helpful. He also made time for play and him and my sister and I hiked and biked all over the desert, exploring trails and discovering wildlife. We had the time of our lives and we'll never forget that family bonding time spent doing our favorite pastime — enjoying God's creation by appreciating the great outdoors!

During this time, my father and I would take long walks at night under the stars and he would point out all the constellations and identify specific stars and planets. He was particularly interested in star clusters called "nebulae" and we would speculate about the nature of these formations. Because of these times, my dad inspired a great curiosity within me that compelled me to embark on a lifelong search for the true nature of reality and the fundamental truths of our existence. I wanted to find out how the universe works and to discover the meaning and purpose of our place within it. His insatiable curiosity and love of science inspired me to write a book about creation and evolution which I have, of course, dedicated to him.

I know that those ten years of his retirement were one of the happiest times of his life and long after they were over, we enjoyed laughing and reminiscing about, what we called, "The Glory Days."

My dad's fascination with science and astronomy ultimately merged with a more spiritual search for truth and in the final year of his life, he began to make the connection between science and spirituality. He knew my sister and I were inspired by spiritual beliefs and practices and so last year, after a close brush with death due to the ravages

of chemotherapy, he came to me and said, "Bring it on. I am ready to explore spirituality. It's time." So I shared many books with him, especially ones that clearly tied the scientific explanation for how things work with the spiritual message of "One Creator" who dearly loves all of his children and offers the gift of life as a blessing. I gave him a book about the life and times of Jesus Christ and he became fascinated with it. He dedicated many hours to reading the historical account but would then just sit and contemplate the deeper meaning and greater significance behind the story.

A couple of weeks ago, my sister called me up and said, "Dad says he met Jesus and that he was surrounded by loving angels." I was thrilled and felt that I had given him the best gift possible at the end of his life. My sister and I both believe in the eternity of the soul and he finally accepted that message as well. In the end he knew that once he left the physical realm, he would be onto much greater adventures in the spiritual one. We also reassured him that we will always be together dancing around each other's souls and celebrating our infinite love with joy and harmony for all of eternity!

Not with too much exuberance though, we must remember the golden rule: "Everything in moderation!"

Dad, I know you are listening to every word so, above all else, I want you to know this one last thing:

First of all, "Hola!" (that's our special greeting). I want you to know that you are loved more than you can possibly imagine and I know you'll still be "taking care of your girls" from heaven. I promise Kimi and I will take good care of "Mom and puppy" and Scott promises he'll "take care of your girls" for you. We will miss you terribly but know you are always with us in our hearts and souls for now and forever. Love you dearly, dad. See ya soon!

Self-Reflection
Time Period: August 2012 – August 2013
Topic: Death and Dying

Memories, Thoughts & Feelings:

I feel blessed to have had the opportunity to spend time with my father "one-on-one" during his visit to my home. It was remarkable that he chose to use this time to explore spirituality. His brush with death had triggered an intense curiosity about "the other side" and my recent experience with Jenny had forced me to come face-to-face with death as well. As a result, we were both searching for deeper answers about the afterlife. This may be common amongst those who confront mortality and are still uncertain about the eternity of the soul.

My path became more illuminated by my father's eager enthusiasm and curiosity. As I saw him gain strength, courage and inspiration from the teachings, I knew I wanted to learn more so that I could share the wisdom and inspire others. A strong desire began to well up within me and I began to focus on how I could express myself through writing.

I was overjoyed at the many positive effects the spiritual teachings were having on my father. He became more determined than ever to get stronger and healthier. It was as if he knew it was important to seek answers before moving on, and I felt privileged to have the opportunity to be his guide. During his final months, he dedicated a great deal of time to reading about the life and times of Jesus as presented in *The Urantia Book*. Shortly before dying, my father told my sister that he saw Jesus surrounded by angels. When she told me this, I was elated and knew I had given him the best parting gift I could have ever offered.

My father's soul ascended with a rich experience of the physical realm and a great curiosity about the spiritual one. I am aware of his presence at times when I need strength and courage. He was a great inspiration to me during my lifetime and now, in his omniscient state, he continues to encourage me when I feel overwhelmed. I will love him dearly for all eternity and am incredibly grateful that he was chosen to be my father in this lifetime.

Suspected Causes:
Related past history

My father had very little exposure to religion or spirituality in his youth; his father was an atheist and his mother, as a subservient wife, followed his lead. They didn't speak about such things in the household and his father, a professor, emphasized academics instead. This explains a lot about my father's approach to creation and evolution during my upbringing. He was firmly committed to the Darwinian explanation of a naturally occurring creation driven by a "survival of the fittest" evolution. This apparently eliminated the need for an Almighty Creator responsible for the intelligent design and progression of the universe. Ultimately however, it left a spiritual void in the depths of his soul which cried out to be filled, once death became imminent.

Even as a child, I knew there was more to the story than science could explain. I believed what my dad had to say about Darwinian evolution and the progression of apes into cavemen, but the mystery of the "missing link" always gnawed at me. During history class, I knew what they were teaching wasn't the entire story either and since we never went to church, that story was vague as well. As I got older, I had the sense that "God was within" and that there was a "oneness" to the universe. I have no idea where I got these ideas from but they felt more like an inner knowledge than an outer teaching. These underlying messages lay dormant until my life came to a point where I would either have a spiritual awakening or a physical meltdown. By the grace of God, I was shown the light of pure unconditional love and my spirit was illuminated at last.

Effects:
Occurring as a result of the causes identified

I believe that my own spiritual evolution was part of a larger plan which included my father. The knowledge and wisdom I had received served as the inspiration he needed at a crucial turning point in his life. As the synchronicity of events unfolded and he moved into my home, we were both enabled to evolve together. By the time he passed, he had a strong conviction about the eternity of the soul and as such, was able to embrace the light with an open heart and mind. For me, his spiritual awakening provided the inspiration I needed to pursue my path.

Lessons Learned:

"When the student is ready, the teachings will appear." I have also become aware how important it is to surrender to the will of the universe, and keep the faith that the forces in motion are part of a divine plan. With that in mind, I realize that I have to do my part and play by the rules if I want the forces to work in my favor. Living from my highest and most virtuous self is the key to opening the door to these positive energies. When I am in a heightened state of awareness and committed to directing my thoughts, words, and actions, I am able to closely monitor myself and redirect if necessary. By doing this, I have learned to recognize the qualities I need to develop based on my interactions with others, and by my emotional reactions. Once I pinpoint a weak spot, I can think back to its root cause and reassure myself that the past is gone and I have the opportunity to redefine my perspective in the present. This is similar to the Buddhist practice of controlling the mind.

I have also learned that my guidance can only be effective when my desire to serve is based on pure intentions. If I become motivated by the need for recognition or reward, my attempts to enlighten will be fruitless.

I have to spend every waking moment focused on my soul's evolution by serving others and generating abundant virtue. This pursuit is the only meaningful use of my life and if I desire a positive afterlife and fortunate rebirth for myself and others, I must remain diligent and apply myself daily.

Lesson Plan:

All I have is the present moment and all I can do is put my best foot forward each and every day. With a strong commitment to serve others and to develop my self-knowledge and self-discipline, I will be making the most of this blessed incarnation here and now.

I will dedicate time every day to my spiritual practices. I will connect with the greater field of consciousness to access universal truth, going within to listen to my own inner wisdom. From what I learn through my practices (and the abundant resources I have gathered) I will focus on developing theories, ideas, and philosophies about the true nature of reality and share it with others. My intention will remain to inspire curiosity and encourage readers to explore, seek and discover. My sincere wish is that by seeking, they will find a deeper meaning and greater purpose to their lives here and now.

Every morning, I will open my eyes and realize how fortunate I am to be greeting another brand new day full of endless possibilities. I will smile and embrace every opportunity to radiate love and light toward myself and others. I will monitor my thoughts, words and actions and remain committed to applying my highest and most virtuous self at all times. I will make every effort to recognize and improve upon problems I still struggle with.

I will never forget my true purpose here on earth, which is simply to evolve toward a higher consciousness. Reconciling my past, harmonizing with the present, and projecting a promising future will help me to fulfill my purpose. Embracing every glorious moment of my life in a heightened state of awareness will give it a much deeper meaning as I recognize the beauty and grace all around me. I will not ignore the ugliness, but will do my best to diffuse and deflect it. Whenever possible, I will intentionally send love and healing to those who are suffering.

Finally, I will relax and enjoy the beautiful forces swirling around me as I surrender to the harmonious flow of the universe and serve with an open heart and mind.

DAY TEN
The Spiritual Essence of Death & Dying
With Spiritual Counselor & Minister, Janet Myatt

SUZANNE: Good afternoon, Janet, and welcome to the last day of our workshop. We have taken such a wonderful journey together over the last nine days and today promises to be one of the most illuminating. Talking about death and dying can make us feel uneasy. But what may seem to be a tragic fate can actually be seen as a new beginning.

JANET: There is nothing to fear about crossing over. If we manage suffering with an open heart and mind, we can remove much of the fear from that process as well.

SUZANNE: During my experience with my mother-in-law, we all recognized when it was time for her to drop the body that was causing her so much pain and agony. It was time for her to transcend it and take the journey into a higher realm. I also observed that she was giving her husband an opportunity to balance his karmic debt; his devotion to her was beyond measure. He was there for her 24/7. There was a period when she was fighting and fighting and then gradually, she gave in. Once she realized that her body no longer had the strength to fight any longer, she became peaceful and quiet. This made it easier for everyone else to accept the inevitable transition.

Then, after she passed, the most remarkable thing happened. A couple weeks after the funeral, I became very aware of a presence in my room. My dog would growl and stare at the corner of the room with his fur all standing on end. I instinctively knew it was her, and I was actually comfortable with her presence. At the same time, I knew she needed to fully cross over for everyone's benefit. When I reached out to you, you were able to look and see that she just wanted to relay a message and then she would be on her way. You reported that she just wanted to say, "Thank you." It was so touching. I was able to share it with Scott and he believed me because he had felt her presence too. Not only had she come back to thank us, but now we knew her spirit was alive and well!

JANET: I was delighted to be able to be of service. My relationship with death is a bit different than most and I'm not afraid of it anymore. I understand it to be a transformation — a movement from one form into another. Death is always happening simultaneously with life; old cells die even as new cells are being born. Humans leave their dense physical bodies even as new humans are born. Stars are born as others collapse and cease to be. The universe is constantly in flux, creating and destroying itself. The law of conservation tells us that energy is never lost, just converted from one form to another. We persist as spirit whether we are incarnated into a dense physical body or not. The forms we use to express ourselves do not persist; they are converted.

When a loved one dies we experience it as a loss but on the other side, loved ones who have already crossed over experience this transition as a birth. I have seen them greeting the incoming spirit with great joy and love, just like we rejoice over the birth of our children when they are born.

SUZANNE: When we became aware that my father was slipping away, we performed a ritual. We all held hands and each of us were able to offer a prayer and say goodbye. I asked the angels to welcome him with open arms and help him transition into the light. It was really quite beautiful, and then we continued to stay there. When the hospice worker arrived, she said, "You know what, you guys need to go because as long you are here in the room, the attachment is too strong and he can't let go. He needs to go. It's time."

So we left and went home. I told my sister "Go ahead, and leave your phone on and I'll stay here with mom if you need to leave in the night." The next morning, I could tell she had left because her car was parked differently. I hugged my mom and told her "You know I think Dad may have passed in the night." Just then my sister came up the stairs and she looked radiant as she shared her remarkable experience.

She told us that she was walking down the dark corridor of the hospital when she saw the most brilliant light emanating from the doorway of Dad's room. She said that when she entered the room, the entire room was filled with light and my father looked peaceful. During his life, my dad worried a lot and suffered from bouts of depression, but now he looked so peaceful.

JANET: I'm so happy to hear that because I know how much you loved your dad. You were an integral part of making that experience as joyful as possible. I'm so happy that you and your family got to experience it that way.

There are two things that I want to mention here. The first is that many people frequently need to pass when they are alone. This transition is a very private and intense transformational experience. When there are a lot of people around, particularly loved ones, the distraction of their presence dilutes or fragments the transition. This makes it incredibly difficult for them to take that final step. It can even prolong their suffering. This is why so many loved ones pass in the middle of the night. They need that privacy and that time.

Second, I want to mention the importance of the ceremonial ritual of saying goodbye and releasing the loved one onto the next phase of their spiritual journey. It will make it much easier for everyone involved if we take a moment to formally say farewell to the person passing over. A simple "I love you, it's okay to go" can be a huge blessing for them. It's also important for us to take this opportunity to forgive them of any unresolved grievance or trespass. Much healing comes to all parties when we let our story with that person end. If each person can do this in a truly heartfelt way, it can make the transition so much easier for the loved one passing over. So many times family members want to stay with their loved one because they don't want them to feel alone when they pass. But, they are not alone. And in fact, it might even be the first time that individual really experiences *not* being alone as they merge with the light and feel the love flowing into them. They are *immersed* in the light and love of God and greeted by all of the spiritual beings they have an affinity for. Often they see loved ones who have passed before, and they welcome them home. Releasing them to this process and then stepping aside helps alleviate any lingering guilt they may have about leaving their current family and loved ones behind. It's a blessing for the person passing and for those remaining.

As a spiritual counselor, I encourage family members and loved ones to manage their own fears about the process and not burden the person passing over with their own guilt, sorrow, or uncertainty. In my opinion, it's important to allow the person facing death to go about their process with all the loving, kind, and optimistic support we can muster.

Life is eternal; only the forms we take are temporary. At the individual, incarnated level, most of us cannot see the larger truth of who we are. But all material things pass; we must accept this. Cast your eyes inward and upward to understand and embrace the larger meaning of Life. Learn how to let go of over-identifying with the physical body and world, and much peace will emerge within you.

SUZANNE: Beautifully said, my dear friend. Amen.

Now it's your turn!

SELF-EXPLORATION #10 – IN REMEMBRANCE
Theme: Death & Dying

Realizing that this is a difficult topic to explore, it may be necessary to close your eyes, take a few deep breaths and gather your courage. Please be reassured that examining your feelings about your own death, or the death of a friend or family member, is an important part of your evolutionary path. Knowing that suffering and dying are natural and necessary within the human experience doesn't make it any easier to handle. Recovering from the tragedy of losing someone requires a great deal of time, patience and ultimately, faith in the divine plan. A dedicated effort must be made so that you can move forward and live your life with the happiness and joy your lost loved one would want you to.

Coming to grips with the idea of your own death may require some serious soul-searching, but it is well worth the effort. Living with the realization of your own impermanence enables you to embrace every moment of your life here and now more fully. It also gives you a much greater motivation to reconcile your past mistakes, come into harmony with your present circumstances, and plan for an abundant future full of meaning and purpose.

Explore your Heart and Mind

If you have experienced the loss of a loved one, it's important to reflect upon the ways in which their death and dying affected your life during the process, and after they departed. If their death was sudden and unexpected, think about the last time you were with them. Try to recall the last meaningful experience you shared and embrace the essence of it. Remember how it felt to be together and recall the laughs you shared and the things you discussed:

_____

_____

_____

_____

If you were present during a long process of dying, think about the love, support and compassion you offered and how it was received. Imagine the gratitude your loved one probably felt, and how important you were to them at the time. Just the presence of a kind and sympathetic person who truly cares can alleviate the suffering of someone in pain. Did it feel good to be able to give of yourself during this time and were you at peace with the process?

_____

_____

_____

_____

Did you have mixed emotions of resentment and anger about the suffering your loved one had to go through, or about the treatment they were receiving? Did you blame yourself or others? Did you take your fear and anger out on anyone else?

_____

_____

_____

_____

Did you hide your feelings and pretend to be alright in an effort to soothe your loved one and give them the reassurance they needed at the time? Or were you truly at peace with the process?

_____

_____

_____

_____

Identify any unresolved feelings that may have been pushed down for the sake of others. Be open and honest with yourself, remembering that you could only give of yourself to the extent that your heart and mind allowed you to at the time. Give yourself and others some leeway, knowing the stress and pressure experienced by everyone. This includes your loved one, if he or she said things that hurt your feelings. Be forgiving. It may be helpful to write down those things that anyone said or did during this time that still bothers you now. Making a note of it, reading it aloud, and expressing forgiveness will help to heal the wounds.

Now let's explore your own mortality.

Whether or not you have experienced the loss of a loved one, you have probably felt sorrow over losing someone due to a break-up, move, or other unexpected change in your life. Realizing you will never have the closeness of that relationship again can be heartbreaking. Now try to imagine that you are the one leaving everyone behind. There may be a sinking feeling of sadness, or more. Imagine what others may feel, based on your own memories of loss in the past.

_____

_____

_____

_____

_____

_____

_____

Now think about never seeing your loved ones again. Imagine never being able to enjoy the sights and sounds of nature again. Think about all the familiar people, places and things in your life that you may take for granted and imagine never seeing, touching, tasting and smelling them again. Imagine knowing you would not wake up tomorrow morning. How would that change the way you interacted with others today?

_____

_____

_____

_____

_____

If you knew it was your last day, what might you do or say? Think about the people in your life that are most important to you. What would you say to each of them to let them know how much their love and support has meant to you?

_____

_____

_____

_____

_____

If you have unfinished business or negative feelings, what would you do or say to mend fences before it's too late? How would you express your appreciation and forgiveness to the loved ones in your life right now, if you knew today was your last day on earth?

_____

_____

_____

_____

_____

Now think about all the things you meant to do but never did. Time has run out and you never took the time to go to those places you always wanted to see, or pursue some dream you always had. What reading or hobbies are you saving for retirement or a rainy day? What recreational activity have you always thought sounded like fun but never tried?

_____

_____

_____

_____

Finally, think about the things you see as being wrong with the world and the things you could have done to help improve upon it. What causes do you wish you would have taken up? What charities could you have contributed more time or money to? What charitable deeds do you feel good about?

_____

_____

_____

_____

Time for your Reflection

Ask yourself: If today was my last day, how would I feel about the life I have lived? Are there things I would have done differently? Do I have regrets about things I did or said or more importantly, about things I didn't say or do? In what ways would I have lived my life differently? What about my attitude? Was it generous and loving or sometimes, selfish and inconsiderate? Who did I help, support and encourage? Who was I always there for? Who did I hurt? Who did I blame?

Performing the "VIS-MED for Death & Dying" will help you sort through all these questions and concerns. Going within will illuminate the truth of who you really are as a loving spirit.

SELF-REALIZATION #10
Meditation on Death & Dying

It's time to progress on your path of self-realization.

Before journaling your experience, please engage in Dynamic Movement Therapy to open and expand your body. Then be seated comfortably and perform the Inspirational Breathing Practices to oxygenate your body and clear your mind of distractions. You can engage in the movement and breathing practices by referring back to the written guidelines in the introduction, or Access the audio download for free at *www.suzannerosstransendence.com/Up!Trilogy/WakeUp!Meditations*.

Now you are ready to go within by doing your visualization/meditation. When we think of death as a new beginning rather than a sad ending, it makes the transition much easier. We can imagine ourselves or our loved ones being welcomed by angels, friends and family. We can imagine a paradise filled with beautiful flowers, flowing streams and luscious landscapes. Freed from form, the spirit is liberated and can fly like a bird or float like a cloud. Freed from the constraints of time and space, the spirit has no limitations. In paradise, everyone is joyful and loving, compassionate and caring. The colors are brighter and the sounds are sweeter. It's a celebration of life — eternal life!

In the Bible it says: *As above, so below*. We can visualize this paradise in heaven right here on earth by rejoicing and celebrating life. We can embrace and appreciate our friends and family every chance we get. We can talk to the angels anytime we like. As we engage in our meditation for death and dying, let's remember our souls are eternal. We can still live each day as if it's our last and still know in our hearts that we are eternal. We can begin to imagine the endless adventures that lie ahead in both the physical and spiritual realms. We can celebrate eternity!

You can download an audio version of this guided meditation by going to my website at *www.suzannerosstranscendence.com.* On the Up!Trilogy menu, select **Wake Up! Meditations** and go to the **VIS-MED for Death and Dying**

DAY TEN
Self-Reflection

Name of the Experience: _____

Time Period: _____

Topic: Death & Dying

Memories, Thoughts & Feelings:

_____

_____

_____

_____

_____

Suspected Causes:
Related past history

_____

_____

_____

_____

_____

_____

Effects:
Occurring as a result of the causes identified

_____

_____

_____

_____

_____

_____

Lessons Hidden Within:

_____

_____

_____

_____

_____

_____

Lesson Plan:

_____

_____

_____

_____

_____

_____

DAY TEN
PRACTICAL SPIRITUALITY

Afterlife: Beyond this Realm

"We live in almost total inward blindness (spiritual unconsciousness) restricted to and limited by our outward senses. Yet, by design, the human soul was created to walk in stereo consciousness - a blended awareness of two cosmic realms: material and spiritual."

— Sean Calvin

Like many truth seekers, I am fascinated by paranormal phenomena including ghosts, UFOs, angels and aliens. I am also intrigued by near-death experiences, past life recall, astral travel, and psychic phenomena. The mere existence of paranormal phenomena implies that there are realities beyond what we observe and interact with every day. We can call these "parallel realities" since they coexist with our physical three-dimensional one.

Let's start our journey into parallel realities by recognizing the simple truth of oneness, and then we can move into the profound concept of multidimensional reality. It's interesting that the term *reality* should even apply to the physical world since we know it is essentially an illusion. The only thing "real" about it is the effect it has on us, particularly on our karma — the accumulation of our soul's experiences. We know by now that the sole purpose of the material realm is that of a classroom — a place to learn and teach. That being said, let's embrace the opportunity to learn from our physical experiences by going beyond them. As evolved beings who are seeking the truth beyond the illusion, we find ourselves straddling both realms. While one foot is still firmly planted in the physical illusion, the other one is exploring higher realms.

In the process of dying, our loved ones will traverse both realms. They will move in and out of their form as they begin the transitional process. When my father was passing, there were times when he did not seem present in his body. One day when we came home from the hospital after seeing him in this state, we were shocked by an unexpected visit. My mother and I were tucked into her bed when suddenly the front door flew wide open and moments later, a gentle nudge slowly pushed the bedroom door open. The dog jumped up and started growling at the door with all of his fur standing on end. My poor mom was frightened but somehow I felt calm. I knew my dad's spirit had come to visit and I said out loud, "Hi Dad, thanks for coming to visit. Mom, puppy and

I are just fine. Thanks for checking on us. We love you." My mom settled right down and we smiled at each other.

Our final practice is two-fold in nature. The first practice is focused on easing the transition for a dying loved one, as he or she moves out of the physical body and into the spiritual realm. This practice is very loosely presented so that you can fill in the blanks with your own spiritual or religious beliefs and practices.

Practice #1 – As you become aware that your loved one is nearing the time of death, gather your family around and individually, collectively or both, say goodbye. Make a point to give your loved one permission to pass. Call on spiritual assistance from the higher realm to guide him or her into the light. Whether you wish to pray, chant, or just express your sentiments, know that your loved one can hear you. Also, be aware that your words or even your thoughts can be heard after death, so try not to express fear in the presence of either the deceased body or spiritual energy. Once you perform a parting ritual, give your loved one the peace and space to pass into the spiritual realm without being drawn to the attachment of your presence in the physical realm.

Practice #2 – This practice of "resonance" can be used anytime to enhance the connection to your spiritual guides and your higher Self. The light of the spiritual realm vibrates at a much higher frequency than the density of the physical one. We need to focus on raising the vibrational frequency of our environment if we want to resonate with spirit. There are a few ways to do this. One is to spin your chakras starting at the base, or root, chakra and moving up your spine until you reach your crown chakra. Once you spin your highest chakra, you will be vibrating at a higher frequency and spirit will enter through the crown of your head. Your crown chakra will become a divine portal through which higher consciousness can flow. Another way is to sing and chant, as this naturally creates a higher vibration in the environment. Lastly, you can use instruments that are musical or vibratory like Tibetan singing bowls, drums, gongs or crystal glasses.

Both of these practices will help you bring the power of the spiritual realm into your physical reality. That is what this entire series on "Practical Spirituality" has been designed to do. Since you are a spiritual being having a physical experience, the most important practices that you can bring into your daily life are those that enhance your connection to both realms. Merging your higher self with your ego identity will help you realize your true identity as a divine expression walking the earth. Stay in-spirit, my friends, and it will serve you well on your journey into the light.

Master Plan

Contemplation

We have all been blessed with the precious gift of life and one day, we will move on. None of us knows exactly when that will be, but it's important to have no regrets. You should feel good about the life that you lived and know that you did your best. It's equally important to come to terms with those things you don't feel good about, and to have forgiven yourself and others. It is good to die knowing you made an effort to help those less fortunate, and have left the world a better place than you found it.

How have you contributed? In what ways did you benefit the lives of others? How did you serve voluntarily and give of your time and resources freely? What more could you have done?

From a Buddhist perspective, you must leave this life with a peaceful mind and a heart full of love in order to have a fortunate rebirth in your next incarnation. That means you must have balanced your accumulated karma from the previous life.

Are you at peace? Is your heart full of love or are there lingering emotions of fear, resentment, jealousy or anger? Are you still holding on to the past? Are you embracing every moment of your day with an open heart full of love and gratitude? Are you projecting visions of the future that are bright and hopeful?

Let's make a plan to learn from the past, embrace the present, and project a positive future. Focus on developing a sense of inner peace by balancing the karma from the past. You can make a list of things that you still need to let go of by verbally confessing them and expressing sincere regret. Follow this up with a promise that you will not repeat these "offenses." This will allow you to forgive yourself so that you can move on with a clear and undisturbed mind. Make a plan to live in a heightened state of awareness, monitoring your thoughts, words and actions very closely. Pay attention to the value you bring to every interaction and make sure your reactions are kind and considerate. This way, you won't accumulate any more negative karma and can focus on gathering virtue. This will benefit you now, and in many lifetimes to come.

We have come here for the purpose of evolving to a higher level of consciousness. We can only do this if we make a sincere effort to learn and grow from every experience. We cannot ascend if we remain stagnant and keep repeating the same patterns. That's why it's so important to identify the key lessons we came here to learn and then make a commitment to master them. That has been the primary purpose of this workshop. Now that you have completed it, it's time to review your lesson plans and combine them into one Master Plan. Map out a step-by-step process that allows you to make daily progress one step at a time. Before you know it, you will be living your life on purpose and with every step, your life will become more joyful, meaningful and abundant.

Congratulations! Through completing this workshop, you have progressed on your evolutionary path. Although this lifetime is only temporary, you are making the most of it. Remember that your soul is on an eternal adventure, and every experience you have in this life will be imprinted upon it forever. Living your life from this perspective, you will develop a strong determination to draw from your highest self at all times.

Live in the light of love, my friends.
It will serve you well now and for all of eternity!
— Suzanne

A Master Plan

List three key points from each lesson plan

Lesson Plan #1: Transformation

1._____

2._____

3._____

Lesson Plan #2: Transition

1._____

2._____

3._____

Lesson Plan #3: Closure

1._____

2._____

3._____

Lesson Plan #4: New Beginnings

1._____

2._____

3._____

MASTER PLAN

Lesson Plan #5: Harmony

1._____

2._____

3._____

Lesson Plan #6: Healing

1._____

2._____

3._____

Lesson Plan #7: Reawakening

1._____

2._____

3._____

Lesson Plan #8: Synchronicity

1._____

2._____

3._____

Lesson Plan #9: Suffering

1._____

2._____

3._____

Lesson Plan #10: Death and Dying

1._____

2._____

3._____

These thirty key points comprise a step-by-step plan for you to master the lessons you came here to learn during this lifetime. I recommend that you make copies of this master plan, or scan and download it into your computer or mobile device so you will always have access to it. In order to master your lessons, it will be necessary to focus on them repeatedly. I suggest that, over a thirty-day period, you pick one of your lesson plan items to focus on and at the end of each day, you can make notes about the success or challenges you had applying it. At the end of thirty days, you will have improved your ability to integrate these key principles into your daily life. This step-by-step process should be repeated until you truly feel like you have applied your lessons in many different circumstances. At this point, they will have become a natural way of being and you will have successfully mastered the life-lessons you came here to learn. You will have fulfilled your life's purpose: You will have evolved to higher level of consciousness!

CONCLUSION

Entanglement

We cannot be free to fully embrace the present moment, or skillfully create our desired future, until we become disentangled from the past. In the Aramaic version of the Lord's Prayer, a simple request is made: *"Untie the tangled threads of our destiny that binds us as we release others from the entanglements of past mistakes."* [1] If we are to liberate our spirit and free our mind, we need to release the entanglements of our past and balance the karma we have created. This balancing act is ongoing.

Our lives are a dynamic evolutionary process.

We are constantly creating new experiences, and each one leads to the next. They build on each other and accumulate. With each new day, our actions cause a series of effects. Sometimes it's hard to keep track of everything we have set into motion, and we have to make lists and schedules. Then there are all the details and interpersonal relationships associated with every transaction and interaction. Most of us have created fairly complicated lives with plenty of commitments and obligations to keep track of. Our head is spinning with all of the details as we make plans, rehearsing and replaying all the actions and interactions in our head. We can get so caught up in this ongoing cycle of cause and effect, or action and reaction, it seems like we are either cleaning up from the previous day, reacting to the events of this one, or preparing for the upcoming events of the next. You might feel, at times, that you wish you could escape from it all. This is exactly what you need to do: escape, breathe and get centered. This will prevent you from feeling so scattered.

Another benefit of this temporary respite is the opportunity to reflect upon the interactions you've had throughout the day. Simply ask yourself, "What have I set into motion today? What actions caused what effects? And most importantly, how have those things I have said and done today impacted others?" You are checking to see if they were conducive to your well-being and to that of others.

Were your thoughts, words and actions kind, considerate and loving? Were you patient, understanding and generous? In other words, are you aligned with your highest Self, and activating your divine potential, as you move throughout your day? Remember the practice of asking yourself, "Ego or spirit?". We have to keep checking to see whose driving the bus! If it's ego, we have to see whom we've impacted with our ego-centered thoughts and intentions. We have to redirect them toward spiritually inspired ones, and make a commitment to reconcile or minimize negative effects. Simply put, we have to clean up our mess and promise to do better the next day. We have to tap ego on the shoulder and say, "My higher Self will be taking over now."

Over the course of this workshop, we have been applying a cause-and-effect analysis to illuminate the lessons hidden within our experiences. Once we identified these lessons, we gained a clearer understanding of how and why things occurred as they did. We began to accept the fact that the lessons were skillfully designed to help us appreciate the value of these experiences, and perceive them as gifts rather than cards randomly dealt to us. We were able to release the blame that we had placed on ourselves and others. With this enlightened perspective, we developed a sense of gratitude toward those people who were our best teachers. We discovered that oftentimes, the most challenging people teach us the most valuable lessons. We discovered that *forgiveness for ourselves and others is the key to becoming "disentangled."*

Now that we are more enlightened, we don't want to create any more entanglements or negative karma. Moving forward, we want to generate abundant virtue instead. We want to accumulate only positive karma so we don't have to look back with regret.

Making sure that we are aligned with our highest Self at all times is the most effective way to keep a clear conscience. This takes practice, however, and we will no doubt be drawn back into the influence of our ego-based thoughts until we get the hang of applying this "higher Self perspective." As we evolve into this higher way of being, it helps to keep in mind that *it's all about the lessons.*

It's all about evolving.

It becomes clear that when we are not resisting or trying to control everything with our ego-based mind, we remain open to the generosity and kindness of spirit. When love and compassion are flowing freely, joyful experiences arise. It's only when judgment and blame enter the picture that the perception of our experiences changes dramatically. Resistance arises and disharmony ensues. It is the difference between an open heart radiating patience and compassion, and a closed heart storing judgment and blame. One makes us feel empowered and unified and the other, victimized and separate.

It's important to keep applying a "karmic cause and effect analysis" to our daily experiences going forward. This way, we can extract the new lessons our higher self is trying to teach us. Remember: *As we master the lessons we came here to learn, we can move on to more advanced ones.* Our soul is compelled to evolve along its path of self-realization. As sentient beings, we have the gift of our senses enabling us to enjoy the texture of the physical realm. Our sense desires are what keep us so attached to the physical realm and as long as we appreciate them fully, without greed or non-virtue, we can use them constructively for our soul's evolution. We are right where we need to be at this point on our evolutionary path. Creation and evolution are the key features of the divine plan and self-realization is the sole purpose. Free will and the freedom to create is an inherent gift that has been bestowed upon us.

Each of us is endowed with the free will to choose our path. Each being is enabled to choose the experiences which will help him grow the most in each lifetime. As lifetimes multiply, the patterns become more complex and the web of entanglement more deeply woven. Becoming entangled in this web is the first step on a new soul's path. The entanglements begin to define the incarnations as each experience in every lifetime weaves its way through and around each other. A tapestry of eternal life unfolds marked by life and death, creation and destruction. Each individual is creating a karmic web of its own within the collective web of the whole. Balancing this karma purifies the experiences and reveals the important lessons. Liberating oneself from this karmic web is the final goal of each soul's evolutionary journey.

Pure love is the root cause of creation and we will all return to it someday. God is love, our origin and destiny, the alpha and the omega, the beginning and the end. When we finally merge with the One Great Self, we will finally experience the blissful oblivion of pure unconditional love.

The good news is that we don't have to wait until we ascend into the heavenly realms to experience the bliss of pure love. Once we reconcile our past and consciously balance our karma, we can engage in the present moment more fully and embrace life in all of its beauty, grace and form. By opening our minds to the endless possibilities just waiting to be explored, we allow them to enter our lives. We begin to live in harmony instead of resistance, thereby allowing the stream of universal abundance to flow.

I opened with a line from the Aramaic version of the Lord's Prayer. It was a simple request just like the one I will close with: *"Do not let us be seduced by that which would distract us from our true purpose but illuminate the opportunities of the present moment."* [2]

It is my sincere desire that every one of you becomes a beacon of light for the rest of humanity. I want you to live your life fully by activating your divine potential at all times and in all places. I want you to experience the pure joy of radiating love and light. This is a new way of being in a world that is becoming enlightened. Congratulations for entering the ascension path. There is a light at the end of the tunnel and you are walking toward it. Once you see it, it will always shine on you. Once you merge with it, there is no turning back.

You are loved more than you can possibly imagine. Enjoy the journey, my friends.

References

1,2. *Himalayan Path: Journal of Yoga Spirituality and Wellness*, Volume 11, Number 2, Spring 2011. Published by The Institute of the Himalayan Tradition.

Acknowledgements

If it weren't for the financial support of my husband, this book would not have been possible. It's only because he works so hard (and because he believes in me) that I had the time and resources to turn my dream into a reality. Without the spiritual inspiration that my sister provided early on, I never would have awakened to my true calling as an inspirational author and motivational speaker. I am grateful to my mother and father who encouraged me to believe that there are no limitations to what I can achieve. I also owe a debt of gratitude to my Spiritual Counselor, Janet Myatt, who not only contributed to this book by offering "The Spiritual Essence", but taught me how to go deeper within my own heart and mind. She made me realize the divine potential we all have within ourselves and showed me how to activate it.

I'd like to recognize Ron Valle and Mary Mohs from The Awakening Center in Brentwood, California who invited me into their spiritual community and introduced me to the ancient Vedantic philosophy and practices. They also introduced me to my spiritual guide, Stoma Parker (aka Dr. Stephen Parker), an internationally renowned teacher of the Vedantic philosophy based out of The Himalayan Institute in Honesdale, Pennsylvania. The personal mantra initiation that Stoma offered awakened me to the oneness of all living beings within the mind of the One Great Self. He helped me see that the life force, or prana, that illuminates all beings is the breath of the One Great Spirit.

I would like to offer my sincere gratitude to Clubsport in Pleasanton, California. They welcomed me into their family with open arms at a time when I needed to be recognized and supported. They helped me reestablish myself as a wellness professional and supported my aspirations as an integrative specialist offering mind/body/spirit programming. The clients that I have taken on during this time have all become dear friends to me. They are all like family to me and each and every one of them has supported and encouraged me to pursue my aspirations as a writer and speaker. I would especially like to thank Tina Onderbeke, my own personal "Dream Catcher", Peggy Prien, my soul-sister and Connie Yi, my partner in designing the app that will support all three books. Thank you for all of your love and support!

I am especially grateful for my Creative Assistant, Mai Tran, who provides all of the technical support I so desperately need. She has helped me create and design my interactive website and get linked to social media. She has made an audio version of all of the guided meditations in this book accessible and is helping me turn live workshops into online webinars. She also helps me produce marketing materials and coordinate events that promote my books and services. I cherish her friendship and would be lost without her technical support and creative assistance. Finally, I would like to thank my editor, D. Patrick Miller, of Fearless Books in Napa, California, for sharing his wisdom and insight about the daunting world of publishing. I am sincerely grateful that he opened the door to self-publishing for me and provided so much guidance and support. Of course, he agreed to edit my book which made me feel like my book was worthy and dedicated a great deal of time to enhancing the text and design. With his patience, knowledge and supreme talent as an author and editor, he helped me transform my manuscript into a book we can both be proud of. For that, I am extremely grateful.

About the Author

Suzanne Ross is an inspirationalist. She has a strong desire to lift the spirits, fill the hearts and improve the health of everyone she meets and has been spending the last 20 years doing just that. She owned a health and wellness center for 13 years in Southern California and for the last seven years has been offering wellness services at a premier Bay Area health club in Northern California. As an Integrative Wellness Specialist, she provides individual and group fitness training along with nutritional counseling and guided meditation. Suzanne also offers a 30-day program called, "Realize your Full Potential", that integrates the mind, body and soul. This program includes "Thought Awareness" workshops, nutritional detoxification, guided meditation and dynamic movement therapy. She has designed a similar program tailored to the needs of corporate employees called "Pure Potential" – A Mind/Body approach to Corporate Greatness."

With her advanced knowledge of health and wellness, Suzanne has empowered hundreds of people to reach their highest potential through improved health and wellness. Not only has she helped them improve the quality of their life from a physical perspective but, through sharing her enlightened message, has inspired many to realize their potential from a spiritual perspective as well. By offering "The Up! Trilogy", Suzanne is expanding her live 30-day programming by bringing it into the lives of many with her interactive books and guided meditations.

She hopes that her message of human empowerment and "Creator-Consciousness" will transform the lives of those seeking to manifest a reality that aligns with their true purpose. Through teaching her signature "Vortex Visualization" and guiding her students through lucid dreaming and contemplative meditation, Suzanne aspires to raise awareness about the power of connecting to a higher consciousness. She believes that anyone can dramatically enhance their experience of life by tapping into the greater field of consciousness that lies beyond our everyday awareness. This connection, she feels, not only reveals a deeper meaning and greater purpose but also empowers seekers to unleash their creative spirit and realize their unlimited potential to do, be and have anything their heart truly desires.

She expresses deep gratitude to all who join her on this journey and hopes that her readers will unite through her website:

www.suzannerosstranscendence.com

Made in the USA
Monee, IL
03 March 2023

29088374R00155